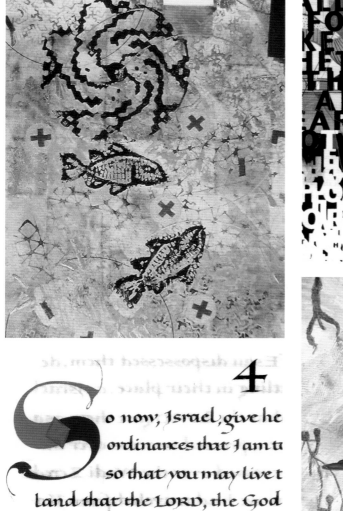

**4**

So now, Israel, give he
ordinances that I am ti
so that you may live t
land that the LORD, the God

*Moses then called Bezalel and Oholiab and every skillful one*
*to whom the LORD had given skill, everyone whose heart was stirred*
*to come to do the work; and they received from Moses all*
*the freewill offerings that the Israelites had brought*
*for doing the work on the sanctuary.*

EXODUS 36:2-3 (NRSV)

# ILLUMINATING THE WORD

# THE MAKING OF THE SAINT JOHN'S BIBLE

BY

CHRISTOPHER CALDERHEAD

THE SAINT JOHN'S BIBLE

COLLEGEVILLE, MINNESOTA

HALF TITLE PAGE: Ancient scribal techniques combine with modern artists' methods to produce a contemporary Bible manuscript. On a table next to Donald Jackson's drafting board, quills, brushes and tubes of paint are arrayed within arm's reach.

PAGE PRECEDING TITLE PAGE: Four details from The Saint John's Bible: *Loaves and Fishes, The Ten Commandments, The Garden of Eden*, and an initial capital from Deuteronomy 4.

TITLE PAGE: A full page illumination from The Saint John's Bible is rendered in gold and color on calf skin. This image is the frontispiece to the Gospel according to John.

*The Saint John's Bible*
Published by Liturgical Press

The New Revised Standard Version: Catholic Edition

Printed in China.

3 5 7 9 10 8 6 4 2

ISBN 0-8146-9050-5
LIBRARY OF CONGRESS CONTROL NUMBER: 2004115579

The Saint John's Bible can be found on the World Wide Web at: www.saintjohnsbible.org
The Liturgical Press can be found on the World Wide Web at: www.litpress.org

# CONTENTS

# PREFACE

THIS WHOLE PROJECT is either utter madness or magnificent good fortune. A whole series of chance circumstances have unexpectedly come together to result in the commissioning of an entire Bible copied by hand. For the first time in about five and a half centuries, since Johann Gutenberg began to sell copies of the earliest printed Bibles, an otherwise entirely sane American institution has ordered a new Bible to be made by a process which most people would assume had been rendered obsolete by the invention of printing.

First of all, the setting is a Benedictine monastery. From the beginning, Christian monastic communities have been patrons of art and sponsors of the production of monumental Bibles. The earliest surviving complete Bible in Latin, the huge *Codex Amiatinus*, now in Florence, was made in one of the twin Benedictine houses of Wearmouth or Jarrow in northern England in the early eighth century. The great Carolingian Bibles of the ninth century were almost all prepared in the Benedictine monasteries of Tours. The vast Bury and Winchester Bibles of twelfth-century England were Benedictine commissions, as were many others, such as the Admont and Stavelot Bibles. The custom of creating and using vast manuscript Bibles runs deeply in the ancient Benedictine tradition.

Secondly, Saint John's is a major contemporary university. Books are and always have been at the core of scholarship. Saint John's has a first-rate modern library, its own publisher, and, most famously, the Hill Monastic Manuscript Library, now with some hundred thousand early manuscripts stored by photography and digital technology. It is equipped with the latest scientific techniques of research. In such a context it is reassuring and valuable to modern students to be able to reflect on the methods of communicating all written knowledge at a period when the universities of Europe were in their infancy. The survival and evolution of modern learning has descended directly through a huge epoch of manuscript culture. To those who have never seen a real manuscript, The Saint John's Bible will open a new world. For the experienced historians of books and of the Middle Ages, who cluster around the Hill Monastic Manuscript Library, the Bible will supply answers to countless practical questions on how medieval books were designed and made a thousand or so years ago.

It is chance too that Donald Jackson was prepared to undertake such a project. This should not be underestimated. He is probably the best-known contemporary scribe and illuminator working in Britain or North America. He is an old friend of Saint John's, which he had visited many times before the commission took shape. He has an almost spiritual feeling for parchment and ink and for the written word which fits well with the nature of a Bible. This is probably the most extensive scribal commission in the western world since the end of the Middle Ages, and it requires an artist of stature with a capacity and a determination for a task of marathon length. It simply happened that this came about at the right moment in the life of the most appropriate scribe.

The timing is also right in a much wider context. We can all see that ancient cultural values are under

דברים

Rejoice, Zebulun, in your going out;
 and Issachar, in your tents.
¹⁹ They call peoples to the mountain;
 there they offer the right sacrifices;
 for they suck the affluence of the seas
 and the hidden treasures of the sand.

²⁰ And of Gad he said:
 Blessed be the enlargement of Gad!
 Gad lives like a lion;
 he tears at arm and scalp.
²¹ He chose the best for himself,
 for there a commander's allotment was reserved;
 he came at the head of the people,
 he executed the justice of the LORD,
 and his ordinances for Israel.

²² And of Dan he said:
 Dan is a lion's whelp
 that leaps forth from Bashan.

²³ And of Naphtali he said:
 O Naphtali, sated with favor,
 full of the blessing of the LORD,
 possess the west and the south.

²⁴ And of Asher he said:
 Most blessed of sons be Asher;
 may he be the favorite of his brothers,
 and may he dip his foot in oil.
²⁵ Your bars are iron and bronze;
 and as your days, so is your strength.

²⁶ There is none like God, O Jeshurun,
 who rides through the heavens to your help,
 majestic through the skies.
²⁷ He subdues the ancient gods,
 shatters the forces of old;
 he drove out the enemy before you,
 and said, "Destroy!"
²⁸ So Israel lives in safety,
 untroubled is Jacob's abode
 in a land of grain and wine,
 where the heavens drop down dew.
²⁹ Happy are you, O Israel! Who is like you,
 a people saved by the LORD,
 the shield of your help,
 and the sword of your triumph!
 Your enemies shall come fawning to you,
 and you shall tread on their backs.

I HAVE LET YOU SEE IT WITH YOUR EYES BUT YOU SHALL NOT CROSS OVER THERE

THEN MOSES THE
SERVANT OF THE LORD · DIED THERE
IN THE LAND OF MOAB
AT THE LORD'S COMMAND

The *Death of Moses* appears at the end of the book of Deuteronomy. This illumination was produced by Donald Jackson in collaboration with Aidan Hart.

threat today from secular pressures and from ideological extremism. It is a striking fact that the great Bible commissions of the past have often corresponded with moments when traditional Christianity seemed most at risk. Several huge manuscript Bibles of around 1100 conclude with references to the reassurance of the Scriptures in the time of the First Crusade, proclaimed in 1095. The Dominicans, early champions against heresy and religious deviation, were the principal patrons of orthodox Bibles in the thirteenth century. Even Gutenberg is known to have taken orders for his new printed Bible at the congress in Frankfurt in 1454, convened in response to military advances of the Turks into southeastern Europe. Any manuscript Bible is written slowly. It is almost impossible to study it in haste. If the presence of The Saint John's Bible causes us to pause and to remind ourselves of a life beyond contemporary politics and the daily frenzy of the world, then it will answer a universal need.

Finally, is it complete insanity to make such a book, by such a method? Yes, it probably is, in the sense that it is not necessary to spend so much time and money on something that could be made mechanically in a few moments. It has not happened for a long time. It probably will never happen again. It may be madness or imagination or simply faith that has driven this project, or a combination. Let us be glad that we live in a world where patrons and artists can seize a chance like this to participate in a book, a Bible no less, which will certainly outlive all of us.

CHRISTOPHER DE HAMEL
Gaylord Donnelley Librarian, Parker Library
Corpus Christi College
Cambridge, UK

other side of the sea for us, and get it for us so that we may hear it & observe it?" [14] No, the word is very near to you; it is in your mouth and in your heart for you to observe. ■ See, I have set before you today [15] life and prosperity, death & adversity. [16] If you obey the commandments of the LORD your God that I am commanding you today, by loving the LORD your God, walking in his ways, and observing his commandments, decrees, and ordinances, then you shall live & become numerous, and the LORD your God will bless you in the land that you are entering to possess. [17] But if your heart turns away and you do not hear, but are led astray to bow down to other gods & serve them, [18] I declare to you today that you shall perish; you shall not live long in the land that you are crossing the Jordan to enter and possess. [19] I call heaven and earth to witness against you today that I have set before you life and death, blessings & curses. Choose life so that you & your descendants may live, [20] loving the LORD your God, obeying him, and holding fast to him; for that means life to you and length of days, so that you may live in the land that the LORD swore to give to your ancestors, to Abraham, to Isaac, and to Jacob.

## 31

When Moses had finished speaking all these words to all Israel, [2] he said to them: "I am now one hundred twenty years old. I am no longer able to get about, and the LORD has told me, 'You shall not cross over this Jordan.' [3] The LORD your God himself will cross over before you. He will destroy these nations before you, and you shall dispossess them. Joshua also will cross over before you, as the LORD promised. [4] The LORD will do to them as he did to Sihon & Og, the kings of the Amorites, and to their land, when he destroyed them. [5] The LORD will give them over to you and you shall deal with them in full accord with the command that I have given to you. [6] Be strong and bold; have no fear or dread of them, because it is the LORD your God who goes with you; he will not fail you or forsake you." ■ Then Moses summoned Joshua [7] and said to him in the sight of all Israel: "Be strong and bold, for you are the one who will go with this people into the land that the LORD has sworn to their ancestors to give them; and you will put them in possession of it. [8] It is the LORD who goes before you. He will be with you; he will not fail you or forsake you. Do not fear or be dismayed." ■ Then Moses [9] wrote down this law, and gave it to the priests, the sons of Levi, who carried the ark of the covenant

Suzanne Moore's special treatment of a text from the Pentateuch appears opposite Deuteronomy 31.

# PROLOGUE

*Every scribe who has been trained for the kingdom of heaven is like the master
of a household who brings out of his treasure what is new and what is old.*

MATTHEW 13:52 NRSV

YOU ARE HOLDING in your hands a printed book. There is nothing extraordinary in that. We are surrounded by printed books. We assume that books exist in editions—thousands of identical copies. If you should lose this book or if by some mischance you should tear a page, you know that you can always find another somewhere—at a bookshop, at a library or on the internet. This book costs less than dinner and a movie for two at the local mall.

If you have just unpeeled the shrink-wrap from this copy, yours are probably the first human eyes to actually see this page. From its birth on a computer disk, through its journey from printing plant to warehouse to your hands, it has been in the grip of machines. Quality control inspectors have perhaps examined one in every hundred copies to ensure the machines functioned properly, that the ink went down smoothly and didn't streak and that the pages didn't get folded and sewn out of order. But no one has seen the pages of *this* book.

Technology shapes the way we look at books and the way we read them. We tend to treat text as a commodity. We read quickly and efficiently. We rarely pause to examine the book itself.

In the era before printing, every book was unique—and enormously expensive. Reading was slow and deliberate; in the first few centuries of the Common Era, it was almost always done out loud. In a manuscript book, you can tell whether the scribe was rushed or took his time. Sometimes you can see him growing tired, as the script becomes cramped or uneven. Every word you read was written by an actual human being—the act of reading is a moment of contact between you and the scribe.

Medieval scholars and monks would sometimes travel long distances to consult a single book. Important biblical manuscripts, like the Book of Kells or the Lindisfarne Gospels, were elaborately illustrated and decorated. The Winchester Bible is as complex as a gothic cathedral—and, like many cathedrals, it was left unfinished. These books were designed to be pored over, meditated upon, treasured.

ON APRIL 28, 1998, Donald Jackson and Brother Dietrich Reinhart, OSB, signed the contract which officially launched The Saint John's Bible. Donald used a quill pen and brilliant red ink. Together they embarked on a collaboration which would last almost a decade.

The Saint John's Bible is a modern manuscript book. It recaptures the spirit of the great medieval Bibles, yet it grows out of a completely contemporary artistic and theological sensibility.

Donald Jackson, one of the most skilled living calligraphers, is the artistic director of the project. From his Scriptorium in Wales he supervises a team of scribes and illuminators. The Bible is being written with quills on vellum, using hundred-year-old sticks of ink. The illuminations are made with a combination of ancient and modern techniques.

Donald Jackson at the
Scriptorium in Wales.

In May 2004 a facsimile of the
first volume of The Saint John's
Bible was presented to
His Holiness, Pope John Paul II, at
an audience in Rome. Abbot
John Klassen, OSB,
Donald Jackson and Dietrich
Reinhart, OSB, hold the book,
which is opened to the beginning
of John's Gospel.

Donald Jackson and Dietrich Reinhart, OSB, sign the contract for The Saint John's Bible.

A committee of scholars and artists guides the work. The Benedictine Abbey of Saint John the Baptist in Minnesota was founded in 1856. It has long been a center for the arts and liturgical renewal. The Saint John's Bible is a reflection of the monastic devotion to the Scriptures. The painstaking work of making the Bible echoes the slow, meditative reading which is a hallmark of Benedictine life and spirituality.

IN THE YEAR 2000 I was asked to begin documenting the making of The Saint John's Bible. For four years I have been interviewing the scribes, artists and scholars involved in the project. I have had the privilege of seeing Donald at work in his Scriptorium and joining the monks in their daily round of prayer at Saint John's. The stories which appear in this book are a distillation of hundreds of hours of interviews. They provide a glimpse of the working process behind the first major illuminated Bible to be produced since the Middle Ages, a Bible for our own times.

God in the details: a tiny slip of paper with Donald's initials is transformed into a thing of beauty.

# ILLUMINATING THE WORD

## THE MAKING OF
## THE SAINT JOHN'S BIBLE

The oak cross fixed in the concrete bell banner in front of the Abbey church was made from wood harvested in Saint John's own managed forests.

# CHAPTER 1

# LIVING THE WORD

THE GROUNDS OF Saint John's were perfectly still just before seven in the morning. The monastic and university buildings stood silent sentinel over the green campus. Behind them Lake Sagatagan was glassy-smooth, disturbed only by the tiny black heads of snapping turtles coming up for air. It was an early morning in the spring. The sun had been up for some while; so had many of the monks, but few were stirring beyond the monastic enclosure. A lone man in a black habit walked quietly along the drive in front of the Abbey church.

A bell began to ring out from the Abbey banner, the imposing concrete structure which holds the bells in front of the monastic church. It was the call to prayer.

I had come to Saint John's with many questions. Why had they commissioned Donald Jackson to write and illuminate an entire Bible by hand? In an era when a Gideon Bible is found in every hotel room in America, when biblical Web sites proliferate on the internet, when the Scriptures get carried about in backpacks and underlined with yellow highlighter in subway cars during rush hour, why spend this kind of time, care and attention making a manuscript Bible?

But now was not the time for questions. Carol Marrin, the director of the Bible project, was waiting for me at the door of the Abbey church. We went in and found places in the guest section. An elderly monk clattered past us, his cane tapping an uneven rhythm on the stone floor. Younger monks strode in with all the confidence of men in their prime.

Each seat had its own complement of service books. Carol and I each pulled out three of the binders and turned the pages to find the day's liturgy, arraying our books in order on the small shelf in front of us. Near us a stranger picked out one book, flicked through it, put it back and pulled out another, unsure what to do. An older monk leaned over and with a few whispered words set everything in readiness.

The bell outside sounded again and without a word we all rose in our places.

"Lord, open my lips," the leader said.

We responded, "And my mouth will proclaim your praise."

After singing a hymn, we sat down and began to pray our way through the psalms of the day. Verses sung or chanted by a single voice were followed by verses sung or chanted in unison by all. Some portions were allotted to one side of the church or the other, spoken in dialogue, back and forth across the sanctuary in orderly progression.

The monastic hours of prayer have a distinct pace. The familiar words are not uttered in haste. We paused deliberately after every verse. At the conclusion of each psalm, we kept silence, leaving time for the words to sink down deep.

A reading, a sung canticle and prayers followed in due course and we were done. The community rose and dispersed to every corner of the campus. Our work day had begun.

As Carol and I walked out of the Abbey church, she began to rattle off a list of meetings she'd set up

The bell banner is silhouetted against a bright morning sky. The cornerstone for Marcel Breuer's Abbey church was laid in 1958. The bold modernism of the church was a confident expression of the monks' commitment to the visual arts. The Saint John's Bible continues that tradition of artistic experimentation.

for me through the day. It was 7:30 in the morning and Carol was wide awake and ready to go. There were no gaps in the schedule. Every hour was accounted for. This was the other side of Saint John's—it is not only a place of prayer and silence. It is also a place of very hard work.

We walked to the dining hall while Carol filled me in about the people I would meet, giving brief descriptions of each person, tidbits of monastic politics and pointers about questions I should ask. A squad of ROTC cadets jogged past us, dressed in black T-shirts and shorts. They broke step to walk into the dining hall together. The last cadet held the door for Carol.

Between bites of sausage and egg and toasted Johnnie Bread (a product of the monastery) I made notes. Around us a steady stream of undergraduates were coming into the dining hall. The university was waking up.

Breakfast done, I headed to my first meeting. Carol called after me, "Oh, by the way, Jo White phoned; she's coming by a bit later with some photographs. Come by my office and we can have a look at them." She waved and disappeared down the path.

## Holy reading, holy writings

ABBOT JOHN KLASSEN, OSB, is a tall man with a gentle demeanor. I met him in his office. He made me a cup of coffee and we sat near the large, sculptural fireplace. The abbot's office fills a small suite of rooms in the wing of the monastery designed by Marcel Breuer. As I settled into my chair I looked eagerly around the room, enjoying every architectural detail. The interior is a perfectly preserved 1950s modernist interior by one of the great masters. That it is intact is a tribute to Benedictine thrift and good stewardship.

Monks gather in the Abbey church for morning prayer. In his Rule, Saint Benedict organized the monastic day around a regular cycle of prayer. The recitation of the Psalms is the heart of the community's worship.

A monk in the black habit of the Benedictine order walks outside the
Abbey church before morning prayer.

Monks are encouraged to develop the habit of reading the Scriptures in
a slow, meditative technique referred to as *lectio divina*. The daily practice of *lectio* draws deeply on the imagination as a key to understanding
the Bible not only with the mind, but with heart and soul as well.

I asked, "How do you feel The Saint John's Bible connects with the life of the monastery?"

He began with institutional concerns. He spoke of Saint John's commitment to the arts, especially to
the book arts, and mentioned some of the other institutions within the community—the Arca Artium
collection and the Hill Monastic Manuscript Library—which are part of that commitment.

We chatted back and forth about buildings, staffing, programs. There were many plans for how the
Bible might be used. Institutional plans, however, rarely light a fire under anyone. I probed to see what
would kindle a flame.

It was peace and justice. The abbot's eyes sparkled. This Bible would be about something new: "It is a
retrieval of the Catholic imagination with Scripture. The Word becomes sacramental. It is not just a text.
It is like the Eucharist: a visual image of the Word." With his own background in applied ethics and peace
studies, he was particularly concerned that The Saint John's Bible should speak for the poor and marginalized. "God's commitment to the poor is embedded in Scripture," he said. "In the prophetic books, in
psalmody and throughout the New Testament. The deeper we are drawn into Scripture, the more we
will be driven to address these issues in our lives." He hoped the illuminations would be compelling wit-
nesses to "God's own awareness of and his standing with the poor."

Throughout their history, Benedictine monasteries
have emphasized the importance of books in the religious life. During the early Middle Ages, they were the
most important centers of book production in
Western Europe. These nineteenth century stained
glass windows from the former Abbey church reflect
the central position of books in the monastic
imagination.

He foresaw the Bible moving to exhibitions around the country, engaging people, especially the young, asking them to encounter the Scriptures in a new form. "What happens when you read the Word together? Things come out of the text—new, exciting things." He saw The Saint John's Bible as a way of sharing the Scriptures in a classic Benedictine way: to encourage *lectio divina,* the slow, meditative monastic method of reading the Bible, on a mass scale. That's what he'd like to see Saint John's do with its new Bible; that's what he'd like to see happen in the broader world, when people see the book and pore over it.

After meeting the abbot I walked over to the Hill Monastic Manuscript Library to meet Columba Stewart, OSB. A spare, thin man, he wore black jeans and a short-sleeved clerical shirt, unbuttoned at the collar. His eyes were sharp and intense. He greeted me with a swift, firm handshake.

We sat down and I made small talk.

At the first pause he said, "What do you want to ask me?" He smiled.

I cut the chitchat. "Tell me about *lectio divina*. I want to know more about where it comes from, how it's done."

"It was part of the return to the sources which happened after Vatican II. The Council's statements on monasticism invited the religious communities to reexamine their ways of life. It was often confusing; everything was up for grabs. Should we wear a habit? What hours of prayer should we keep? How are we to translate our worship from Latin into the vernacular?"

The Council forced monasteries to consider afresh the roots of their traditions. Monks and nuns around the world looked at their life with new eyes.

"What does it mean to be a Benedictine, a Trappist, a Franciscan?" he continued. "What are the deep roots of our communities?"

For Benedictine houses like Saint John's, this inevitably meant returning to Saint Benedict's Rule, the very foundation of their tradition. Written in the early sixth century, it presents a simple, balanced life of prayer and work. Steeped in biblical images, much of its text is directly quoted from the Scriptures. It presents a monastic life which is permeated by the Bible. The central practice of the community is the recitation of the psalms, and monks are directed to "listen readily to holy reading" and devote themselves to prayer.[*]

In the 1970s as the community explored the foundations of its life, it began to recapture a deeply personal, imaginative reading of Scripture. The practice of *lectio* is slow. The earthy image most frequently used to describe it is that of a cow chewing the cud. Ruminating on the Bible rather than analyzing it is the key. The reader pauses whenever a word or phrase strikes him. He sits with that word, letting it sink in. Reading passes into contemplation, which passes into prayer.

Cassian, the fifth-century monastic writer, describes this kind of attentiveness in reading and reciting the psalms. The monk who recites the psalms is like a deer feeding in the pastures of Holy Scripture—

> Being endued, by the strength and succulency of this divine nourishment, with all the affections which are expressed in the psalms, he receives their impression and recites them, as if they were no longer the songs of the Bard of Zion, but his own warm effusions, and that from the depths of a contrite heart, he was really pouring forth his own prayer to God. He believes, at last, that the psalms were made expressly for him, and that the truths they contain were not accomplished in David alone, but are daily accomplished and verified in himself personally.[**]

A charismatic teacher, Donald Jackson lectures to the participants of the Calligraphy Connection. His bold, fluid writing fills the large panel behind him.

[*] Rule of Saint Benedict 4:55

[**] Cassian, *Conferences*. Trans. Father Robert of Mount Saint Bernard's Abbey. London: Thomas Richardson and Son, nineteenth century (no date). Conference 10, Chapter 10, pp. 528–529.

The practice of *lectio*, Father Columba said, was central to the practice of the community. If a monk had trouble with this deliberate, meditative reading of Scripture, then he probably wasn't suited to the monastic life.

I wondered if that wasn't a bit harsh, but I didn't say so. It was certainly a realistic and practical appraisal of the monastic vocation. And Columba struck me as practical to the core. The monks' days are ordered around morning, noon and evening prayer. The Mass is celebrated daily. Monks are expected to build in private time for *lectio divina* every day. They recite and read the Scriptures all day long.

I came away from our meeting with a richer sense of how central the Bible is in monastic life. And a reading list.

## *Calligraphy at Saint John's*

Jo was waiting for me in Carol's office. Short, white-haired and feisty, Jo is a force to be reckoned with in the calligraphy world. She'd brought a packet of photos, brochures and journals which illustrated the history of calligraphy at Saint John's.

She greeted me with a warm hug and kiss. Carol pulled out some new prints of Bible pages to show her.

"How's it going?" Jo asked me with her flat Minnesotan vowels.

I gave her a rundown of my visit so far.

"Good, good. Mm-hmm. Yes." Jo likes to keep track of things.

Carol stepped out of the office and Jo reached into her bag and pulled out a box to show me. It held an album of calligraphy samples which she'd been given. All the calligraphy stars were represented—there were pieces by Sheila Waters and her son, Julian, by Donald Jackson and Thomas Ingmire. An exquisite little manuscript by Ann Hechle was tucked into a corner of the box.

The Calligraphy Connection held at Saint John's in 1981 gathered lettering artists from across the world for the first summer calligraphy conference. The Connection spawned a tradition of annual conferences in the United States which has lasted for a quarter century.

"I'm going to show these to Columba," she said, "I want to have them appraised."

Without Jo White there would be no Saint John's Bible. She has promoted calligraphy at Saint John's for more than twenty-five years. As Carol remarked to me after she left, "Jo gets things done. I've seen her stand up in meetings when people are not coming to a decision and say 'Well, who's in charge?'"

Jo organized the Calligraphy Connection at Saint John's in 1981. It was the first conference of its kind, gathering lettering artists from across the United States and Europe for an intense week of practical teaching. The Connection spawned a calligraphy institution, the annual summer conference. Every year since 1981 a conference has been held in a different city in the United States. Saint John's has hosted the annual gathering three times.

In 1988, she collaborated with Jane Borchers to bring a traveling exhibition of Donald Jackson's work to venues across the country. As she likes to say, "Two middle-aged housewives got that show into thirteen cities."

Jo White was also instrumental in planning a symposium entitled *Servi Textus,* designed to initiate a conversation between calligraphers, scholars and collectors. Jo hoped that their deliberations would help create a market for works of calligraphic art, and begin to develop ties between curators and lettering artists.

It was during the planning for *Servi Textus* that the idea of The Saint John's Bible was first proposed.

Once Jo had shown me her lettering samples, she packed them away and headed off the down the hall to see Columba.

A happy group gathers at a diner in St. Joseph, near Saint John's. From left to right, Jo White, Donald and Mabel Jackson, Rebecca Cherry and Jo's husband, Bob.

## A Bible is born

WITH A FEW MINUTES before my next appointment, I looked over my notes. The week before, I had phoned Donald Jackson and Eric Hollas, OSB, to ask about the day they first discussed the Bible project.

Memories differ about the details. It was Saturday, November 27, 1995. Father Eric was then in charge of the Hill Monastic Manuscript Library. He was in Chicago with Donald Jackson to promote *Servi Textus.*

Donald remembered, "It was part of the warm up for the conference. Saint John's felt they had to pay court to the calligraphy community. I offered to give a talk at the Newberry Library. It was the first time Eric and I had gone on the boards together. The next day before we went our separate ways we went to the Art Institute to see the Monet exhibition. Lots and lots of haystacks. Afterwards we went out for a late lunch in the Loop. It was a cold day and I bought a fedora at Marshall Fields to keep out the cold."

Eric said, "It was hard to find a place to eat in that neighborhood on a weekend. We went into a little Italian place. It was half empty and dark."

"Eric likes Italian," Donald recalled. "So we ordered pasta and a bottle of red wine. There was a busy lunchtime crowd."

Donald bided his time as they ate their lunch.

"The wine was very good. I waited until we were two-thirds of the way down the bottle and then I popped the question: 'What are you doing to celebrate the millennium?'"

Eric told him Saint John's had no plans in particular.

Donald continued his pitch. "The Archbishop of Canterbury likes to say, 'Whose birthday is it anyway?'"

An illumination from a Book of Hours shows John the Evangelist writing with a quill on a small scroll extended across his knee.
Book of Hours. Sarum Use. France (Rouen), end of the fifteenth–century. Manuscript on vellum. Kacmarcik Collection of Arca Artium, Saint John's University.

He suggested to Eric that Saint John's should commission him to write a book of Gospels to mark the two-thousandth anniversary of Christ's birth.

"Donald always says he proposed Gospels," Eric recalled. "I'm sure he said Bible."

Donald sticks to his guns. "I swear to this day I said Gospels. Anyway, Eric, like a good Benedictine, immediately said, 'How much?' I said 'A million dollars.' I wasn't expecting him to ask so I just named a figure."

Eric remembered, "Donald asked me to take the idea back to Saint John's. I thought to myself, 'This will never happen.' But I don't like to say no, so I said I would."

They went their separate ways and Donald went back to the hotel where he and Jo White were staying. She knew he had intended to make his proposal over lunch.

"When I got to the hotel where Jo White and I were staying, she took a two-dollar bill. We wrote the time and date on it and she tore it in half. She handed me one half and she kept the other. She said to me, 'When this project comes off, we'll reunite the two halves.'"

Eric returned to Saint John's and waited to mention the idea to Dietrich Reinhart, OSB, the president of the University.

"It was much later," he recalled. "Dietrich and I were driving one day to the Twin Cities and I had a whole list of items to bring up. When I mentioned my conversation with Donald and the idea of making a Bible, he said immediately, 'We have to do that.' It wasn't a logical response. It came from the gut."

Monasteries make decisions slowly. The men who make up the community have to live with the decisions they make. Brother Dietrich presented the Bible project to the monastic community in 1997. The community debated, argued and wrestled over the idea for a full year. At last they voted yes—the project had the green light. Donald and Jo reunited the two halves of their two-dollar bill.

Jo White's two dollar bill. On the day Donald Jackson first proposed the making of The Saint John's Bible to Eric Hollas, OSB, Jo wrote the date on the bill and tore it in half. The two halves were reunited when the contract was signed.

## A celebration of the non-linear

I WANDERED DOWN to my next appointment, lunch with the president of the university.

Dietrich walked me down to the student dining hall. As president of the university, he had been the driving force behind The Saint John's Bible. I'd never met him before although I had seen his picture many times and had spotted him around the campus. His manner was easy-going; he was quick to smile. As we walked through the dining hall he greeted undergraduates and staff as they passed by him. We sat down with our trays and he asked me how my visit was going, about my own career, about the people I'd

Brother Dietrich Reinhart, OSB, the president of the University, chats at a press briefing.

Saint John's University was founded by the monks in 1857, immediately after the Abbey itself was established. Many of the monks teach or work at the university. The ceremonies and rhythms of academic life interweave with those of the monastery.

met. I found myself chatting amiably about my own hopes and fears, my desires for the future, my journey of faith. Twenty minutes into lunch, I suddenly stopped and said, "Wait a minute: you're doing a fantastic job of interviewing me!"

Dietrich smiled back. "It helps me feel at ease," he said and I realized it made us both feel at ease. Our talk felt more like an amiable conversation than an interview.

We began to discuss how the Bible project had come about as well as its impact on the community as a whole. In the midst of this he remarked, "As a historian, I don't want to live in the past." Perhaps that was the key to the whole enterprise for as a historian he has a keen sense of the past. He talked movingly about parts of Saint John's property where you could still make out an Ojibwe burn area, a place where Native Americans had burned away the underbrush to create a better hunting ground. That sense of place was enormously important to him; it was both about knowing what had come before and about having a sense of gratitude for the generations of people who laid foundations to build on. He had a strong feeling that we all "rely on the love of people we never knew. Think of Jesus of Nazareth. People knew him—and they passed it on."

The collections at Saint John's include many important printed and manuscript books. Eric Gill's *The Four Gospels* was printed in England at the Golden Cockerell Press. A convert to Roman Catholicism, Gill tied image and word together into a seamless whole. His design for *The Four Gospels* blends typographic sophistication with a deeply theological sensibility. His refined style was marked by modern simplicity and a keen appreciation for tradition. His work influenced the liturgical arts for more than a generation.

lots upon them, what every man should take. And it was the third hour, & they crucified him. And the superscription of his accusation was written over, THE KING OF THE JEWS. And with him they crucify two thieves; the one on his right hand, and the other on his left. And the scripture was fulfilled, which saith, And he was numbered with the transgressors. And they that passed by railed on him, wagging their heads, and saying, Ah, thou that destroyest the temple, and buildest it in three days, Save thyself, and come down from the cross. Likewise also the chief priests mocking said among themselves with the scribes, He saved others; himself he cannot save. Let Christ the King of Israel descend now from the cross, that we may see and believe. And they that were crucified with him reviled him. ✶ And when the sixth hour was come, there was darkness over the whole land until the ninth hour. And at the ninth hour Jesus cried with a loud voice, saying, Eloi, Eloi, lama sabachthani? which is, being interpreted, My God, my God, why hast thou forsaken me? And some of them that stood by, when they heard it, said, Behold, he calleth Elias. And one ran and filled a spunge full of vinegar, and put it on a reed, and gave him to drink, saying, Let alone; let us see whether Elias will come to take him down. And Jesus cried with a loud voice, and gave up the ghost. And the veil of the temple was rent in twain from the top to the bottom. And when the centurion, which stood over against him, saw that he so cried out, and gave up the ghost, he said, Truly this man was the Son of God. There were also women looking on afar off: among whom was Mary Magdalene, and Mary the mother of James the less and of Joses, and Salome; (Who also, when he was in Galilee, followed him, and ministered unto him;) and many other women which came up with him unto Jerusalem.

124

NOW WHEN THE EVEN WAS COME

Eric Gill. *The Four Gospels.*
Waltham St. Lawrence: The Golden Cockerell Press, 1931.
Kacmarcik Collection of Arca Artium, Saint John's University.

He explained something of the history of Saint John's. "On the 1500th anniversary of Saint Benedict's birth, Cardinal Basil Hume came to Saint John's. He said while he was here, 'I have studied medieval monasteries; I think this is the first living one I've visited.' I think what Hume was sensing was that Saint John's, like so many medieval monasteries, had determined the pattern of settlement for the whole area."

Dietrich described how the German monks who had built the monastery had served local parishes in this area of Minnesota and how the place names themselves reflected the German Catholic piety of those founding monks. Then he explained that the founding vision had given way to a new vision. In the 1940s with the entrance of the first African American monks and with the growing importance of the monastery as a center for liturgical revival and ecumenical and interfaith activities, Saint John's began to see itself as a cutting-edge place. By the 1960s, there were more than four hundred monks. The new, modernist church designed by Marcel Breuer reflected the optimism of that time.

This strong legacy had built a large and important complex of buildings; it had given rise to a host of other institutions, the university foremost among these, which were grouped around the monastery. But the legacy also had its shadow side. The liturgical renewal which Saint John's had helped pioneer had borne fruit. This was a good thing, but it meant Saint John's no longer had a cutting-edge position. The Church at large had adopted the reforms and changes the monastery had advocated. The late sixties also saw the decline of monastic vocations and the departure of quite a few monks. Perhaps, Dietrich suggested, the institution had been grieving. And perhaps not all that grieving was resolved. Was there a way of finding a project which would give Saint John's a new vision, something which would refocus its energies, excite people and shift the focus toward the future?

The original Abbey church was built by the monks themselves using bricks made at the monastery. When Breuer's modern Abbey church was built, the spires of the old building were removed and it was converted for use as the Great Hall. It is seen here through the parabolic arch of the bell banner.

When The Saint John's Bible was first mentioned to him he thought perhaps this was something they could rally around.

"If it was an anachronism, I wouldn't be interested," he said. He wasn't going to live in the past. This project with very old roots just like Saint John's—or the monastic tradition itself—could be a way to light a new fire.

"It wouldn't work if it was clichéd or if it was some project out there in cloud cuckoo land. No. It had to be great art. It had to be about the real world today. It had to resonate with Catholic tradition but not in a dogmatic way. It had to connect to the curriculum."

He began to describe all the ways a project like this could involve different parts of the community, how it could engage the imaginations of people over a period of many years.

Ultimately the project was about huge issues. "What would happen if we took seriously when we say, 'I can treat every person I meet as Christ.' If we took that literally, think how transforming it would be. Each person I meet has a word of salvation for me." He paused to let that thought sink in.

"But the thing is, we're *guys*. We're living a middle-class lifestyle. We're part of a mainline tradition. So we don't like to wear our faith on our sleeves. We need props. We need vestments and an altar to say sacred words. We need a curriculum to discuss ethics. We need roles to allow people to open up and ask advice. But when you look at the discussions which take place around The Saint John's Bible, people allow themselves to say they were moved. People who aren't ordained find themselves talking about Christ. Very practical, down-to-earth people ask, 'What about religious art?'" It was just that potential which had made Dietrich such a strong advocate of the project.

"The Saint John's Bible is a celebration of the non-linear," he said with a broad smile.

## Scope of the project

"So take me through step by step," I said to Carol back in her office. "What goes in to making The Saint John's Bible?"

"The aim of the project," she said, "is to ignite the spiritual imagination. We want to develop programs around the Bible in spirituality, art and education." These programs will continue to grow long after the Bible is finished.

The thick binders on her shelves are filled with documents relating to the Bible project. She took one out and placed it on the table in front of us.

"Certain values guide The Saint John's Bible," she said, pointing to one of the sections in the book. Bold face headings listed a set of goals.

"We set these values down at the very beginning of the project. Some of them are self-explanatory: ignite the imagination; glorify God's Word; foster the arts. Others are more complex, like this one." She pointed to the words "Revive tradition."

She explained, "Monasteries of the Middle Ages were places where books were made. In some periods of history they were the only centers of book production." Since printing took over the book trade this tradition of hand-written manuscripts has been almost entirely absent from the Christian world. The Saint John's Bible revives the link between monastic communities and the hand-made book.

"Here's another one: Discover history. Who has made a manuscript book of this scale in the last five hundred years? We hope that the experience of writing out The Saint John's Bible will throw light on workshop practices and craft techniques."

"What about 'Give voice?'" I asked. "What do you mean by that?"

"The Scriptures speak forcefully for the excluded and underprivileged. We hope that The Saint John's Bible will be a voice for the marginalized in the true spirit of Christianity. The subjects which have been selected for illumination emphasize this important theme throughout the Bible."

Carol went on to explain that the Bible would be composed of seven volumes—Pentateuch, Historical Books, Wisdom Literature, Psalms, Prophets, Gospels and Acts, and Letters and Revelation.

"Are they being made in that order?" I wondered.

"No. Donald began with Gospels and Acts, which is the most heavily illuminated volume. Then he wrote Pentateuch and Psalms. In fact the making of each volume overlaps with the making of the others. The production schedule is complex to say the least."

The choice of translation was up to Saint John's. They selected the New Revised Standard Version (NRSV) as the most up-to-date, scholarly translation available. The order of the books reflects the Roman Catholic canon. The "Deuterocanonical" books, which Protestants refer to as the "Apocrypha," are included among the other writings in the Old Testament.

"Donald is the Artistic Director of the project," she continued. "He's gathered a team of scribes and illuminators to help him complete the manuscript. He could never have made the entire book by himself. He is creating most of the illuminations but he often collaborates with other artists. Quite a few illuminations are done by guest artists working under his direction and most of the text is written by the scribal team using a script Donald has designed with them."

The robust physicality of early books is beautifully expressed in this Latin printed Bible of 1491. A small, thick book in an *octavo* format, its tooled leather cover is ornamented with metal detailing and clasps. When The Saint John's Bible is completed in 2007, it will be bound between stout oak boards. The large vellum pages will recapture the physical grandeur of early books.

Bible. Latin Version.
Basel: Johann Froben, 1491.
Sixteenth century stamped pigskin binding with clasps and metalwork (dated 1536).
Kacmarcik Collection of Arca Artium, Saint John's University.

The Gospel of Saint John.
Wenner Manuscript: Eth. Ms. 1.
Ethiopia, 1918.
Parchment bound with wooden boards, in a
two-part leather case. Hill Monastic Manuscript
Library, Saint John's University.

In some cultures the tradition of writing Bibles by hand has survived into the modern era. This small Ethiopian manuscript of John's Gospel, made in the early twentieth century, was designed to be carried in a small leather pouch.

"And how does Saint John's contribute to the design process?" I asked.

"Two monks, David Cotter, OSB, and Michael Patella, OSB, worked up something we call the 'schema.' It lists the passages which will be illuminated in the Bible and it sets out major themes in each volume. It functions as the master plan for the project."

The schema provided an outline for the detailed theological briefs which were then written for each illumination.

"The Committee on Illumination and Text was formed to work with Donald. Father Michael is the chair and the members are drawn from the wider Saint John's community. Many of them are monks from the monastery. Others are scholars connected to the university. It's an interesting group. There are both academics and artists on the committee. They wrote the briefs and they see Donald's working sketches. They give him feedback and direction as he works."

There will only be one copy of The Saint John's Bible; that's the nature of a manuscript book. It is a singular object. I asked Carol how people would be able to see the Bible.

She answered, "It will be on display here at Saint John's. We will also be publishing an expensive, full-size facsimile of the manuscript. There will be a smaller trade edition as well so people can have a copy at home. Right now we're planning for an exhibition at The Minneapolis Institute of Art."

"The project isn't finished though, is it?"

"Not yet. We have the first three volumes which will be shown in the exhibition. Donald is still working on the last four volumes. The whole Bible will be finished in 2007."

"But that's just the beginning, isn't it?"

"Oh yes. Once the Bible itself is finished, then it will take on a life of its own—The Saint John's Bible will be here long after we're gone."

I looked at my watch. It was time for my next appointment.

## Taking tea

A CLUE TO THE ETHOS of Saint John's can be found at the pottery studio Richard Bresnahan maintains in the basement of Saint Joseph Hall. Trained in Japan, Richard has imported the tradition of taking tea in the workshop each afternoon with his apprentices, students and guests. A hearth stands near the front end of the studio. Surrounded on four sides by a low wall topped with beautifully finished wood, the center is a hollow filled with sand. A single gas ring supports the iron kettle.

Richard greeted me at the door. His head was wrapped in a printed bandana; he wore practical work clothes. He shook my hand warmly.

"Do you know Sister Johanna?" he said.

"Oh yes, we've met," I answered turning to her and shaking her hand.

Johanna Becker, OSB, has been Richard's great mentor through the years. Her academic field is East Asian art, specializing in ceramics. When he finished his undergraduate degree at Saint John's, she helped arrange his two-year Japanese apprenticeship. When he built the largest wood fired kiln in North America, which stands across the road, he named it after her.

Sister Johanna had brought a friend of hers, a priest, who filled out our party. Richard turned to his apprentice, a young man with a beard and a ponytail, and instructed him to fetch Johanna a comfortable chair. The rest of us sat on stools while Richard made the tea. The tea pot, water jug and cups were all products of his studio. We chatted as the water boiled softly on the gas ring.

Richard established his pottery on campus in 1979. The ethos of the studio combines Benedictine values of sustainability and self-sufficiency with Japanese workshop practices.

"In America, we're making up our culture," he commented. "Some of the things I do here would never happen in Japan." He showed us a tea pot with an elegant woven reed handle. "I work with the weaver to make these pots." In conversation with the weaver, he creates new ceramic forms which complement the exquisitely twining handles. He explained that in Japan the pottery traditions are more fixed. Each region produces its own varieties of pottery based on local materials and centuries of workshop practice. In America, by contrast, the field is more open; there is no tradition to guide—or limit—his work.

Richard is creating a new tradition at his studio. He uses local materials and sustainable methods. His clay comes from a site nearby; he has enough clay in store to last the rest of his and several other lifetimes. Many of the glazes are made of agricultural byproducts from farms in the region.

"I couldn't do this at an ordinary university," he said. "We fire the Johanna kiln once every twelve months. Who's going to wait twelve months for a grade?" It isn't economical in the narrow sense of turning a quick profit. To run a pottery like this one has to take the long view. Like the monastery the pottery is designed around distant time frames longer than any one person's lifespan. The forest which surrounds Saint John's is managed in a sustainable fashion; the buildings are meant to last. The land is husbanded rather than simply exploited.

Conversation turned to lighter topics. Tea cups were filled and refilled. Soon it was time for Johanna to go; her ride was waiting to take her back to Saint Benedict's, her monastic home in St. Joseph. We all rose to say goodbye.

When the other guests had left, Richard gave me a tour of the studio. Opening a large vat he plunged his hand in and brought up a handful of wet, grey mud.

Benedictine crosses decorate windows on the towers of the old Abbey church, now the Great Hall.

The imagery of The Saint John's Bible makes reference to many world traditions. The Arabic Bible shown here was printed in Italy in 1590–91. It is an example of a cross-cultural Bible from the European Renaissance made for Christian communities in the Middle East.
*Evangelium Sanctum Domini Nostri Iesu Christi Conscriptum A Quatuor Evangelistis Sanctis.*
Rome: Typographia Medicea, 1590–91. Saint John's Rare Books, Alcuin Library, Saint John's University.

"The glazes we use are all natural."

I reached my hand in and felt the fine silt between my fingers. It was cold and smooth.

"I've been to so many funerals of my peers. When we were students no one told us not to plunge our hands into the chemical glazes—yellow cadmium and cobalt blue."

"Heavy metals," I said, making the connection.

"Exactly. I've been experimenting with glazes made from local materials. This is made from navy bean straw."

We walked down to the Johanna kiln across the road. Richard's apprentice followed close behind. Housed in a large shed, the kiln was cold, empty. The shed is built over a steep part of a hill; the kiln rises in three large chambers, each with its own set of flues and doors for stoking the fires. Along the vaulted top of the central chamber, a series of small holes with lids can be opened in a precise sequence during the firing.

The bricks were recycled from demolished buildings at the monastery. "The monks made all these bricks by hand on site."

A deep appreciation for the land, for the work of those who have come before and for future generations informs Richard's working practice. We went back up the hill to his studio where he showed me some of his wares.

The Stella Maris chapel, built during World War I, stands on a rocky outcrop jutting into Lake Sagatagan. It can be seen from the lakeshore behind the Abbey church.

The Abbey church in the snow.

"The ceramics which survive are those which find multiple uses," he said. He tries to make forms which can be adapted to many functions—the best hope that his work will continue to be used and valued far into the future.

It brought to mind something Eric had said to me: "The Saint John's Bible could last longer than any of the buildings at the monastery. Think about the great manuscripts of the past. They have survived long after the monasteries which produced them have disappeared."

I took my leave of Richard and walked up the grassy hill to the Abbey church. Undergraduates were playing catch on the lawns around their dorms. The bell rang out six p.m.

## The close of day

AT NINE O'CLOCK the bell does not ring for Compline, the service of night prayer. The Abbey church is dark. A small group of ten or twelve monks walks silently into a pool of light around the altar. They form a wide semi-circle and begin to sing.

> Lord, now you let your servant go in peace;
> your word has been fulfilled.
> My own eyes have seen the salvation
> which you have prepared in the sight of every people,
> the light to reveal you to the nations
> and the glory of your people, Israel.

The day is ended. The monks disperse to their rooms and to bed.

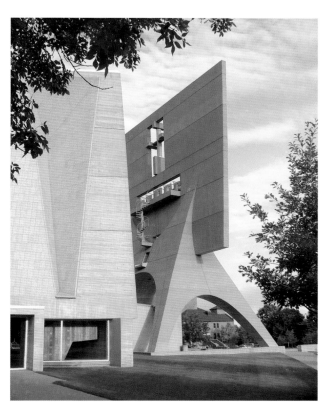

The bold, sculptural forms of the Abbey Church dominate the monastery and university grounds. The bell banner looming above the entrance can be seen for miles around.

# THE SAINT JOHN'S BIBLE

## PENTATEUCH

*158 pages · delivered in September 2003*

Genesis
Exodus
Leviticus
Numbers
Deuteronomy

## HISTORICAL BOOKS

*319 pages · scheduled to be delivered in August 2006*

Joshua
Judges
Ruth
1 Samuel
2 Samuel
1 Kings
2 Kings
1 Chronicles
2 Chronicles
Ezra
Nehemiah
Tobit
Judith
Esther
1 Maccabees
2 Maccabees

## WISDOM LITERATURE

*102 pages · scheduled to be delivered in November 2005*

Job
Proverbs
Ecclesiastes
The Song of Songs
The Wisdom of Solomon
Sirach (Ecclesiasticus)

## PSALMS

*80 pages · delivered in April 2004*

## PROPHETS

*272 pages · scheduled to be delivered in April 2005*

Isaiah
Jeremiah
Lamentations
Baruch
Ezekiel
Daniel
Hosea
Joel
Amos
Obadiah
Jonah
Micah
Nahum
Habakkuk
Zephaniah
Haggai
Zechariah
Malachi

## GOSPELS AND ACTS

*136 pages · delivered in September 2002*

Matthew
Mark
Luke
John
Acts of the Apostles

## LETTERS AND REVELATION

*93 pages · scheduled to be delivered in July 2007*

Romans
1 Corinthians
2 Corinthians
Galatians
Ephesians
Philippians
Colossians
1 Thessalonians
2 Thessalonians
1 Timothy
2 Timothy
Titus
Philemon
Hebrews
James
1 Peter
2 Peter
1 John
2 John
3 John
Jude
Revelation

| Page No | Gathering/ folio | Description | Allocation | Time for Text | Date of Text Comp. | No of lines (Text) | No of lines (poetry) | Rubrication & footnotes | Chapter nos & caps. etc | PROOF READ | COMPLETION | Chapter & Verse |
|---|---|---|---|---|---|---|---|---|---|---|---|---|
| | | | | | | 2028 | 76 | | | | | |
| Matthew 25 | C1 (h) r. | Text | Brian | ✓ 10 hrs. 30 mins | 29.2.00 | 102 | 3 | ✓ 2 hrs | | ✓ | | 26:35-75 27:1-5 |
| Matthew 26 | C1 (f) v. | Text | Brian | ✓ 9 hrs. 30 mins | 2.3.00 | 108 | | ✓ " | | ✓ | | 27:6-56 |
| Matthew 27 | C2 (f) r. | Text + decoration | Brian | 8 hrs | 7.3.00 | 65 | | ✓ 1¼ hrs. | | ✓ | | 27:57-66 28:1-20 |
| Mark frontispiece | C2 (h) v. | Illumination | DJ | | — | | | | | — | | |
| Mark 1 | C3 (h) r. | Incipit + Text | DJ | ✓ | 16.1.01 | 30 | | ✓ 1hr. | | ✓ | | Mark 1:1-30 |
| Mark 2 | C3 (f) v. | Text | Sally | | 28.6.01 | 104 | | | | ✓ | | 1:31-45 2:1-28 |
| Mark 3 | C3 (f) r. | Illum. (Sower + Seed) + Text | Sally | | 1.7.01 | 76 | | | | ✓ | | 3:1-35 4:1-4 |
| Mark 4 | C3 (h) v. | Text | Sally | | 26.6.01 | 102 | 3 | | | ✓ | | 4:5-41 5:1-13 |
| Mark 5 | C2 (h) r. | Illum. (Two cures) + Text | Sally | | 27.6.01 | 69 | | | | ✓ | | 5:14-43 |
| Mark 6 | C2 (f) v. | Illum. (loaves Fishes) + Text | Sally | | 2-04-02 | 80 | | 11½ hrs | | ✓ | | 6:1-34 |
| Mark 7 | C1 (f) r. | Illum. " + Text | Sally | | 08-4-02 | 76 | | 10½ hrs | | ✓ | | 6:35-56 7:1-15 |
| Mark 8 | C1 (h) v. | Text + decoration | Brian | ✓ — | 06-05-00 | 98 | | ✓ 12½ hrs | | ✓ | | 7:16-37 8:1-25 |
| Mark 9 | D1 (h) r. | Text | Brian | ✓ — | 10-05-00 | 106 | | ✓ 13 hrs | | ✓ | | 8:26-38 (9:1-32) |
| Mark 10 | D1 (f) v. | Illumination (Transfiguration) | Sue | writing/one first | — | | | | | — | | |
| Mark 11 | D2 (f) r. | Text | Sue | | 22-05-01 | 106 | | 8 hrs 30 | | ✓ | | (9:33-50) 10:1-31 |
| Mark 12 | D2 (h) v. | Text | Sue H | ✓ 6hrs. 40 | | 101 | 6 | ✓ 2 hrs | | ✓ | | 10:32-52 11:1-23 |
| Mark 13 | D3 (h) r. | Text + decoration | Sue H | ✓ 6 hrs | 28.2.00 | 86 | 4 | ✓ 1¼ hrs | | | | 11:24-33 12:1-27 |
| Mark 14 | D3 (f) v. | Sp. Treat. + Text | Sue | writing first | 25-05-01 | 77 | 3 | 5 hrs 15 | | | | 12:28-44 13:1-15 |
| Mark 15 | D3 (f) r. | Text | Sue | — Sue | 01-06-01 | 100 | 6 | 6 hrs 50 | | | | 13:20-37 14:1-20 |
| Mark 16 | D3 (h) v. | Text | Sue H | ✓ 6 hrs 30 mins | 29.2.'00 | 102 | 3 | ✓ 1¼ hrs | | ✓ | | 14:35-72 15:1-7 |
| Mark 17 | D2 (h) r. | Text | Sue H | ✓ 6 hrs | 18-04-00 | 105 | | ✓ 2 hrs | | | | 15:8-47 16:1-8 |
| Mark 18 | D2 (f) v. | Text + decoration | Sally | ✓ Sally | 16/03/01 | 37 | | ✓ | | ✓ | | |
| Mark 19 | D1 (f) r. | Decoration | DJ | | | | | | | — | | |
| Luke frontispiece | D1 (h) v. | Luke Illumination | DJ | | | | | | | — | | |

Brian & Chris – 6.4.'01

3758   108

24.10.00  9 completed – 15 to comp.

Pages from the Allocation Book detail each stage a Bible page passes through during production. The columns record the page number, a gathering/folio reference, a description of each page, the scribe allocated, time allowed for writing, chapter numbers, whether the page has been proofread, whether it has been completed and the chapter and verse of each page.

Sketches for the *Loaves and Fishes* illumination are spread out on a table. Early Christian mosaic fish, Native American baskets and Islamic filigree patterns combine to form a dense, interwoven texture, reflecting the diversity of images incorporated into The Saint John's Bible.

# CHAPTER 2

# A VISIT TO THE SCRIPTORIUM

O N February 24, 2000, I looked out the window of a train heading westward across England. The landscape was bare, brown and grey in the soft winter daylight. We passed villages with ancient church towers. Electric pylons marched across the countryside. At one point the train stopped right next to a huge industrial site. Great concrete cooling towers loomed over us. A few miles on, in the distance I could make out a prehistoric chalk carving in the side of a hill: a huge white horse. The people next to me on the train were talking about university admissions. I was on my way to Wales to visit Donald Jackson's Scriptorium. The train ride provided a clue of what I would find: something completely modern with roots in something very old indeed.

Mabel, who is married to Donald, picked me up at the station. We trundled my bags into the back of her old, beat up Volvo and headed off to The Hendre Hall.

"It's been quite a week!" Mabel said and then laughed. A team of four calligraphers had arrived and begun the work of writing pages for the Bible. Only two of them were still there; the other two had decided this project wasn't for them. As we drove on, Mabel told me about the ups and downs of managing a household full of people. The Saint John's Bible is the collaborative effort of a whole team. Sally Mae Joseph is in charge of running the studio. She is Donald's only in-house scribe and illuminator. There is the team of scribes, a computer consultant, an office manager, and a whole cast of characters including the gardener, the cleaning lady, and various members of Donald's extended family. Mabel helps keep this team together by managing the household and logistics. She does it with great humor and patience.

As we traveled through the Welsh countryside, we left behind the bleak industrial landscape surrounding Newport and began to move up through hills and valleys. Soon we were deep in the countryside. The landscape is rugged and the road hugs the contours of the hills. Centuries of cultivation have left their mark on the land. We came to a crossroads where we waited for a single passing car so we could cross over. "Oh, there's traffic," Mabel said to herself.

I was arriving in the midst of a drama. Production was shifting into high gear. The preliminary design work was finished, and now Donald was training his group of scribes to begin writing out each page of the actual manuscript. The number of people working on the project was growing, and what had been a small and rather intimate process was now becoming a humming industry. The mood at The Hendre was changing as new people and new personalities were added to the team.

Mabel continued her story. Four calligraphers had come to The Hendre to take up the work. They were all professionals with great skill, but The Saint John's Bible is not like any calligraphic project any of them had worked on before. The sheer size of the project and the demands of working in a team had proved quite a challenge.

Mabel said, "One of the calligraphers actually disappeared at one point—we had to ring the police!"

"The police? Why?" I asked.

"Well, it was very worrying. He just went off one day and no one knew where he'd gone. He was struggling, I think, with the writing."

What had happened was this: the calligraphers had arrived several weeks before. Originally Donald had intended to train them for a week and then immediately set them to writing full pages of the manuscript. It had proved difficult to get the team ready to work so fast. Their different personalities had to mesh. They had to adapt quickly, not only to using new tools and materials but also to the script Donald had devised. One week of training became two and the scribes were still mastering Donald's technique. This was much more complex than anyone had thought. Not only was there the question of a large leap in skills but also the scribes were being asked to practice their craft in a collaborative workshop setting. None of the team had ever worked in a major scriptorium like this. In fact, there are no scriptoria like this—and there haven't been since the invention of movable type revolutionized book production in the fifteenth and early sixteenth centuries.

One calligrapher decided to opt out early on. Another scribe was working hard to master the script but was finding the whole set up difficult. This task was not suited to everyone's temperament and abilities. So one day he decided to take a walk, perhaps to think things through.

An hour passed and no one took much notice. Then two hours passed. The rest of the team began to get concerned. Finally, everyone set off on a search-and-find expedition and the police were called.

"He showed up hours later," Mabel said. "In the end, it was nothing; he'd just taken himself off for a walk and a breath of fresh air. We were very relieved."

He too decided to leave the project. Suddenly I knew why Donald had said to me on the phone, "You're writing about the setting of the Scriptorium? The real story is what's going on here with the calligraphers." I was to hear much more about this drama in the days which followed.

The Hendre Hall where Donald Jackson lives and works is nestled in a hollow in the Welsh countryside near Monmouth. Across the road from the Hall is a compound of working buildings where The Saint John's Bible is being made.

## An industrious household

THE CAR PULLED into the house at The Hendre Hall. Donald and Mabel live in a converted village hall, a rambling half-timbered building, beautiful against the hills which surround it. Donald keeps his own office in a wing of the Hall. Across the small road there is a group of small sheds and outbuildings, loosely grouped around a gravel courtyard and a grassy lawn. The main building is the Schoolroom, a converted mechanics' shed, which has been renovated to make a fine scriptorium. It is full of natural light with a row of desks for the scribal team. In the back are a kitchen and the space where Sally works. There is also a little room where visitors can stay.

Across from the Schoolroom stands the Black Iron Shed, built, as its name implies, of corrugated metal. It serves as a storage area. In one corner of the shed, there is a small electric griddle, filled with sand: a place to cure quills. Across the lawn, the New Shed serves as a place to prepare vellum skins for writing.

The Hendre Hall was originally part of the Rolls estate—that's the Rolls as in Rolls Royce. In the old paternalistic days of large estates, the building had been built to serve as the village hall. The people of the village lived in houses belonging to the estate. In the 1970s, before they bought and converted it, Donald and Mabel remember going to the Hall for village events, for fêtes and pantomimes. When the estate was still thriving, the outbuildings across the yard had served as sheds for mechanics who tinkered with cars. This old paternalistic world has now passed away and the estate has been broken up and sold off.

The Hendre Hall is a huge Tudor revival style building. The main space—the Hall itself—has been transformed into a large and comfortable living room. All around there remains evidence of the communal life The Hendre Hall had once hosted. Huge wooden rafters in dark wood support the tall ceiling. Small heraldic shields are carved into the woodwork. At one end there is a large raised platform to serve as a stage. All around are large windows which admit the constantly changing sunlight. The stair rails are worn smooth by decades of hands, coming and going to village events. In its present incarnation the

Donald Jackson and Sally Mae Joseph walk in the woods behind the Schoolroom. The delicate iron bridge in the foreground crosses a small brook.

* "Scrutch" rhymes with "butch."

Brian Simpson, one of the scribes, writes in the Schoolroom. The desks are carefully positioned to receive natural light from the scribe's left so his writing hand will not cast a shadow on his work.

Sally Mae Joseph, the project's senior artistic consultant, is Donald Jackson's only in-house scribe and illuminator. She uses a small knife in her left hand to hold the undulating vellum down as she writes. A small sheet of paper under her hand protects the writing surface as she works.

room is filled with couches, tables and comfortable chairs. It is a lush environment and I wanted to wander through and look at all the collections which were displayed on every surface. A set of old inkpots in cut glass caught my eye; but it was time to put down my bags in my upstairs room and head over to see The Saint John's Bible in the making.

I walked into the Schoolroom, where I found two scribes writing at their desks. The room was hushed, filled with that silence which comes of people sitting together in total concentration. Over the shoulders of the calligraphers, I could just glimpse fine columns of beautiful writing, even and clear and black against the off-white vellum.

Donald beckoned silently to me to follow him over to the New Shed, where Sally was preparing a vellum skin. It's messy work. The skins have to be sanded with several grades of sandpaper and the dust gets everywhere. Sally wore work gloves and a mask as she labored over a large calfskin. Donald's brother, who is a furniture maker, was jury-rigging a fan device to catch the flying dust. We stopped the fan.

"What do you call this process?" I asked.

"It's called 'scrutching,'" came the answer, and they all laughed. "Scrutching"* will not be found in any dictionary, but it is a perfect word to describe the scratchy, sweaty job.

Donald's eye suddenly shifted to the skin Sally was preparing. Chatting amiably one moment, he stopped. There was something amiss about the skin on the table. Sally stood aside as he picked it up.

"I think a hole is developing in the skin," he said.

He picked up the skin, running his large hands across the surface.

"Yes, I think there must have been a particle of dust underneath; there's a small flaw. You'll have to be careful of that spot."

He looked at the surface of the formica table on which Sally was working. A fine layer of dust had accumulated on the tabletop. Perhaps indeed a small lump of vellum dust had sat under the surface and the sanding had thinned the skin a trifle too much.

"Every skin is just a bit different," Donald said. "It's a living thing. It's not like this table top." He tapped the formica surface. "This is the kind of perfection we're used to, mechanical, cold, flawless." He continued drumming his fingers along the tabletop. "We can't achieve that here. It's not what we're about."

"Perfection is not an option," Sally said and everyone laughed. This had become their watchword. The perfection of the craftsman is something we're not used to anymore, living in a formica world.

The Bible is being written in the ancient manner on calf skins. These come to The Hendre uncut: large, flat skins with rough edges. They never sit perfectly flat, but always retain just a bit of flexibility. Part of Sally's job is to select a skin for each folio of the book. All of the skins are of the highest quality available, smooth, off-white and without blemishes, holes or markings. The thickness of the vellum can vary, both between skins and even within each skin. Sally selects thicker skins to take large illuminations; the thicker skins are more stable and able to withstand paint and gilding better. Each skin has to be sanded to raise the fiber a bit, giving the skin a soft, almost velvety nap. This gives the scribe a surface with some 'tooth' to aid the writing. Areas which will be illuminated need less of this nap and are sanded more delicately.

Unlike a printed book in which a kind of slick perfection is sought after, a manuscript begins with a material which is organic, variable and has a life of its own. Over time, once The Saint John's Bible is bound, the vellum pages will slowly mold to each other, creating a gently undulating regularity. Making the Bible is more like gardening than engineering; it is about working with materials which have personalities of their own. Donald's task is to work with these natural materials, to make them work in harmony, just as he has to pull his team of scribes into a kind of harmony.

At lunchtime I went up to the Hall to eat with Donald and the family while the scribal team ate down at the Schoolroom. The kitchen at the Hall, like the living room, is filled with objects. His daughter Carmen has painted an inscription along the top of the walls in an art nouveau style listing various English foods. Mabel laid out a simple lunch of soup, bread and cheese. It felt very—as the English would say—homely. As we chatted over lunch, I could sense how special this place was. There are not many households like this one anymore, in which work and family, labor and meals hold together as an organic whole.

## Creating a contemporary Scriptorium

AFTER LUNCH, I asked Donald to tell me more about the work with his scribal team. His cheeks puffed slightly as he let out a long, steady stream of air.

"The thing is," he explained to me, "calligraphers aren't trained for this kind of work. Who are the great calligraphers? Thomas Ingmire, Denis Brown. Great personalities, unique personalities. But here on this project I want people to understand, 'It is not my idiosyncrasies which are valued, but my consistency and the group harmonic.'"

Donald compared the task at hand to the work of professional musicians. If you are hired to be part of a band, you know how to pick up your instrument and join in. You adjust to the rhythms of the group and you're ready to play on an afternoon's notice.

Donald Jackson and Sally Mae Joseph examine a small computer printout of the first volume. Visual references and sketches for the illuminations are spread out on the table in front of them.

During the design process small-scale mock-ups of each volume help Donald Jackson and his team make visual decisions and keep track of production. During the design process this print out of Gospels and Acts was pinned to the studio wall. It was used for the allocation and distribution of guest artists' work and then served as a visual record of the completion of written pages and illuminations.

The Gospels and Acts studio working dummy, a large printout arranged in folios and gatherings, was used to guide the selection and ruling up of skins, and for recording finished capitals, chapter numbers and running headlines. It is decorated with a photocopy of Aidan Hart's sketch for *The Sower and the Seed* and a tiny image of a monk reading. Donald Jackson has splashed Sally Mae Joseph's name across the top in a spontaneous and vigorous italic hand.

Calligraphers by contrast usually work by themselves. Their training is often based on a careful, detailed analysis of the letterforms they are trying to use. This leads to a great deal of examination of pen angle, the width of the strokes, the shapes of the arches and all the minutiae which make up a well thought-through calligraphic script.

"I am also looking for a team which can be responsive to me. They need to show a willingness to empty themselves, so I can take them where we need to go together."

Donald turned to the working habits he wanted people to develop in the Scriptorium.

"All movements have to be efficient. I watched some of them at the beginning. They put their ink over there," he said, gesturing to his left. "Then they would pick up their pen and brush, lean over to put the brush in the ink, readjust themselves in front of their writing, load their pen and then begin to write." His body became more and more contorted as he acted this out; his back and shoulders swayed back and forth as he mimed this complicated set of movements.

"That's three or four steps before you even begin writing. Instead, I asked them to put their ink right near by where they could dip the pen in a single gesture and carry on writing."

I had seen the arrangement he'd made for himself at one of the desks. It was a small chair with two cardboard boxes, one duct-taped to the seat and the other to the back of the chair. Elegant it was not; but it was very, very practical. There is another kind of elegance which comes of a craftsman setting up an efficient workspace. It was sturdy and it held everything he needed to write with. Everything was within arm's reach, without the writer having to move from a writing position.

Donald turned to the attitudinal shift he was trying to develop in his team.

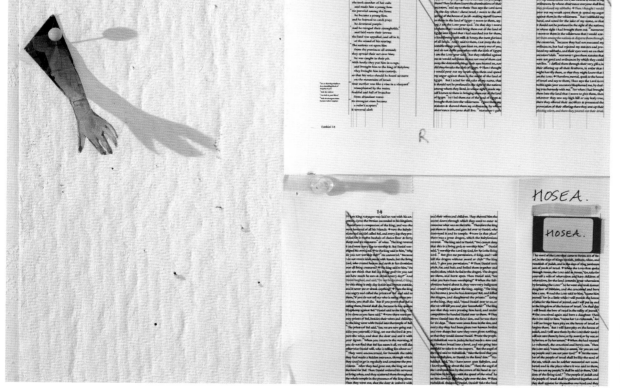

A tiny drawn hand, left over
from the rough drawings for the
*Resurrection* illumination, is pinned
to the wall near a computer printout of the books of the Prophets.

"I'm looking for a deeper perfection. Not superficial perfection. They have to let go of what makes them feel safe," Donald said. We were back to the subject he'd mentioned while drumming on the Formica table in the New Shed. The fact is we are so used to mechanical perfection, the flawless regularity of the machine age, that we have to reaccustom ourselves to working in a pre-industrial manner.

"I would watch people go back into an analytical mode. It's just not appropriate here," Donald said. The analytical approach in which most English calligraphers are trained has a lot to do with trying to achieve a mechanical kind of perfection.

Donald continued, "The problem is, you can't sustain the analytical approach over time. When you have a whole page to write, you can't continue analyzing what you're doing. Sometimes the vellum skins are dodgy; they have rough parts and smooth parts, and you just have to keep going."

One of the problems in setting up this Scriptorium is that there isn't a large pool of people to draw from. This has a lot to do with the difficulty of earning a living at calligraphy. Without a large, sustainable market for the work, people aren't used to functioning in this kind of sustained way. Donald is one of the few scribes who have pushed their craft far enough—and who have brought enough business savvy to the enterprise—to be able to make a career of it.

"Calligraphers simply aren't paid enough for what they do," he said. He was right. The average calligrapher barely makes a living at professional lettering. It is often treated as a passionate vocation rather than as a profession.

Donald continued, "As a result, it's very hard for most calligraphers to sit down and turn out the work." They are used to taking a long time over projects, doing it as much for the love of the craft as for any hope of being paid for it. Calligraphers on the whole work alone in a studio at home. This makes it particularly hard for them to come in and immediately slip into the collective work of a major scriptorium. The Saint John's Bible demands a kind of collaborative effort which just doesn't happen elsewhere.

I wandered back down to the Schoolroom. Chattering came from the back kitchen, where the scribes were taking a break with Olivia Edwards, who was the office manager at the time. Sally made me a cup of tea and I sat down at the table. Sue Hufton, one of the scribes, plopped a bag of dried figs onto the table along with a bag of dried sunflower seeds. A box of liquorice appeared and made the rounds. Brian Simpson, the other scribe, joined us. The room was full of happy energy, a well-earned break from the intense concentration of several hours of writing.

"How's it been going?" I asked.

"It's not perfect, but we just have to keep going," Sue said.

Olivia from the office added, "I think we all have to. I hit a moment about two weeks ago when I really needed reassurance."

"I know," said Sally. "I just felt totally useless."

"Well, I'm the only one who *is* totally useless!" Brian chimed in and everyone laughed. Brian is much older than the rest of the team and brings a lifetime of craftsmanship and good sense to the job. He often drops the right remark into a conversation to lighten the tone and set people at ease.

We began to talk about how the work had progressed.

Sue said, "It's not easy to be put back into a student role when you've been working for a long time. I noticed when we got here that Donald slipped automatically into the teacher mode, and I think some of us had a hard time with that; but we had to be receptive to Donald and what he was doing."

The tiny desiccated body of a newt rests atop Chris Tomlin's sketchbook and a sheaf of writing samples.

Originally all the scribes were to have been given a sample of the script to look at before they arrived. Ten days before the team arrived at The Hendre everyone had been given a paragraph of writing to study but Donald had said, "This isn't resolved. It's not an exemplar." Donald had been designing the script as he went along; it was not fixed, but evolving. This fluidity in the script had given a lot of the team a hard time.

"But Donald is very forgiving of mistakes. He gave each of us a lot of rope; but he also always left the door open," Sue commented.

When the team had arrived to begin its training, some of the scribes had tried to analyze the hand, but it was inconsistent. The writing varied, with different shapes of arches, different strokes at the end of the letters, and all sorts of variants. I could see on a table the study sheets he had worked out with them. They were a mass of small fragments of letters, mere notations of a living practice of writing.

And yet, looking at sample pages Donald had written, I saw the texture of the script was remarkably even, while the writing remained incredibly alive, fluent and spontaneous. I could see how hard it would be for the calligraphers on the team to capture this spirit. Learning to write in this way was about learning to follow Donald's adage: "Thinking doesn't happen from the neck up." I remembered what he had said to me: "It's not about pen angle, nib width or the structure of arches. It's about achieving a certain feeling." In a lively mixed metaphor, he said, "In a hundred years, when they look at the manuscript, it's the feeling they're going to hear."

That night Donald and Mabel took everyone out to the pub for dinner. The name of the local pub is "The Halfway House," which sounds rather dire, until you realize that it is halfway between Monmouth and Abergavenny. We gathered around the log fire and had drinks before dinner. We sat down to a simple and hearty meal, and talked about everything but the Bible.

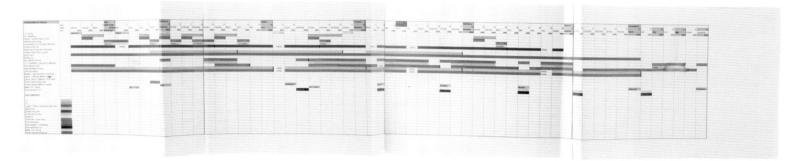

## *Perfection is not an option*

THE NEXT MORNING, I wandered around the Schoolroom as everyone worked, watching the scribes writing, examining the finished pages and reading through some of the theological briefs for the illuminations prepared by the Committee on Illumination and Text at Saint John's. Glancing up from these, I saw that each person sitting at their desk had their own body language. Brian sat absolutely still, perfectly calm, with a relaxed but concentrated expression on his face. Sue looked serious, deeply pensive and her body seemed ever so slightly tense as she wrote. And Donald—how can I describe it?—although he was sitting in the same position as the others, his eyes intent on his work, he exuded a physicality I didn't sense in the others. His large hands seemed to caress the vellum. From time to time he would stop and run his hands across the skin. I could see, looking at him, that he wasn't thinking "from the neck up." Years ago, he described to me writing with a quill on vellum as having the feeling of "running the flat of your fingernail softly down a baby's back." And here he was, doing just that—gently working the quill across the skin with enormous control and equal vitality, bringing this Bible to birth.

Not wanting to disturb the work which was going on, I sat down in the kitchen of the Schoolroom, made myself a cup of tea, and spent some time looking at the computer layout pages and the theological briefs which set out themes for the illuminations. The computer printouts were interesting. Most calligraphic books in this day and age are fairly simple affairs, and once the basic formats have been determined, the writing can be done without further planning. In the case of The Saint John's Bible, because it is such a huge undertaking, the layout for every page has to be determined before any writing can take place.

With the precision of a battle plan, a flow chart details the various stages of production for the entire Bible project.

Another record book holds details of the folios taken away by scribes after each visit to work on in their own studios.

One reason for this careful formatting is the set of exacting requirements demanded by the committee which holds the copyright of the New Revised Standard Version (NRSV). They set stringent guidelines for layout which have to be respected, even in this unique hand-made book. Formats need to be prepared and proofread to make sure all the NRSV requirements have been met on each page.

There is another reason formatting has to be done first on the computer. In order to parcel out pages to individual scribes on the team, the text has to be fixed, down to each line break. This also allows pages to be written out of sequence. Once the team had mastered the script, they would begin taking pages home with them; the bulk of the writing would be done on their own and they would return at intervals to compare and examine their work and to pick up fresh sheets of vellum. The layout had to be completely fixed beforehand.

"Vin" Godier is the computer expert who produces the layout pages. He uses Sanvito, a multiple master typeface, which very closely approximates the spacing of the manuscript hand. Twenty-first century technology serves the ancient art of writing by hand.

So I settled in to look at these computer printouts, comparing them to finished pages of the book. As I sat there over my cup of tea, Sally and Donald quietly came into the room and went over to Sally's desk. They put a page of the manuscript onto the desk, and began discussing what they saw. They talked in hushed tones for about half an hour before I noticed something was amiss.

"That's right," Sally said.

"Yes, but this is about a centimeter out of line," replied Donald.

Sally frowned without saying a word. Donald was very calm but it was clear something had gone wrong. I watched from the kitchen table, not wanting to interrupt. I slowly realized that Donald had written a whole page, only to have Sally discover that she had ruled the columns ever so slightly off square. The lines themselves were perfectly square and true. But the columns, which are long, weren't quite at ninety degree angles to the straight lines of writing. The cumulative mistake meant that while the columns lined up at the top, they were five to ten millimeters from where they should be at the bottom. Visually, this was so minor that it was hardly noticeable, except that the pages had to be ruled up on the opposite side. Vellum being slightly translucent, any writing shows through slightly; this would highlight the fact that columns on either side of this sheet didn't line up properly.

Because vellum is a natural material, it never sits completely flat. Any turning of the page means it settles on the desk differently. Ruling up such a supple material is almost as subtle and difficult as ruling up a piece of fabric—it just doesn't stay still. Moisture also affects the skins, which swell and stretch in high humidity and shrink in dry weather. Even if a skin were perfectly ruled one day, by the next it might have slightly moved.

Silence fills the Schoolroom as scribes write at their desks with complete concentration.

Computer printouts on the wall of the Schoolroom show the layout of the first volume at a glance. Each row of sheets is a single book from the volume—Matthew, Mark, Luke, John and Acts of the Apostles. Blank spaces indicate where the illuminations will appear in the finished manuscript. Small colored rectangles mark the position of small decorative details.

Sue came in after a while and pointed out that, having spent the better part of an hour and a half discussing the problem, perhaps it would be better just to re-rule a sheet and do the page over. I noticed no one took her up on this offer. After a bit Donald went back up to the main house. He wasn't angry; he knew this was simply part of the learning curve.

Sue might have repeated the mantra "Perfection is not an option," but probably thought better of it under the circumstances.

Sally came over to the table, clearly not pleased with what had happened.

"I suppose it was good that it happened to one of Donald's sheets rather than to Sue or Brian. That would have been worse," I said.

"You're telling me," Sally answered, as she reached for a rice cake. She munched on it silently as the rest of us chatted about other things.

Later, at lunchtime, Sally waited for Sue and Brian to be out of the room and she went from desk to desk, measuring the line ruling on everyone's pages. There were slight variations in their columns, but none were as far out of square as those on the page Donald had finished. Sally's relief was palpable—it was she who was responsible for the ruling up of all the pages.

An ivory-handled erasing knife sits next to a small jar containing a sample of Japanese sumi ink. If his supply of antique ink sticks ran out, Donald Jackson would have been obliged to find a modern ink to complete his seven volumes.

## Treasures

LATER THAT AFTERNOON, I asked to talk with Donald about the tools and materials he was using. I had seen the skins, but I was curious about the quills and the inks. In particular I was curious about the precious ink sticks with fine gold Chinese writing stamped on them.

Donald unwrapped a clean, black stick of ink. These needed to be ground in water in a slate inkstone

Donald Jackson works at his tilted desk in the Schoolroom.

to make each day's portion of writing ink. Donald had more than one hundred of these, from a shop in Camden Town, London, called Roberson's.

Donald told me, "Roberson's were old-fashioned artist's colormen whose shop had been open since 1810. They supplied famous Victorian artists like Lord Leighton (the academic painter). In fact Lord Leighton's palette, which he had signed and given to the shop, still hung over the counter."

When Donald shopped there in the sixties and seventies, the proprietor was already old. The sticks had been brought over from China by sail with shipments of tea in the time of his father. Donald bought a large supply of ink sticks at two shillings apiece.

Once the project was underway, it became clear there would not be enough ink sticks to complete all seven volumes. Donald had some research done. The ink sticks turned out to be extremely valuable collectors' items. There was no way they could afford to buy more.

During one of Sally Mae's Bible presentations, she showed a picture of the stick ink and talked about its unique qualities and the problems of supply. From the back of the room a voice spoke up "I think I have some of those sticks." It was the voice of a calligrapher who had worked with Donald some years before. He had given her a quantity of the sticks but she had never used them. So she donated them to the project.

Later two other calligraphers to whom Donald had given ink sticks donated theirs as well. Those sticks sat in drawers around the world waiting to come home to complete The Saint John's Bible—a valuable gift to the project.

The vermilion Donald uses comes from another artist's supplier. The firm which manufactured the vermilion cakes closed in 1867, and the shopkeeper who had this rare supply was wary of parting with too many at a time.

"I used to go in and buy just enough not to arouse his suspicion. Then I'd send one of my friends in to buy some. But then you had to wait a decent time before going in again, or he would refuse to sell you any." Eventually, when the shop was to close, Donald offered to buy the lot at seven-and-six per cake (which is seven shillings, sixpence in the predecimal English coin) and was refused. After the shop closed Donald tracked down the whereabouts of the remaining stock to find that the old man had been hoarding over two-thousand cakes of the precious color and he was able to buy the lot for a fraction of the original cost.

These cakes were exquisite. Brilliantly red-orange, they were pressed into molds and were as clean and shiny as mint coins. Each was carefully wrapped in paper. Donald has enough in reserve to last him the remainder of his professional life.

## Breaking the tension

BRIAN AND SUE went home in mid-afternoon on Friday. They would return the following Monday to continue work. The last event of my visit was the Friday afternoon planning meeting with Olivia, Sally and Donald.

As we settled into comfortable chairs in The Hendre Hall, everyone was relaxed and there was a lot of laughter in the room. Olivia led the meeting, raising the various subjects for discussion and decision. There were many logistical issues to resolve. Donald was preparing to go to America for a major promotional tour—how was he going to balance that with the need to spend time working on the project itself? They discussed ways to handle the film crew which was about to descend on them to shoot a documentary. As they worked out a plan for the American tour, they also discussed the progress report they would file with Saint John's that afternoon.

The conversation began to wander from the agenda. Someone mentioned that the illumination of the Baptism of Christ included a full-length portrait of John the Baptist—how would Donald handle the image, they wondered?

"I bet he was thin," someone said. "He was probably in pretty good shape, with his healthy, outdoor lifestyle."

A light moment at the Scriptorium. Team members assemble for a group shot, holding a folded printout of one of the Bible volumes.

Someone else pointed out that his hair shirt was probably a rather slinky number. This idea of John the Baptist as a New Testament Leonardo DiCaprio set Olivia and Sally off and everyone laughed. It was good for them to break the tension of the morning and put the problem of the slightly skewed columns behind them.

In the two days I spent at The Hendre, Donald introduced me to a community of people who were being molded into a team to produce a work of great craftsmanship. They are using all the resources available to make something which is grounded in the ancient tradition of calligraphy, yet which is also entirely up-to-date. There's nothing at all nostalgic about it—it's hard work, with production schedules, computers, visiting television crews and tight deadlines. And yet it is also a place where they are rediscovering the techniques of the medieval scriptorium. It is a place of quills, vellum, rare vermilion and hundred-year-old sticks of ink. What better setting could there be to create a twenty-first century, living Bible?

A hanging flower basket stands out against the grey stone wall of the Schoolroom.

The technique of manufacturing vellum has remained almost unchanged since the Middle Ages. All of the great medieval manuscripts—the Book of Kells, the Lindisfarne Gospels or the Winchester Bible, for example—were written on such skins. In our modern era, there is still no better surface for fine writing. This room at William Cowley Parchment and Vellum Works in Newport Pagnell, England, is filled with hundreds of finely prepared skins.

# CHAPTER 3

# IN SEARCH OF
# THE PERFECT WRITING SURFACE

I ASKED Donald why he chose to write The Saint John's Bible on vellum.

"I've thought of all the possibilities," he said. "I considered setting the whole thing in type and let-ting the hard, metal letters press sculpturally into soft paper. Or writing on mylar plastic—I've done it; it takes writing beautifully."

So why vellum? Some calligraphers use vellum because of the sheer weight of tradition. Vellum has always been considered the most exquisite writing material. Others choose vellum because of their arts and crafts movement convictions. It is an anti-industrial statement. It harks back to a simpler time of indi-vidual scribes using organic tools and materials in a holistic way. It connects them to something founda-tional in the western tradition and evokes a kind of spirituality of work.

For Donald the question is more open. What effects does he want to achieve, and what material will let him do those things best? If this means a return to the most traditional of writing surfaces, he needs to know it is because that surface can do things no other surface can. Deeply imbued with the ethos of the working craftsman, Donald needs, nonetheless, as a contemporary artist, to use whatever means he can find to make work of his own era. This means that despite years of working on vellum, he still had to explore the question of why this particular surface was right for The Saint John's Bible.

I remember talking to Donald once after he'd done a large manuscript book on paper. "I have a new respect for calligraphers who work on paper," he said. "Paper is so much more demanding— scary, even. If you make a mistake, you're finished." Paper, with its more fragile surface, can withstand only the gen-tlest of corrections; erasures leave rough patches, which can only be smoothed with painstaking effort. Its clean, hard finish leaves the letters isolated against the background. The surface itself, lacking any vari-ation of tone, gives no visual anchor for the text which sits on it. Paper can also raise problems of sharp-ness, especially with small writing. The natural absorbency of paper resists the scribe's efforts to produce perfectly sharp, crisp stroke endings.

Vellum, by contrast, while it is a most demanding material, responds as no other surface can to the ministrations of the pen. The quill and ink cut gently into the fine, raised nap of the prepared vellum sur-face, allowing the writing to be sharp and subtle. In its own way, vellum guides the movement of the pen in the scribe's hand. It allows just a hint of writing to show through from one side to the other, creating a gentle grid which lightly ghosts through from one page to the next. At the same time, it is enormously strong, and able to withstand the work of many hands. What sheet of paper could take the kind of labor expended on a single page of The Saint John's Bible? Many hands work their way across the surface of every page, writing text, adding marginal notes and small colored capitals, illuminating and gilding.

Vellum comes in many varieties. Heavier skins are useful for bookbinding, while thin-ner skins are best for making the pages of books. The Saint John's Bible required very large unblemished skins. Donald Jackson tried the products of several makers before he found the best source.

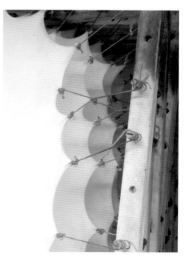

Skins stretched on frames dry taut at Cowley's.

Paper would require enormous care not to be creased or discolored in the process of passing through the hands of so many craftspeople. On vellum, mistakes can be erased with a sharp knife, leaving a surface only marginally different from surrounding areas and which can still take fine writing.

Vellum as a material is also beautiful in its own right. Its soft, variable surface is to paper as alabaster is to frosted glass. Every sheet of vellum has its own character, its own quirks, its own slight variations in tone and thickness. The incredible translucency of vellum catches the light. This is not a hard, mechanical surface but an organic substance which gives richness to the page no other material can reproduce.

Donald turned the options over in his mind. The durability of vellum is unquestioned—every major medieval manuscript is written on it. But most importantly no other material could have given him the surface qualities he needed for the book he was creating. "I've been there. I know all the disadvantages. But just like a cabinet-maker who chooses to work in elm—the grain goes crazy, and it's hard to work but he does it anyway—I choose to work in vellum. I do it for the way it responds to my hands or the work of my hands and to my senses. That's it. That's why I do it."

It is one thing to decide to use vellum; it is another thing altogether to find a reliable supply. Having settled on vellum as his material, Donald set out on a search which would put him in contact with vellum makers in Israel, Canada and Ireland before he finally found a supplier in England who was able to produce what he needed. "It's like looking for the Holy Grail," Donald says, reflecting on his quest for just the right kind of vellum for the Bible.

## The manufacture of vellum

IT IS MANY YEARS, even many centuries since vellum has been produced in the vast quantities needed for the writing of a major book like The Saint John's Bible. Even in the Middle Ages, it was no small thing to get appropriate skins. The craft of making vellum requires great skill and is very labor intensive. It requires vast amounts of water and a large supply of animal skins. Slowly but surely, the commercial suppliers of vellum and parchment have been disappearing, along with centuries of insight into the niceties of preparing skins by hand. The economics of vellum manufacturing become more tenuous every year as commercial uses of the product disappear. There was a time when legal documents throughout the western world were written or printed on vellum. Many musical instruments, especially drums, had vellum components. Gradually paper and plastics have reduced the need for the material, leaving fewer and fewer commercial outlets to suppliers. Perhaps most importantly, in a world which values economic efficiency over every other value, there is less and less room for a traditional craft which is entirely based on the one-to-one relationship between a maker and his material.

Vellum is made of the skins of calves. Any animal skin may be used—I have seen examples made of kangaroo and even ostrich. Some very fine small Books of Hours in the Middle Ages may even have been produced with squirrel skins, which could be why they are so thin and fine in texture. In contemporary practice, the most common animal skins are calf, goat and sheep. Most calligraphers today reserve the term *vellum* (related to the word *veal*) for calf skins, using the word *parchment* for other skins, especially those of sheep. In common practice the words *vellum* and *parchment* are often interchangeable, as a quick peek in the Oxford English Dictionary will demonstrate.

The basic technique of making vellum has remained unchanged for almost two thousand years. Some

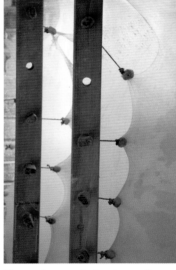

The translucency of vellum is one of its great appeals. In a manuscript book, the writing shows slightly through the page. In printed books, this would be considered a fault. In manuscripts, the show-through creates a light shadow which calligraphers value.

Donald Jackson prepares a skin using sand paper. A deep sensitivity to the qualities of the skin is essential. Every skin is unique and careful attention is required not to crease or damage it.

illuminated medieval manuscripts contain beautiful illustrations of the vellum making process which remain recognizable today. Today's makers may wear jeans and Wellington boots to work and they may have tattoos on their forearms but they still use essentially the same tools and materials that their forebears did a thousand years ago. The medieval illustrations show us exactly what still takes place.

The process starts with skins soaked in a solution of lime and water for up to two weeks.* The hair mostly falls off; what remains is scraped from the surface. They are then reimmersed in the lime solution for another fortnight. After this treatment the skins are stretched on a wooden frame. These frames are large and rectangular with pegs around all four sides. The skin is suspended in space with little cords which join the frame's pegs to small gatherings around the edges of the skin. As the skin dries, it stretches taut and flat. It is treated with pumice and water and is carefully scraped with a special knife called a *lunellum*. This knife (as the name suggests) has a crescent-shaped blade; its handle is set at ninety degrees to the plane of the blade. If the blade nicks the surface of the skin, a small hole will open up; in some manuscripts, like the Book of Kells, the scribes simply wrote around the holes. If a blood vessel has burst during the soaking process, the skin can become blotched with a deep purple bloom. Many skins bear the maker's marks of the person who scraped them. Breaking off the tines of a fork to produce a unique pattern, the maker pokes his distinct mark into the edge of the skin.

The aim of the vellum maker is to drain the skin of grease and to prepare the surface for writing. Vellum, unlike leather, loses its suppleness and becomes taut and stiff. Depending on the thickness of the skin, its stiffness can vary. Thick skins are as unyielding as cardboard; thin skins fold and bend easily.

When the skin has been repeatedly scraped, wet down and dried out, it is cut from the frame. Skins are sorted by color, weight and size. They are stacked or rolled and put into storage.

The finished skins have two distinct sides: the hair side and the flesh side. The hair side, from the exterior of the animal, has a fine, slightly slick texture and generally a soft cream-color. If any markings from the

* For the technique of manufacturing vellum, I have drawn on Christopher de Hamel's, *Illuminated Manuscripts* and on Sam Somerville's article "Parchment and Vellum" in *The Calligrapher's Handbook*.

When handled properly, vellum is enormously strong. Donald Jackson erases multiple lines from a Bible page using a sharp knife. He literally scrapes away the surface. After an erasure has been made, the skin is prepared again and new writing can be added. Paper would not easily stand up to such intrusive treatment.

animal remain, they sometimes show on this side either as a network of very fine black dots or as soft, cloud-like areas of light brown or grey. The flesh side has a somewhat rougher texture and is generally a purer white than the hair side. Good skins for writing are slightly velvety to the touch; the issue of "raising the nap" of the skin is of crucial importance to the scribe. The vellum manufacturers prepare the skin to various degrees, some offering skins almost ready for writing, others leaving the finish, especially on the hair side, slightly greasy and slick, allowing for the calligrapher to make his or her own adjustments.

The skins in their rough-cut state retain the overall shape of the animal. To a calligrapher with a trained eye, the roughly rectangular shape betrays the places where neck, tail and limbs once extended from the hide. Along the spine the skin is often slightly thicker; sometimes slight stretch marks indicate the underbelly. The skin is also subtly variable in its thickness from one end to the other; the shoulder end is generally thicker than the tail end. Along the edge of the rough-cut skin, the margins can become almost translucent. This horn-like area is useless for writing and must be trimmed from the final page.

Among its quirks as a material for writing, vellum is very susceptible to moisture. In dry weather it shrinks, becoming hard and stiff, even brittle. In damp weather it expands, becoming soft and supple. When soaked in water, it returns to its original state as a completely limp, flexible hide; it needs to be restretched if the calligrapher wants a flat writing surface. Because it reacts so strongly to moisture, it needs to be stored in rooms with stable humidity and the calligrapher has to be very careful about the amount of liquid which comes into contact with the page. This is a particular concern when illuminations or gilding are called for.

When using vellum, the calligrapher needs to know the material intimately with all its strengths and weaknesses. As the scribe writes, he or she becomes involved closely with the surface, aware of its every shift in thickness and texture. The pen glides across rough areas and smooth. It reacts differently on either side of the skin. Every skin is unique, individual. The calligrapher learns over time to react to each idiosyncrasy of the page and to accept the inevitable variations which the surface dictates in their writing.

The raw skins are soaked in a solution of lime and water for several weeks. The hair falls off and fat is drawn out of the skin.

## The search for vellum makers

BEFORE HE COULD BEGIN The Saint John's Bible, Donald needed to find a reliable source for large amounts of vellum. For the ordinary scribal job the task of finding the right skin is simple. Going through the available skins, the calligrapher usually only needs to find a single sheet which meets the task. But this job was different. Donald needed to supply his Scriptorium with a huge number of skins, all of which had to be of a matching standard. There were to be no markings on the hair side. All the skins had to be even in texture, thickness and color. There could be no holes in the skins (despite the example of the Book of Kells!). In addition, Donald had decided on a huge page size—fifteen and seven-eighths inches wide by twenty-four-and-a-half inches tall. This meant that the skins had to be at least twenty-seven-and-a-half inches by thirty-five inches in order to allow each sheet to be folded once, as well as allowing a small working margin of one-and-a-half inches all around. This large measurement put Donald's requirements right at the outer limit of available skins. But it was not simply a question of finding the right number of skins or of finding skins of the right size. More pressing was to find a supplier who was still making skins which were acceptable for writing at all.

"What about the Irish source?" I asked Donald in a conversation at The Hendre. I knew there was a maker in Ireland who was very popular with students at the Roehampton Institute, one of the few places which exist to train professional calligraphers.

"I'm afraid they're basically making vellum for musical instruments; it's hit or miss when it comes to writing. They don't think like calligraphers at all. The students like them, but that's because they're not experienced enough."

Donald continued, "I tried a source in Canada as well. I have to say, he made some of the finest skins I've seen since my student days."

"Why didn't you go with him?"

A sodden skin is completely pliable.

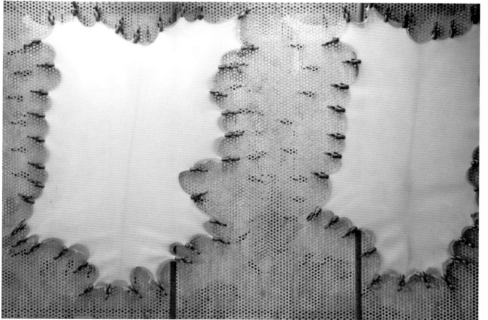

Even when the hair has been removed and the skins are ready to be scraped they recall the shape of the calf from which they came.

The skins are stretched onto wooden frames before scraping. Tiny balls of vellum off-cuts or newspaper are wrapped into gatherings made at the edges of the skin. These are then tied to the adjustable pegs lining the frame. Care is taken to ensure the tension across the skin is even so it dries perfectly flat.

"He does it in his spare time and I just wasn't sure he could produce skins in the quantity I needed them."

While the writing quality of the Canadian skins had been excellent, the samples that he'd been sent weren't quite the right size. He needed to consider other makers, people who could produce two-hundred-fifty skins of uniform quality at the large size required.

The next logical step was Israel.

Israeli Jews produce a massive amount of vellum to satisfy the religious market; Judaism requires the use of vellum for a huge range of ritual goods. The Torah must be written by hand on scrolls of vellum, as must the tiny *mezuzot* which hang on the doors of observant Jewish homes. Tiny inscriptions on vellum are wrapped in the phylacteries used for prayer. With this religiously sanctioned tradition in place, Jewish artists also produce wedding contracts and other Judaica on fine skins. There is a massive demand for calligraphy on vellum, and a working, living tradition of the *soferim*—ritual scribes[*]—to meet this demand. In addition to the *soferim* who work within the religious community under the strictest guidelines, there is a wider community of Israeli artists in Jerusalem who draw inspiration from the formal calligraphic tradition and use vellum in painting, drawing and lettering.

Donald went to Jerusalem where he was guided around the calligraphic scene by Izzy Pludwinski, a *sofer* in his own right. Together they went to the religious neighborhood of Mea Shearim. Located within walking distance of the Old City, its streets are narrow and not very clean. The buildings are mostly less than a hundred years old. Sometimes it is hard to believe you are still in Jerusalem; the streets could almost be in Crown Heights in New York or in any dusty, gritty Levantine city. And yet there is a very unusual air about the place. Large signs posted about the streets ask women to dress modestly out of respect for the religious views of the people of the neighborhood. Most of the women in the street are dressed in dark clothing, their hair carefully covered even in the heat of Jerusalem. The men, from various sects of Eastern European Jewry, wear long beards and wide-brimmed black hats. Their curly forelocks dance as they rush down the streets. Their coats come in many forms, from long black formal coats, reaching mid-calf, to robes of striped grey, almost like dressing gowns. The streets are filled with specialist shops, mostly tiny and dark, selling religious books and supplies. Ritual silver and beautiful prayer shawls are for sale. Heavy tomes for Talmudic scholars fill shop windows. If you are a man without a *kippeh*, or *yalmulke*, and you enter one of the small shops, small children may come and stare.

Everywhere you turn, there are the *yeshivot*—schools for studying Torah according to the various traditions of the neighborhood. Earnest men can be seen through the windows, poring over scrolls and massive copies of the Talmud. Mea Shearim is a place where religious observance is the dominating fact of life, a place for a people who have set themselves apart in order to pursue their particular understanding of what life should be.

Izzy led Donald into this foreign world, taking him to two of the more important parchment outlets of Mea Shearim. As they arrived at one outlet, so did Izzy's friend Mala, an artist who often works on vellum herself. They walked into the first of the outlets, and Donald was amazed at the scene.

"Here was a living tradition," Donald said. "Shelves were stocked with turkey quills, and there were rolls and rolls of vellum around. It fitted. I felt like I was at home. Calligraphers were scurrying in and out, paying for their supplies. Unlike going to western art shops or vellum suppliers, here I felt there was a real understanding of what I, as a scribe, was looking for. The skins *looked* right; they had an authentic

[*]The singular of the Hebrew word for scribe is *sofer*; the plural is *soferim*.

feel; they looked like the old manuscripts. There's also the whole question of secularity. I go to a western vellum supplier, and he says to me, 'I'm making this for cricket bat handles.' By contrast I go to Israel and here people are saying, 'In God's name, I'm asking you for this; it will be a Torah.' It felt more comfortable, more like what I'm after."

Izzy introduced Donald to the owner. The shop was a family business and several generations worked together there. Mala spoke up and wanted the owner to know that this was a *very important* western scribe he was dealing with. Speaking in Hebrew, she laid it on thick, playing up Donald's many commissions for the Queen of England. The old man behind the counter was unimpressed. "So?" he said, "Okay, I'll give him *two* chairs to sit on!"

These preliminaries done with, they quickly set to business. Skins were pulled from the shelves. They were very fine. The Israeli skins are prepared for writing on only one side, on the flesh side, but the parchment dealers said they could prepare both sides if need be. They could also arrange for skins large enough for Donald's needs.

"Where do the skins come from?" Donald asked.

"From Chicago," came the answer. The Israeli vellum makers import the raw skins from the huge abattoirs of the American Midwest; local supplies are too meager for their needs. The untanned skins arrive from Chicago, packed in brine and ready for processing.

The conversation was fruitful and the parchmenters[*] were very helpful but Donald had some qualms about what he saw. Many of the skins on offer were so specifically made for their Jewish context that they wouldn't work in the way Donald needed them to. Israelis design their vellum with the *sofer* market in mind. They even supply some skins pre-scored for *mezuzot*—saving the *sofer* time in ruling up.

"In the end, though I liked the skins, I couldn't use them," Donald said to me months later. "They are culturally specific. They don't give me the qualities I need in a skin. They seemed too rough on the flesh side and too absorbent on the hair side."

He continued, "The Israeli vellum is sanded in one direction. This matches the strong horizontal stroke of Hebrew calligraphy. The nap runs in a single direction and you are writing against the nap.

"The most serious problem was that the parchmenter told me the skins couldn't take any moisture; moisture leads to extreme cockling. When I got home and we tried it, it was true. The skins reacted strongly to the painting and cockled. Gilding worried me most. I suspected it would just pop off the skins."

In the Jewish religious tradition these parchmenters served, there is no need for decoration. The skins simply aren't prepared with the idea of illumination and gilding in mind. Donald suggested that the Israeli skins were stretched more tightly than the western skins and thus when they were exposed to moisture, they reacted more strongly.

"Also you must remember," Donald told me, "that there is a relationship between quill, ink and vellum. These three elements have to work together. The Israeli skins were designed to work with Israeli ink. Working on the flesh side of the skin with its heavy nap, they use an ink with a high gum content. The viscosity of that particular ink works well on skins with a strong nap.

"I also had two questions about the Israeli ink. One was very basic: is this archival? Is it acid? I couldn't guarantee that it wouldn't eat into the skins over time. The second question was aesthetic. The *sofer* ink is shiny, and it dries raised; it doesn't lie flat on the page. It wasn't the look I wanted to achieve."

[*] "Parchmenter" is an old English term for a person who deals in vellum and parchment; it is the primary term Donald used to describe the vellum dealers of Mea Shearim. Interestingly, when talking of his English suppliers, Donald rarely uses the term. The traditional scribal atmosphere of the shops in Mea Shearim evokes that lost world of stationers who once supplied western calligraphers and scriveners with vellum. By contrast the more industrial world of western vellum makers seems one step removed from scribal lore and practice.

So Donald was back to square one.

The next logical place to try was also the closest to home: Cowley's in Newport Pagnell, a three-hour drive from Wales. They had the largest available selection of skins prepared in the western manner Donald was accustomed to. Having made the decision to go with Cowley's, Donald had to consider very carefully what kinds of skins he needed. This wasn't just a scouting expedition; it was time to get very particular about the skins that would be chosen.

"I rang them up and told them what we were looking for," Donald told me. His first concern was the size of the available skins. At the large size he was looking for it was hard to find skins that were thin and supple enough; large skins come from large animals and they tend to be thicker and tougher. Then the skins had to be free of markings on the hair side and without structural weaknesses; there had to be no evidence of overstretching or any thin patches in the skin.

Donald and Sally made two visits to Cowley's. In order to speed up the selection, they brought with them a flat wooden frame which they used as a template. The frame was several inches larger than the trimmed page size of the finished book. Fine threads stretched inside the frame indicated the trim margins. Laying the frame on top of each skin, they could see immediately whether it had the right dimensions. They could also see if any flaws in the skin appeared within the trim area. They were especially concerned that none of the "horny" areas of skin would intrude; these areas, besides standing out with their different texture and color, also absorb moisture differently. If they are included within the final trimmed area, they produce a structural weakness in the book. As the rest of the page expands and contracts with changes in humidity, these areas remain stubbornly unyielding, leading to a progressive cockling in the page over time. They also looked to make sure that the two thin patches which tend to develop near the neck would not be included; these tend not to lie as flat as other parts of the skin.

The stretchers are taken to a heated room where the skins dry drum-tight on their frames.

"On our first visit, it became clear we hadn't been selective enough. We went through quite a few skins and made our selection but when we brought them back to the Scriptorium, we saw all sorts of little details we hadn't seen at Cowley's." The showroom at Cowley's—if one can call it that—is simply a space attached to the vellum factory; the light is not strong and sometimes it is hard to see every detail of the skins. On their second visit he was able to go through about one hundred skins. He chose thirty skins. Of these thirty, seven had to be sent back later.

"We were fortunate to be able to have so many skins to look at," Donald told me. Cowley's produces vellum for the British Parliament which prints a vellum copy of every law as it becomes official. In a bid for modernization, the Labor government had been looking into printing the official statutes on paper and had put all the vellum orders on hold. This gave Donald a rare opportunity to select from a huge backlog of skins. Now that Parliament has decided to continue printing its laws on vellum sheets, Donald faces stiff competition for the available skins.

It could be frustrating. "The best skins always seemed to be just a quarter inch too small," Donald said. Still, one by one the skins piled up and he had a good selection of skins with which to begin the book.

## The art of scrutching

BACK AT THE SCRIPTORIUM, with a sheaf of skins to work with, the hard job of preparation had to begin. Skins come from the vellum factory prepared to a certain extent, but it's up to the calligrapher to do a final preparation before beginning to write. This stage has traditionally been called "pouncing" and involves rubbing down the skin with a mixture of abrasives to create the appropriate texture for writing. Old law scriveners used to keep a pouncing bag at their desks. This contained a mixture of powdered pumice (an abrasive), whiting (a slaked chalk which absorbs any remaining grease) and sandarac (which repels water, helping control ink flow and preventing the letters from bleeding into the skin). Dusting down the skin with this mixture, they would rub it in before starting to write. In Donald's Scriptorium, modern materials have replaced some of these elements but the principle remains the same.

Each skin is carefully examined and assigned a particular position in the book. As the pages are folded, each opening has to match—that is, hair side must be opposite hair side, flesh side opposite flesh side. Illuminations should be on slightly thicker parts of the skin than areas of pure writing; the extra thickness supports paint better. Since the vellum tends to be thicker at the neck and shoulder area and thinner at the tail end, the skins can be positioned within the manuscript to make sure that full page illuminations appear on the thicker parts of the skins. Areas to be illuminated need less preparation, while areas to receive writing require more sensitive preparation.

In the middle of our interview, Donald turned to me suddenly and said, "You know, if you're going to write about this, I think you need to experience what it's like to actually write on the vellum we're using. It's the only way to really understand what we're after." He took out a large practice sheet and prepared different areas of the skin in various ways so I could feel for myself how the writing worked. The sheet of vellum in front of me seemed huge, a full page. Just physically managing such a large skin was an issue in itself. I had to be careful not to crease it as I leaned forward to write. He prepared several areas, and encouraged me to try the hair side first, then try the flesh side. Some of the areas were carefully prepared; some over-prepared; some left almost as they came from Cowley's.

The special knife used to scrape the skins is referred to as a *lunellum*. The crescent-shaped blade is set at a ninety-degree angle to the handle. Scraping the skin is highly skilled work. A small mistake in the use of the *lunellum* can tear or cut the skin, ruining it. Exactly the same process is illustrated in medieval manuscripts.

The aim of the preparation is to create a soft, raised surface. Before it has been prepared, the skin can be too slick and shiny; the pen can get no purchase on the skin. If an area is prepared too much, however, the writing becomes difficult; the pen drags and the letters break up. Donald handed me a quill and prepared a little pool of ink, and walked off, leaving me alone to see what I could discover.

I began on a slick, horny part of the skin right at the edge. The pen had no purchase on the surface; it slid around and every quaver of my hand produced little glitches in the edges of my letters. As my pen skittered across the page the ink refused to adhere properly.

On a more thoroughly prepared section, Donald put gum sandarac on one part and left it off another part. Where the gum sandarac had been rubbed in gently, the writing was beautiful. I could feel the quill bite gently into the raised nap of the skin, slowing my hand just enough to give me control over the writing. In the area without the sandarac, the pen again skidded around and felt too loose against the surface. In one area the sandarac was purposely applied too thickly. Here, though the writing felt good, the ink didn't sit properly on the page. As it dried, a tiny white hairline appeared down the center of each stroke of the pen. The sandarac, which repels water, wouldn't allow the ink to settle in the tiny channel created by the pen.

It's an extremely delicate balance to achieve. The skin has to be sanded to raise just the right amount of nap; if it is sanded too much, the skin begins to break up, becoming too fibrous for the writing. The sandarac has to be added in just the right quantity to give a bit more tooth to the page and to keep the writing crisp and sharp. But if too much sandarac is used, the letters break up. Add to this subtle balance the fact that the skins are of different textures on hair and flesh sides and that they are also variable from one end of the skin to the other and you have an incredibly subtle and delicate job on your hands.

A mortar and pestle are used to grind the sandarac "pounce," a fine powder which is dusted onto the skins during their preparation at the Scriptorium. The little cloth pouch holds the pounce, which sifts evenly through the mesh of the fabric.

* The term 'scrutching' describes
the act of rubbing down a skin in
preparation for writing. The word
was invented by Donald's brother,
Barry.

That delicate job went first to Sally. Later other assistants took over the work of preparing skins. Work-ing in the scrutching shed,* the scrutcher first examines the whole surface of each skin. Every sheet of vellum is from an individual calf and it must be held up to the light to see where the skin is thick and where it is thin. The light shows through any tiny pin-prick holes which are already in the vellum. Then it is examined in raking light. This shows how much the nap is already raised. Are there places where the skin is "breaking up"; that is to say, are there places where the surface is already so textured that further preparation would be unwise?

The skin is then placed flesh side up on the smooth table. It is rubbed with a relatively heavy grade of sand paper (grade 240 silicone carbide), using a good deal of elbow grease. The action is very much like that of planing a piece of wood—an infinitesimally fine layer of the skin is rasped off. This raises the nap and removes any trace of sheen or chalkiness from the skin. The scrutcher checks her work as she goes, running her thumb along the surface and bending down repeatedly to see how the finish is developing. Turning the skin over to work on the hair side, she repeats the process, but this time a bit more gently.

The next step is the addition of gum sandarac. This resin has been ground with a mortar and pestle and sits to one side, wrapped in a fine-weave cloth bag. Dusting the surface with the bag causes the tiny grains to sift evenly across the surface. With a finer grade of sandpaper (grade 400 silicone carbide), she gently rubs the skin down again, this time using a circular motion. This is delicate work and she pauses more and more often to check the result. The skin should take on a soft, velvety finish. If particles of the san-

Sarah Harris at work in the scrutching shed. She works at a Formica table and sands the skins with progressively finer grades of sandpaper. The mask she wears protects her from inhaling fine particles of vellum dust.

darac build up, they can sometimes leave scratch marks. As the work proceeds, the rubbing becomes ever gentler, until the skin is absolutely ready for the scribes.

As the project continues, this process is being slowly refined. Donald feels that the sandarac should not be rubbed in with sandpaper, while the scribal team has asked on occasion for a heavier dose of sandarac. Slowly as a team they are working out the details. It may well be that each volume will be treated somewhat differently, as the best practice develops through trial, error and growing experience.

The search for the perfect writing surface is perhaps less like looking for the Holy Grail than it is an attempt to find a series of balances. Donald and his team of scribes are trying to realize an ideal. It is only when the pen begins its slow dance across the page that human skill is united to its chosen tools and materials in a way which produces something truly splendid, wondrous and yes, even holy.

The suppleness of the vellum page is apparent in this detail from an early design proposal. Properly cared for, a vellum manuscript will last for centuries.

out of the mouth that defiles." [12] Then the disciple

approached and said to him, "Do you know that

the Pharisees took offense when they heard wha

you said?" [13] He answered, "Every plant that m

heavenly Father has not planted will be uproote

[14] Let them alone; they are blind guides of the blind

And if one blind person guides another, both wil

fall into a pit." [15] But Peter said to him, "Explai

this parable to us." [16] Then he said, "Are you als

still without understanding? [17] Do you not see tha

whatever goes into the mouth enters the stomac

and goes out into the sewer? [18] But what comes ou

of the mouth proceeds from the heart, and this i

what defiles. [19] For out of the heart come evil inte

ions, murder, adultery, fornication, theft, fals

witness, slander. [20] These are what defile a person

but to eat with unwashed hands does not defile

# CHAPTER 4

# THE WORD TAKES FLESH

ORGET OLD Hollywood historical dramas and their floppy ostrich plume pens. That's not how it works. Turkeys, geese and swans provide the raw material. The barbs of the feather have to go first. All you need is the clean shaft of the quill. Nothing must interfere with the writing. Then you take a sharp quill knife and make a scooping cut on the underside of the quill. Cut the slit; cut each side; slice the end to its proper shape. Finally, cut the very tip off absolutely straight, leaving yourself a chisel-edged end. The chisel edge is the key to the whole enterprise.

Your pen doesn't look like much. It's about the size of the average pencil. It's the color of your fingernails. It weighs next to nothing. But with that clean-cut chisel-edge, you can make the most subtle and satisfying letters. Holding the quill naturally in the right hand, the writing flows with grace and ease: thick stroke, thin stroke, sliding back to thick. Undulating, modulated lines compose themselves into letters and words and sentences, knitting the page together. The words text and textile share a common root—the Latin *texere*, to weave.

## *A practice of writing*

I HAVE IN FRONT OF ME a sheaf of photocopies from the Scriptorium. They are covered with variants of the text, attempts to define the characteristics of the script. More than at any point in this project, Donald was very reticent when I tried to get him to talk about the design of the writing. Perhaps this is where the process of design is most elusive. The expectation is that he will produce a script like a typeface: something you can put a name to, something you can analyze and take apart and perhaps even license and sell. Donald just doesn't work that way. Not with script. It is not about putting a formula in a machine and producing page after page of standard output. It is about an organic process building a team and setting in motion something which in the end, will result in a script. It is a practice of writing, not a branded, saleable typeface. Donald's reticence was a protection of the space where that practice could grow and develop.

It is fashionable these days to co-opt the counterculture to sell things. Fancy brands of sneakers try to be bearers of counterculture, just as national chains try to reproduce beatnik espresso bars on a vast world-dominating scale. But the practice of writing which the scribes have joined is, in fact, really countercultural, setting all of our assumptions about script on their head. The script of The Saint John's Bible is emerging from a process of collaboration and consultation in which the scribes are recreating the ethos of an ancient scriptorium. Under Donald's leadership and tutelage, they are watching the script evolve together. Donald shapes the evolution; he doesn't have a fixed end-point. It's a setup that would make a systems analyst have a coronary. But it may be the best way for a script to take on a life of its own. That liveliness shows in the final product.

Quills stand at the ready, arrayed on a shelf in front of sketches for the script. The large blue capitals are prototypes for the initial letters which mark the beginnings of chapters. On the wall behind is an article on healthy posture for calligraphers.

As the scribe writes a Bible page with a carefully cut quill, the vellum page is held down with a knife or a bone tool held in the left hand. The computer printout above provides the scribe with his text. The green sections on the printout indicate which lines have been squeezed to fit the column width; the scribe must condense his text accordingly as he writes. A guard sheet under the writer's hands protects the vellum. The little scratch sheet on the left allows the scribe to test his ink flow before writing on the actual page.

## Building a scribal vocabulary

CALLIGRAPHY, like every trade or craft, has its own vocabulary. Anyone who has taken an evening calligraphy class will be familiar with the names of the various styles of writing offered—italic, roundhand, carolingian and so on. A professional calligrapher will not usually call these *styles* of writing, still less *fonts*, a purely typographic term whose misuse has been popularized by the computer. The professional will refer to them as *scripts* or *hands*. A professional also knows that these seemingly distinct scripts are actually variations on a theme. There are infinite varieties of italic, just as there are multiplicities of roundhands or gothics. And the distinction between the hands is not sharp either. A particular italic hand can slide into a gothic with only small variations of pen handling and letter shape. The names of various scripts serve, then, as shorthand descriptions rather than closed classifications.

All of this reflects the history of writing. Edged-pen calligraphy is based on the writing practices of Western Europe between about 300 and 1500 AD. In that period, scripts were in constant flux. Thousands of people writing documents over a period of centuries produced a living tradition which grew and developed with time. For grand books like Bibles, there were formal, carefully written scripts; for quick letters between friends, there were cursive ("running") scripts. With time, cursive elements would creep into formal writing, and formal writing would decay into a quicker cursive form. Over a thousand years, this flow back and forth between formal and informal writing produced innumerable variations on the basic scripts in use. Add to that shifts in taste and fashion, and you have a complex and rich tradition of writing.

When we come back to look at all these varieties of script, we inevitably begin to spot certain key landmarks: the rigidly parallel lines of a high gothic script with its strong, diamond-shaped terminations; the round and lush forms of the Book of Kells, referred to in the trade as an "insular semi-uncial;" the elegant flow of a Renaissance italic. These are just the highpoints of a tradition largely without boundaries. And the more deeply you explore the history of western writing, the more it becomes clear that few of these scripts have clean endings or beginnings. The shift from the round and open carolingian script to the angular and compressed gothic took place in four hundred years of small incremental steps.

To talk intelligently about a script, then, calligraphers need more precise words to describe the act of writing. The terminology can become very technical. The most basic term is *pen angle,* an often elusive concept for beginning students. Imagine a page of lined paper. You hold an edged pen in your hand. You place the pen on the page. If you drag it in one direction, you will get a thick line, using the full width of the chisel edge. If you drag it in another direction, you get a perfectly thin, fine line. The thicks and thins of the writing emerge from the edge of the pen held at a constant angle to the baseline on which the letters sit. This is the pen angle. The italic hand is usually described as a script written at forty-five degrees; roundhand is described as having a thirty degree pen angle.

Were it so simple. Pen angle is rarely as fixed as it seems. *Pen manipulation* is the practice of twisting the pen during the act of writing, varying the pen angle within the letters themselves. In point of fact, everyone manipulates the pen slightly. It's not humanly possible to hold the pen at a mechanically constant angle to the page, even if it were desirable. But there are certainly scripts which seem to keep a relatively consistent pen angle and others which require twists and turns of the pen.

*Slope* describes the angle of the upright strokes of your script. Look at the **h** or the **d**. Does it lean forward, anticipating the movement of the script? It can be described as having a slight forward slope. Usually this is no more than about three to five degrees off the vertical, a gentle tilting of the letters. This is often barely conscious on the part of the writer; it is a natural tendency to lean the letters in the direction of the writing. Left-to-right scripts tend to lean to the right, while right-to-left scripts like Hebrew or Arabic tend to lean to the left. To the untrained eye the slope may not be apparent until ruler and compass are used to check the uprights. Slope affects pen angle as well.

*Weight* describes how dark a line of writing appears to be. A gothic hand, for instance, is considerably darker and "weightier" than your average italic. It's easy to see the difference between the two but it is very difficult to master all the variables that give the writer control over the weight.

In addition letters have parts. The top of the **h** which breaks above the rest is an *ascender.* The long tail of **y** which drops below the line is a *descender.* Letters like **e** and **g** have closed circular shapes called *bowls,* while the **n** and **m** are capped with neat *arches.* Some strokes end with little wedges or thin terminations called *serifs.*

This is the vocabulary of the trade. Donald's team came ready to use this language in thinking about the script. How wrong they were.

Sue Hufton practices the Bible script.

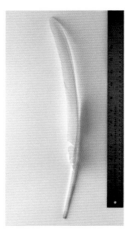

## Starts and false starts

I LAID OUT MY PHOTOCOPIES of the writing on a coffee table before Donald. Light scripts and dark scripts, spiky ones and round ones covered the table. All of them were in the standard column format he had chosen. It was obvious from the samples that small changes in the shape or size of the script had an enormous effect on the appearance of the columns.

Donald pointed to one of the samples. "The problem is retaining the line-ness of the line of writing; if the script is too open, the linear quality goes."

He pointed to a column of handsome script. It was a tall italic. "Look," he said, "it becomes visual mush." He waved his hand up and down, showing me how the lines of text were too light to make a contrast to the interlinear white spaces. The result: a tall column with an even grey texture. Mush.

His trials to develop a Bible script were guided by an interlocking matrix of factors. One basic issue was creating a script which would sit properly within the two-column format he'd worked out. It had to be weighty enough to produce that "line-ness" he was looking for. Like any book script the Bible hand needed to be fairly formal as well as relatively simple in construction. Legibility and ease of writing were both important. Because of the huge amount of text, the writing would have to be small. Those were the technical concerns. Other, less easily defined issues also guided Donald's thinking. The script had to feel worthy of the sacred texts it was being used to transmit. And while it might draw from the tradition, it could not look antiquarian. It had to be a script of today.

One large sample stood out from the rest. It was a page of large letters made with a felt tip marker. In the middle of the page the words "speed flexibility—juice" summed up their lively personality. Lower down on the page, the serifs of some of the letters were circled, as though he had been explaining different ways of ending strokes of the pen. Labelled in Donald's flowing handwriting "Demonstration to prod. Committee" it was dated March 1999.

"This is lively. What were you trying to do here?" I asked.

"I was looking at the Cnut Charter," he said. This famous manuscript was written in the year 1018 and is kept in the British Library (Stow Charter 38). The script is full of interesting idiosyncrasies involving pen manipulation. It is elegant and highly legible. Like any historical script, it could only provide a starting point for a modern script. For one thing it doesn't include all the modern English letters, being written in medieval Latin. For another it's full of obsolete forms and conventions. "I discarded it because it didn't modernize." No matter how he tried to adapt his model, it retained its "archaic aura." "The Cnut hand has to disavow its antiquity," Donald said. "In any case, it's too jumpy for the two column format."

The Winchester Bible had also provided a possible model. Produced in the twelfth century at the monastery connected to Winchester Cathedral, it remains in the Cathedral library to this day. It is one of the most splendid medieval manuscript Bibles and would prove a major source for Donald as he designed the pages of The Saint John's Bible.

On the table in front of us there were some handsome samples of Donald's version of the Winchester script. One thing immediately leapt out from these samples: the Winchester Bible—in Latin—benefits from the even texture of that language. The same script used for our own language becomes much more spiky, the smooth ms and ns of the Latin giving way to the staccato hs, fs and ys of English. Where Latin creates a naturally flowing rhythm, English breaks the line more, throwing many more ascenders and descenders into those interlinear spaces above and below the lines of writing. But that wasn't what killed it. "It defies modernization." There's no more to say.

We looked at the spiky italic again. "Much of this writing was designed with the computer in mind. I was trying to get a word count—a consistent number of letters per line." All the time he was designing a script for his team of calligraphers, Donald was also aware that it was on the computer that the final layouts would be made. His script had to have enough consistency to allow the computer to process the text in preparation for the work of writing. It was an unusual process for a hand-written Bible, made necessary by the complexity and size of the project.

"But this italic isn't just a response to the computer, is it?" I asked.

"It's trying to do something more consciously modern," Donald replied. "But I thought it was too pared down. It would be cloying over a long period, like eating nothing but frosting."

The sketches from 1998 and 1999 were extremely varied. By 2000, the script had begun to settle into shape. Its basic weight and scale were set, and it had even acquired a name: "Jacksonian #2." By now, too, people were beginning to be invited to be part of the scribal team. The script would have to be resolved and soon.

## Collaboration

WHEN THE FIRST TEAM of scribes met at The Hendre, they arrived at the Scriptorium to find a script in development, a work in flux.

This was not just an omission. There was a method in it. The next stage of development couldn't happen without the team in place. The calligraphers' initial visit in February 2000 has been dubbed "the master class." The rest of the project was put to one side as Donald and his scribes studied the script together. The whole process of writing was examined, tested, pulled apart and put back together again. The script would gel along with the group.

"It's not a question of copying a shape," Donald said, "but adopting a shape as your own child—nurturing it—making it your own. It should be open for the scribes to do what they'd hoped they'd do with it."

The challenge he was setting them was enormous. What was this script he presented to them? It was a complex creation.

Brian Simpson described the hand. "It was more different from other scripts than I thought. I looked at it at first and said, 'Oh, it's a rounded italic.' But it's not. It is difficult."

Sue Hufton had a stab at describing it. "It is not conventional. Not roundhand, italic or foundational. I got myself in a muddle early on with these terms. It's not even a mixture of these terms. It's not easily defined. It's to do with the movement of the pen. It's rounded, but not a wide round. It's based on an oval rather than on a circle. The action is similar to round letterforms and to cursive, italic, whatever."

This was a script which challenged the easy classification the scribes might have been used to. I asked Sally Mae to describe it: what was the pen angle? what were the proportions?

"It's not to do with that. No pen angle, no x-height, no exemplars. At the end of the day, I had to throw all that out the window. You have to trust yourself, and you have to trust DJ."

Sue echoed Sally: "I was presented with a script that in a funny kind of way made me set aside everything I knew about letter forms, the relationships between letters—put to one side all my preconceptions

Before it can be cut, a quill must be soaked and softened in water. It is then cured in hot sand in order to harden the shaft. Sarah Harris works in the Black Iron Shed with an electric skillet. With a spoon she pours hot sand into the cavity of the quill, which she then plunges into the sandy skillet.

about letterforms. And yet this is the thing—I needed every scrap of knowledge and experience I could draw from."

The notes for the master class found their way into my sheaf of photocopies titled "The script as it was explained to the calligraphers." A block of eighteen lines of Bible script appears at the top of the first page. It is a loose, even casual version of the script. It is dotted with small annotations. Below this, enlarged letters and parts of letters give evidence of a detailed discussion of the Bible script. These, too, are marked with small checks and x s. This is not an exemplar. It looks like the kind of thing you see on a blackboard in school after a long and complicated lecture. Donald told me he had to stop doing the large demonstration writing; it altered the motion of the pen, so it didn't reflect the subtleties of the writing at the smaller scale of the actual text.

Sue remarked, "I would not have done it this way. This is what I am required to do. But then it becomes my own." She paused for a moment before correcting herself. "No. It becomes ours."

The team aspect quickly became important. Sue said, "When we go down to The Hendre, we feel part of a team, even if we haven't met all the team members—especially the illuminators. We refine the script together. Donald doesn't have any one set way. You want the security of an exemplar. But it's good we never had one. The evolution has been allowed to happen."

Now that they had been writing for the better part of two years, Brian said to me, "Two years in, and we're just beginning to understand the script. It feels better, it looks better." Sue agreed. "It amazed me how much we've been pushed to our limits."

## The scribes

IN AN ENTERPRISE like this, then, the members of the team are all important. The script took shape in an atmosphere of learning and cooperation where personalities could come to the fore. So who were the scribes?

Brian Simpson studied at the Central School of Arts and Crafts in London at the same time as Donald. Bearded and avuncular, his manner is gentle and self-effacing. As Sally says, "Steady Brian. Honest. Steady. Reliable. His whole heart is in it. Lots of care goes into his work. Very careful he—he's not a reckless man, I don't think. Brian picked up the script right away."

At the Central School he had two days a week of calligraphy, one with Irene Wellington, the other with M.C. Oliver. Unlike his classmate Donald, who had moved to London to go to the school, Brian commuted down from his native Leicester. He worked three days a week doing commercial lettering—"brush work for printing"—to pay for two days of calligraphy class. He said to me, "Sue and Sally trained together. It shows. I think their writing is similar. Donald and I studied together. Our writing is similar."

"What makes your writing similar, do you think?" I asked.

He thought for a moment before answering. "I think it's pen manipulation. We use the corner of the pen more. When the pen lifts [off the page], it tends to go on to the corner. Sue and Sally, perhaps they use the flat of the pen more."

"Do you think this has to do with how you were trained?"

"Maybe it was. Irene always wanted you to come up with a project of your own, and she'd let you loose. Then she made gentle suggestions—well, not gentle. But she didn't say this is an **A** and this is the way it's done. She encouraged you to think for yourself."

"How was that different from M.C. Oliver?" I asked.

"Perhaps it says something that we called her Irene, and him Mr. Oliver. He was more dogmatic. This is the way to do it. And that's what you did." His tone changed when he spoke of Irene. "Irene was an excellent teacher, sympathetic. She took it to heart. She was sensitive to people."

I wondered how he felt working with Donald. "I've worked with him a lot over the years. It's helped me knowing Donald so long. As a youngster, he was just the same as now." He chuckled a bit. "He can be frustrating." This last word he drew out in his Leicester accent: froos-trat-ting. "That's Donald. But he comes up with the goods, gets the results. That's what matters in the end. Donald does it by the seat of his pants. It harks back to Irene."

"How was it when you began the writing of the Bible?" I wondered.

"On the first page I wrote I started three-fourths of the page down the first column, so the shaky, tentative writing would not be right at the top."

"I notice you retouch your work sometimes."

"Yes, sometimes. On the tails of the **y**s, sometimes the two ends of the nib catch. I scrape it clean. The

The quill is an exquisitely precise tool working in concert with the vellum surface. Unlike a metal pen it is supple and allows the ink to flow freely producing fine hairlines at the end of strokes. The raised nap of the vellum with its velvety texture gives the page some "tooth." Note the tiny scale of the writing.

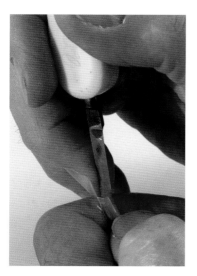
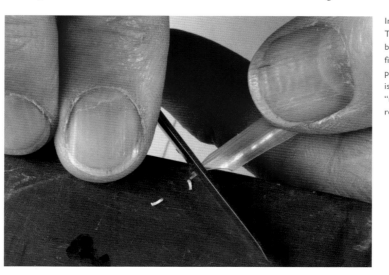

In the hands of a master, a quill is quickly cut. The quill knife must be razor sharp. The barbs on each side of the quill are removed first. A simple sequence of cuts produces a pointed end with evenly curved sides. A slit is then made at the tip. The final step, the "nibbing," produces a chisel-edge shape ready for writing.

# A SERIES OF SKETCHES SHOW HIGHLIGHTS OF DONALD JACKSON'S DEVELOPMENT OF THE SCRIPT

This sample of script was used in the "dummy" Donald Jackson presented to Saint John's. Executed in 1997, it uses the King James translation. After many trials, Donald would eventually come full circle; the final script has a character very much like this first trial.

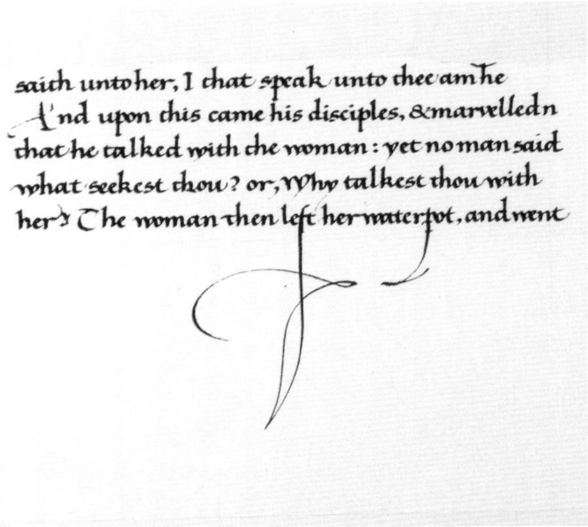
saith unto her, I that speak unto thee am he
And upon this came his disciples, & marvelled
that he talked with the woman: yet no man said
what seekest thou? or, Why talkest thou with
her? The woman then left her waterpot, and went

A self-consciously modern vertical compressed italic from 1998. Donald Jackson felt there was not enough substance or complexity in the script to sustain the message over a thousand pages.

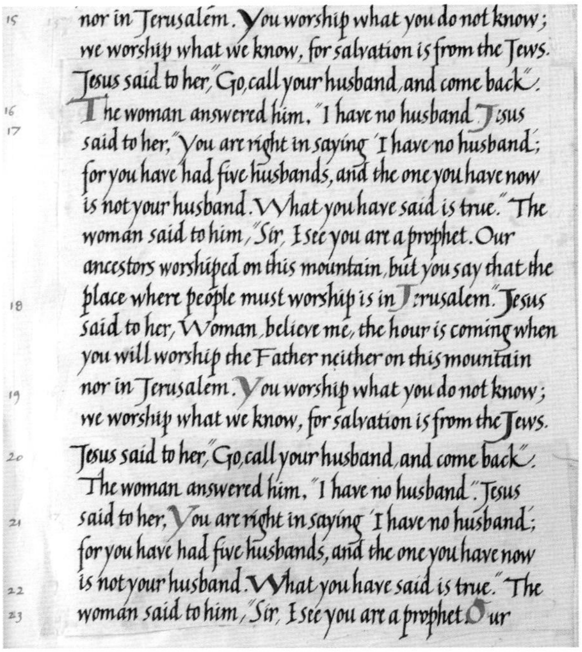
nor in Jerusalem. You worship what you do not know;
we worship what we know, for salvation is from the Jews.
Jesus said to her, "Go, call your husband, and come back".
16 The woman answered him, "I have no husband." Jesus
17 said to her, "You are right in saying 'I have no husband';
for you have had five husbands, and the one you have now
is not your husband. What you have said is true." The
woman said to him, "Sir, I see you are a prophet. Our
ancestors worshiped on this mountain, but you say that the
18 place where people must worship is in Jerusalem." Jesus
said to her, "Woman, believe me, the hour is coming when
you will worship the Father neither on this mountain
19 nor in Jerusalem. You worship what you do not know;
we worship what we know, for salvation is from the Jews.
20 Jesus said to her, "Go, call your husband, and come back".
The woman answered him, "I have no husband." Jesus
21 said to her, "You are right in saying 'I have no husband';
for you have had five husbands, and the one you have now
22 is not your husband. What you have said is true." The
23 woman said to him, "Sir, I see you are a prophet. Our

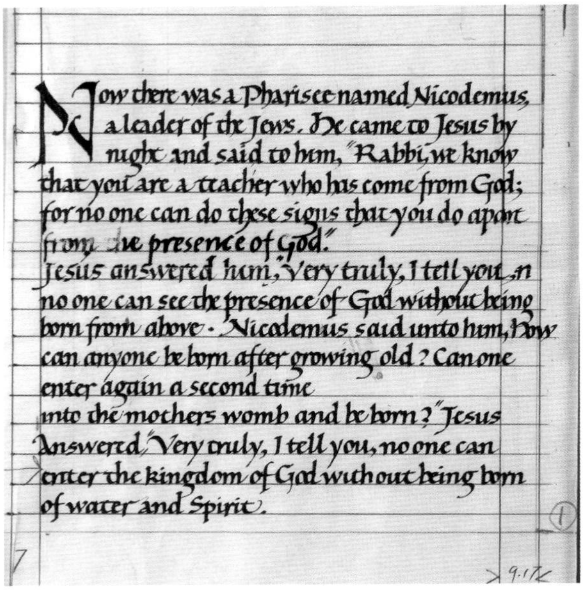
Now there was a Pharisee named Nicodemus,
a leader of the Jews. He came to Jesus by
night and said to him, "Rabbi, we know
that you are a teacher who has come from God;
for no one can do these signs that you do apart
from the presence of God."
Jesus answered him, "Very truly, I tell you, no
one can see the presence of God without being
born from above. Nicodemus said unto him, How
can anyone be born after growing old? Can one
enter again a second time
into the mothers womb and be born?" Jesus
answered, "Very truly, I tell you, no one can
enter the kingdom of God without being born
of water and Spirit.

Another script from 1998 with a strongly vertical quality. The column width was still undecided at this stage. Donald Jackson describes this sample as "mush." Rather than achieving a pattern of dense lines with clear interlinear channels of white, the letters blend into a solid grey mass.

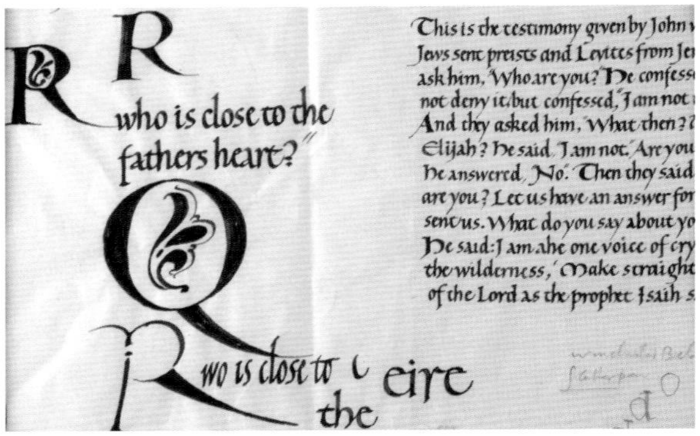
R R
who is close to the
fathers heart?"
Q
R who is close to the
eire
This is the testimony given by John
Jews sent priests and Levites from Je
ask him, "Who are you?" He confess
not deny it, but confessed, "I am not
And they asked him, "What then? A
Elijah?" He said, "I am not." "Are you
He answered, "No." Then they said
are you? Let us have an answer for
sent us. What do you say about yo
He said: I am the one voice of cry
the wilderness, 'Make straight
of the Lord as the prophet Isaiah s

Donald Jackson flirted with a script based on the Cnut Charter, an English document of the early eleventh century. This, too, he rejected. The writing could not be purged of its archaic flavor.

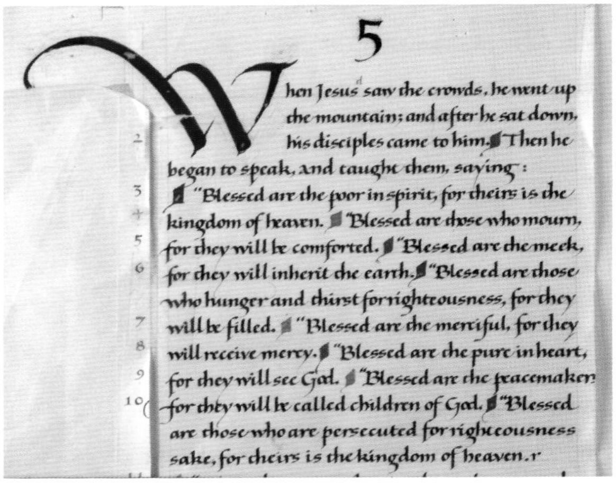
5
When Jesus saw the crowds, he went up
the mountain; and after he sat down,
2 his disciples came to him. Then he
began to speak, and taught them, saying:
3 "Blessed are the poor in spirit, for theirs is the
4 kingdom of heaven. "Blessed are those who mourn,
5 for they will be comforted. "Blessed are the meek,
6 for they will inherit the earth. "Blessed are those
who hunger and thirst for righteousness, for they
7 will be filled. "Blessed are the merciful, for they
8 will receive mercy. "Blessed are the pure in heart,
9 for they will see God. "Blessed are the peacemakers,
10 for they will be called children of God. "Blessed
are those who are persecuted for righteousness
sake, for theirs is the kingdom of heaven.

A sample from January 2000. "This is getting there," Donald Jackson said. "It has a classic feel. The spaces between lines and letters are as important for harmony as the letters themselves." This sample became an important model for the scribes.

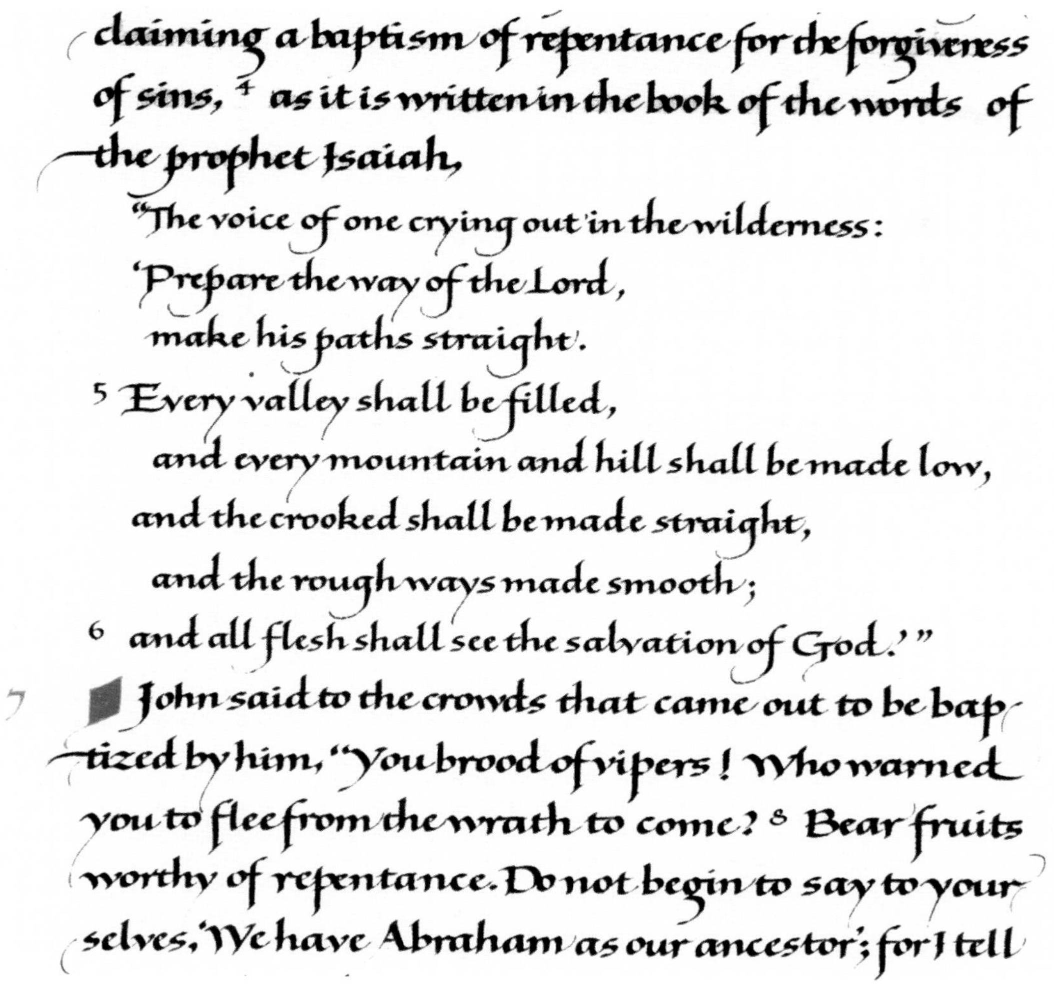

claiming a baptism of repentance for the forgiveness of sins, ⁴ as it is written in the book of the words of the prophet Isaiah,

"The voice of one crying out in the wilderness:
'Prepare the way of the Lord,
make his paths straight'.
⁵ Every valley shall be filled,
and every mountain and hill shall be made low,
and the crooked shall be made straight,
and the rough ways made smooth;
⁶ and all flesh shall see the salvation of God.'"

⁷ John said to the crowds that came out to be baptized by him, "You brood of vipers! Who warned you to flee from the wrath to come? ⁸ Bear fruits worthy of repentance. Do not begin to say to yourselves, 'We have Abraham as our ancestor'; for I tell

Passages of poetry are written in a lighter variation of the standard Bible script. The sample shown here is actual size.

counters of the **e**s also fill in. When that happens I make a little tick mark in the margin, and come back and fix it later. With the knife."

If you look at his pages, you will see some of the tails of the **y**s carefully scratched along their edges to make neat, clean flourishes.

Brian knows his trade. And he knows how to get out of a tough spot. "That's what makes a good craftsman," he said. "It's not that you don't make mistakes. It's knowing how to get out of a mess."

Sue is as lean and precise as her work. There is an air of seriousness about her. She weighs her words before she speaks. "My background emphasis was on drawn, painted and carved letters. I didn't like calligraphy. I felt a bit of a fraud when I was asked to be part of the team." This, she explained, had everything to do with her tools. She was writing with metal pens on paper. But the Bible was a completely different thing—writing on vellum with quill pens was a pleasure. The pleasure had not come, however, without significant struggle. The mastery of the quill was a huge issue. "The script itself is very nice to write now. You do relax: but I have to say relaxing does not mean speeding up. I've actually been trying to slow down. Brian takes twelve to thirteen hours to write a page. I do it in almost half the time: I'll take seven hours."

I wondered if it began to flow more easily as she gained practice. No. It didn't. The writing is demanding. "I am always thinking about how to get the line to fit into its space. Vin (the computer layout technician) is getting a lot better with the typesetting of the computer drafts for the scribes; he's becoming a better judge of the spacing. Sometimes you have a line with fifty-five characters to fit in, followed by a line of forty-five characters. You have to make the lines look the same on the page, have the same color and consistency."

I asked her, "Now that you have really internalized the script, how would you describe your writing?"

"I keep a more consistent pen angle than the others. I do not do manipulations easily. At Roehampton, I wrote the Cnut Charter hand without pen manipulation."

I expressed surprise—at the Roehampton Institute, where we both trained, the study of the Cnut Charter hand was almost entirely designed to teach us about pen manipulation. "I know, I know," she said. "It just came out differently. That's all. It was a different thing."

"Do you think there's a difference in the way each of you write?" I wondered.

"It's less obvious now. Brian and Donald write similarly. Sally and I write similarly. It's to do with our training. Or maybe it's the time when we trained. We trained at different times with different tutors; perhaps that's what makes the difference."

The first group of scribes gathered in February 2000 to begin writing Bible pages. Instead of being handed an exemplar to copy, they were plunged into a detailed examination of the evolving Bible script. These jottings are a record of that conversation showing different strategies for making the letters.

Some things, however, did not come down to training. "Brian does a lot more pen manipulation. Sally does, too."

I asked Sally Mae if her writing was similar to Sue's.

"No, it's not," she said definitively. "Sue wasn't even doing calligraphy: she came more out of drawn and painted letters." There was a hint of fire in what she said. Sally is energetic and enthusiastic, ready to get stuck into a project, with more than a touch of a wild streak. She is quick-eyed, with a wicked laugh. As the studio manager she was involved in the project long before the other two. Unlike Brian and Sue, who do most of their work at home, Sally is at the Scriptorium all the time. She moved to Wales to take up the job. Although she was involved in the design stages of the script, she didn't start writing Bible pages until well after the other two had begun.

Brian Simpson, Sue Hufton, Donald Jackson and Sally Mae Joseph examine and discuss finished Bible pages. The four scribes who work away from the Scriptorium write most of the pages at home, returning at regular intervals to The Hendre. Working in isolation, the scribes find that their writing gradually deviates from the standard script. By meeting together with Donald and Sally Mae they continue to bond as a team and bring their writing back into harmony.

Brian Simpson unrolls the pages he has written at his home in Leicester.

"I've been involved in so many aspects of the Bible," she said, listing all the tasks she'd done or overseen. The reality of meetings, devising work schedules, keeping everyone and everything moving along, as well as being involved in vellum preparation and illumination, means that she doesn't have the chance to write as much as the other two.

"I rarely get the chance to sit and write smoothly and without interruption." But she knows the script. "Even though I started later on the writing, I was part of the master class and the development of the thing. So I picked it up faster."

She also had experience doing peerages—the legal documents Donald produces for the Crown Office at the House of Lords. She was used to writing Donald's house style. It wasn't a far leap into Bible script.

In October 2002 two new scribes joined the team: Susie Leiper and Angela Swan. Unlike the first calligraphers, who were involved with the creation of the script, the two new scribes were learning to adapt to something which had already taken form.

Susie Leiper laughed when I asked her where she had trained. "I came into this sideways," she said. "I didn't go to Roehampton. My very first western calligraphy teacher was in Hong Kong where I was living at the time. Sally tells me it's an advantage coming from a different background."

When she arrived for her first week at The Hendre, there were three other newcomers. Their training lasted five weeks: three weeks at the Scriptorium, interspersed with two weeks at home to practice on their own.

"The very first thing we learned was how to sit properly," she said. "We divided the day up, with a bit of quill cutting every day. The days just disappeared!"

At the end of the third week, two of the four were selected to continue with the project. "It did become quite tense," she said. "There was that awful moment when Donald said, 'Two of you are ready.' And he named them. I was surprised to be one of them."

When she began to write actual Bible pages, she found it daunting. "I felt so unsure. I have never shaken so much in my whole life. But the earthquake subsided into simple fear after the first line or so."

Dozens of practice vellum pages document the growing confidence of the scribes as they master the Bible script.

Soon she settled into a rhythm. She remarked, "I disappear into another world. It's an otherworldly experience." She usually writes for about three-and-a-half hours at a stretch, preferably in the mornings. "I shut myself off from the rest of the world. If it's a Bible morning, I look forward to it."

The other newcomer was Angela Swan who had studied at Roehampton and who had, in fact, worked as Donald's studio assistant from 1988 to 1991. This project was very different from her previous experience at The Hendre. Back then, "I was filling in lots of certificates." Good, skilled calligraphic grunt work. The Bible is a much more intense and involved project.

Mastering the quill had challenged her. "This is the first time I've come to grips with cutting the quills. I have good days and bad days. But at least now I know which is a bad quill day and which is just a bad day."

Some of the recent batch of quills have gone soft very quickly; all the scribes have remarked on the change. The earlier quills were harder and easier to use. "My fourth quill was a little beauty," she crooned. "I wrote twenty-four pages with it. I've kept it hanging in my workshop with a little label:

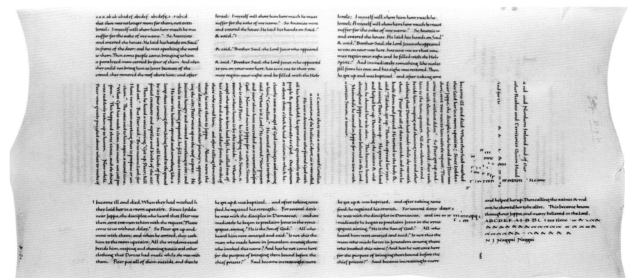

No scrap of the precious vellum is allowed to go to waste. This practice sheet has been used front and back.

"Best Quill—24 pages." It kept its edge; it never split; it never misbehaved."

Like the other scribes, Angela struggles to maintain a consistent script while working at home. "You can lose the goalposts," she said. "I have a little square example of script of about twelve lines. It has the right weight and was okayed by Donald. But even when I'm using this sample, I can stand up and look at what I've written, and say 'Oh no! It's smaller and lighter.' It may only be off by a hair's breadth, but over a whole page it makes a great difference."

The camaraderie of the team has helped a great deal. "We have such a lot of laughs. We understand what one another have been going through. We share the joy of doing it as well. There's a lot of mutual respect and understanding. Because it isn't easy."

And then, as Sally likes to say, there is "The Man," Donald himself. His main preoccupation is the illumination; compared to the others, he has written relatively few whole pages.

Sue remarked, "It's a consensus. It is not purely Donald's script. All he gave us was the starting point of an idea—all four of us have developed and changed." At the same time, the script is not decided by committee. She continued, "He's still in charge. He's got the responsibility." She pauses for effect: "He's the man who said 'yes.'"

Brian was of a similar mind. "Donald's style has shifted as well. We've all fed off one another during this project. For instance, my **g**s. Donald saw them and said, 'I like that. I'll do that.' It's an ensemble. It has to be. No one could work for long under other conditions." Still, "Donald is the master. Happy for us to make suggestions. But he is the linchpin."

The Man who said "yes" had a lot to say about the act of writing: "It's very physical. It's not about 'what alphabet?' but instead it's about the way of sitting, the alignment of the desk, breathing, position. This doesn't come up unless you say you're going to write for many years in a team."

Donald looked at a page of writing. "I see wayward sheep: a healthy development? Or do they betray a lack of understanding?" Their first pages, he told them, were "Wonderfully good enough: you will get better."

## Touchstone

A MEDIEVAL MONASTIC SCRIPTORIUM was made up of people who lived, ate, prayed and worked together. Their writing naturally held together because they rubbed shoulders day by day. After the master class, Donald's scribes scattered. Sally and Donald stayed at The Hendre, but Sue took her pages back to Sussex and Brian took his back to Leicester. In order to keep the team together, the scribes must meet at The Hendre at regular intervals. Given the organic approach of script-building Donald had opted for, regular meetings are the only way to keep wayward sheep from striking out on their own.

Sue told me, "Donald doesn't define things at all. His is the so-called 'intuitive approach'—definition is not easy for him. When you don't pin it down, it changes easily. And anyway, we all need someone to look and say, 'Come on, what can you see?' If you don't have that you can't progress, develop. Each time Donald picks out aspects of form: What am I doing? Why? The point is not to be slipshod in any way. Tiny things: how the serif goes at the bottom of **f**."

How often did they meet?

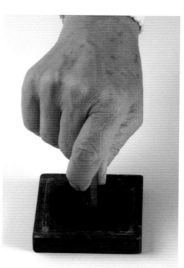

Chinese ink sticks are ground in an ink stone with distilled water. The scribe has complete control over the density of the black and the viscosity of the ink. The quill is dipped into the well of the ink stone. A small lid covers the liquid ink to prevent evaporation when the scribe steps away from her or his desk.

While most of the text is written with black Chinese stick ink, a few elements are written using vermillion. This paint is mixed with egg yolk and water and is of a thicker consistency than the stick ink. A brush is used to load it onto the quill.

Susan Leiper, who joined the project as a
scribe in 2002, writes at a desk in the
Schoolroom.

Angela Swan also joined the project as a
scribe in 2002.

"It varies," Sue said. "We last met back in October: That's about three months ago. Normally, it's about every six to eight weeks. And now it's stretched out. We're scheduled to go back in three months' time."

Brian mentioned the pitfalls of working so far apart. "With Sue and I working away from the Scriptorium, it's hard. That's why it sometimes goes in different directions. Gradual changes creep in. As soon as we unrolled our pages at the Scriptorium, I was horrified with mine. It struck me immediately—a big change. I've lived with mine for weeks. You get used to your own writing. Yesterday, we were laboring away to produce a small sample, just half a dozen lines to take back with us." A touchstone.

Sue said much the same thing. "You think you've got it, but if you're slightly off, each page degrades. From page to page there is a slow shift. We're searching for some kind of standard: there isn't one."

Brian continued, "You do one page and you like it. Then you do another and you compare it to the first. It may have gotten just a bit lighter in weight. Then you do a third page and compare it to the second. It's slightly lighter but not enough to jump out at you. If you do that for enough pages, and you come back to your first page, then you're shocked to see how far you've come from your original page."

"There are so many variables, quill, light, ink," said Sue. "This time we looked at weight—the pattern on the page. Not form. We've looked at forms. When the weight goes, then the linear quality goes.

"Donald photocopied pages from three months ago and from a year ago, and blew them up," Sue continued. "The change was remarkable."

"How so?"

"My writing is consistent in size and shape and form."

"So what had changed?"

"It's about flow. Sally 'knits' the script. It's about the way the **t** and **r** join in, about ligatures and overlapping. It's to do with the way one letter leads into another, especially along the top of the line. There are elements of cursive in it: then you get a good strong line."

When they looked at Brian's writing, they saw his too had changed. Why?

"Is it the slope?" Sue asked. "The pen angle?"

They debated the possibilities. It didn't seem to be any obvious thing. Sue said, "We thought perhaps it was the angle at which he had cut the right oblique edge of his nib: a slight change in angle produces a change in the movement of the quill, which changes the dynamic of the writing." Exquisite nuance of tone: this is the level at which the team is working.

Sally said the conversation had revolved around the organic "feel" of the script. Donald drew a contrast between a "medieval" quality of a line of writing and a "Renaissance" sensibility. The medieval line, it seemed to him, had that strong "knittedness, and richness." The Renaissance tendency was, he said, "more like a copy book or a printed page: it was typographical." He wanted the calligraphers to aim more for the rich, organic feel of the medieval line and move away from the rigidities of the Renaissance.

Sally said, "Brian's writing is closer to the medieval look, but it's gotten smaller and lighter in weight." Perhaps this had to do with the change in the vellum. As the studio assistant Sarah Harris gets more expert at preparing vellum, the writing sharpens up. The thins are better, and so Brian ends up with more fine lines. It shifts the balance of the writing in a lighter direction.

The variables are endless. The conversation goes on. The writing shifts back and forth within the nar-

A computer sheet with annotations provides the fully prepared text for the scribe. In the upper left, the note "DJ text" indicates that Donald Jackson will be writing this page. The faded rubber stamp of a cherub in the upper right shows that this is a calligrapher's copy sheet. The three roughly written lines in the top left column indicate a passage to be written in free capital letters used for the beginning of each Gospel. In the bottom left, the code "A1 (F) V" refers to the Allocation Book. The same reference appears at the bottom of each vellum sheet. The scribe is responsible to check that he or she is writing the text on the correct sheet. The code lists the folio number (A1), and specifies that the script appears on the flesh side of the skin (F). The page is on the left hand side of an opening—in scribal terms, the "verso" (V).

row range Donald has set. The personalities shine through, yet the whole book holds together. "Marvelously good enough?" Better than that.

Brian said in January 2002, "It got quite exciting—we laid our pages all out like a book—we could see the thing as a whole. It came to life. The weight, texture, appearance of the script all held together. It was all from the same book. Personality is important. It does not stifle personality. It's a harmony. The individual struggles fade away."

When they step back from their work they can enjoy what they have made. I asked him about how the ink sat on the page. "The ink dries well. It's almost shiny. You can see that it stands just proud on the vellum." He paused for a moment. "It's a lovely thing," he said with a sigh.

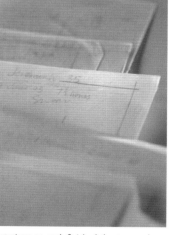

Notations on each finished sheet record who did the writing, how long it took and where the page will fit within the finished manuscript book. These small notes will be cut from the sheets at the end of the project when all seven volumes are trimmed and bound.

# THE GOSPEL ACCORDING TO JOHN

IN THE BEGINNING WAS THE WORD AND THE WORD WAS WITH GOD, AND THE WORD WAS GOD. HE WAS IN THE BEGINNING WITH GOD. ALL THINGS CAME INTO BEING THROUGH HIM, AND WITHOUT HIM NOT ONE THING CAME INTO BEING. WHAT HAS COME INTO BEING IN HIM WAS LIFE, AND THE LIFE WAS THE LIGHT OF ALL PEOPLE. THE LIGHT SHINES IN THE DARKNESS, AND THE DARKNESS DID NOT OVERCOME IT. THERE WAS A MAN SENT FROM GOD WHOSE NAME WAS JOHN. HE CAME AS A WITNESS TO TESTIFY TO THE LIGHT, SO THAT ALL MIGHT BELIEVE THROUGH HIM. HE HIMSELF WAS NOT THE LIGHT, BUT HE CAME TO TESTIFY TO THE LIGHT. THE TRUE LIGHT, WHICH ENLIGHTENS EVERYONE WAS COMING INTO THE WORLD. HE WAS IN THE WORLD, AND THE WORLD CAME INTO BEING THROUGH HIM; YET THE WORLD DID NOT

KNOW HIM. HE CAME TO WHAT WAS HIS OWN, & HIS OWN PEOPLE DID NOT ACCEPT HIM. BUT TO ALL WHO RECEIVED HIM, WHO BELIEVED IN HIS NAME, HE GAVE POWER TO BECOME CHILDREN OF GOD, WHO WERE BORN, NOT OF BLOOD OR OF THE WILL OF THE FLESH OR OF THE WILL OF MAN, BUT OF GOD. AND THE WORD BECAME FLESH & LIVED AMONG US, AND WE HAVE SEEN HIS GLORY, THE GLORY AS OF A FATHER'S ONLY SON, FULL OF GRACE AND TRUTH.

15 ( John testified to him and cried out, "This was he of whom I said, 'He who comes after me ranks ahead of me because he was before me.'") [16] From his fullness we have all received grace upon grace; [17] The law indeed was given through Moses ; grace and truth came through Jesus Christ [18] No one has ever seen God. It is God the only Son, who is close to the Father's heart, who has made him known.

19 ❡ This is the testimony given by John when the Jews sent priests and Levites from Jerusalem to ask him, "Who are you?" [20] He confessed & did not deny it, but confessed, "I am not the Messiah." [21] And they asked him, "What then ? Are you Elijah? He said, "I am not." "Are you the prophet ?" He answered, "No." [22] Then they said to him, "Who are you? Let us have an answer for those who sent us. What do you say about yourself ?" [23] He said,

"I am the voice of one crying out in the wilderness,
'Make straight the way of the Lord,'"

24 as the prophet Isaiah said. ❡ Now they had been sent from the Pharisees. [25] They asked him, "Why then are you baptizing if you are neither the Messiah, nor Elijah, nor the prophet ?" [26] John answered them, "I baptize with water. Among you stands one whom you do not know, [27] the one who is coming after me ; I am not worthy to untie the thong of his sandal." [28] This took place in Bethany across the Jordan where

29 John was baptizing ❡ The next day he saw Jesus coming toward him & declared, "Here is the Lamb of God who takes away the sin of the world ! [30] This

a **or** *through him. And without him not one thing came into being that has come into being.* * *In him was life*

b **or** *He was the true light that enlightens everyone coming into the world.*

c **or** *to his own home*

d **or** *the Father's only Son*

e other ancient authorities read: *It is an only Son, God,* *or, It is the only Son*

f **Gk** *bosom*

g **or** *the Christ*

h **or** *the Christ*

# CHAPTER 5

# THE ARCHITECTURE OF THE PAGE

THERE IS A WELL-WORN paperback book which sits near Donald's writing desk. It is about the Winchester Bible, one of the great medieval manuscript Bibles. It is full of notes and measurements written in the margins. On the inside back cover in Donald's handwriting these words have been quickly jotted down:

> ignition · spark · divinity · divine harmonic · pure quality · all this happens to [an] intellectual but that is quality of an idea · grasps or strives to produce an idea · the artist creates a thing

The writing is rapid, the lines jumbled, word jostling against word. What was Donald trying to work out? I went and asked him.

The Winchester Bible, a twelfth-century manuscript, came from a highly developed scribal culture. The elements of the page work together to produce the kind of flow—the spark—which Donald wanted to achieve in his manuscript Bible. Looking at the reproductions in his book, Donald was convinced there was a "visual harmonic" operating—but what was it? What were the components of that underlying harmony he could see on the page?

"I took out a ruler and I began to measure the proportions," he said. "I felt there was something there, some system underlying the whole book." Was there some practical method, now lost to us, that gave the book page its inherent order and its "divine harmonic"? Donald measured the page, the text area, the spaces between lines of writing, the gutter between the columns. He was looking for some repetitive element, some recurring relationship between the components of the page.

"Was there some proportion which would crop up in other permutations? I was looking for a common denominator measurement. I was switching between measuring in inches and centimeters. Oddly enough, in centimeters it began to have more sense—more coincidences than when I measured in inches. I seem to remember that some pattern of thirty-three millimeters recurring, something to do with the gutter."

He tried to tease out the system—but there was no system, no magic formula which he could apply. In the end, the artist is left with the problem of making an object. The scholar seeks an explanation, a mathematical relationship. For the artist, there is simply the fact of the thing.

"In the last line of those jotted notes, I was thinking of Edward Johnston, how he talked about making a *thing*," said Donald. Johnston, the founder of the twentieth-century calligraphy movement in Britain, always talked about the importance of practical work for the scribe. Theoretical debate and analysis have their place. Rough drafts and samples of writing also have their place. But in the end, "practicing," Johnston said, "teaches you to practice." In his foundational work on calligraphy, *Writing & Illuminating & Lettering,* first published in 1906, he advised his students: "Only an attempt to do practical work will raise practical problems, and therefore *useful practice is the making of real or definite things.*"*

The cryptic notes on the flyleaf of a book in the studio point to a realization. Donald would not find the answers he was looking for in a theoretical system; he would not try to impose an external notion of order or harmony on the book. Instead, the answers would grow out of the problem of working with matter in front of him: the ink, vellum, paint and gold. His ideas, unlike those of the scholar or theoretician, would emerge from an engagement with the physical reality of the thing. Following the lead of his hand, eye and instinct, and guided by his training and knowledge of the manuscript tradition, he would give shape to the Bible in the craftsman-artist's way: the artist creates a thing.

## A vision

In 1996 Donald was at a conference at Saint John's. Entitled *Servi Textus,* it brought together scholars working on manuscripts, people who made books and patrons interested in the book arts. Donald says, "I remember the defining moment of the conference for me. There was a ceremony in the Abbey church— perhaps a funeral or a solemn profession; I don't actually remember. In the middle of the ceremony, a monk carried a large book down into the congregation. He read from it, and then I saw him hold it up, and say, 'This is the Word of God.'" In the midst of a conference about books and artists, here was a book which was unlike all others. In the conference hall they were talking about books. In the church, they were actually using a book. For just a moment during a long ceremony that book became the focal point of a living belief, a meeting point of the human and the divine. The book as an object had to be a thing of sufficient dignity and beauty to live up to its high purpose; the form of the book had to grow out of its role as the expression of belief. For an artist who makes books, here is the heart of the craft: how do you make an object which can embody this living tradition?

"I always had an idea that The Saint John's Bible would be used in ceremonies," Donald says. "It would be a ceremonial object, not simply a utilitarian thing. I have little knowledge of liturgy. The symbolism attracts me—a book like this is about the importance of the words and of the object which holds them. Making The Saint John's Bible is a restatement of the value we place in the words themselves. It's not just about reading the words. These are special words: and it's worthwhile to sweat and to labor to make the words go down on the page."

For Donald there has always been a dual purpose in making The Saint John's Bible. On the one hand the book will be read from in public liturgies. On the other hand it is designed for display as well, to communicate by its size and scale and by its nature as a hand-made object, that this is a unique text: it contains the Word of God.

To say that such a project is unusual is to understate the case. We are so used to printed editions of the Bible and so far removed from the manuscript tradition that there are few guideposts along the way for the craftsman. When I asked him about printed Bibles, Donald sniffed. The Bible translation Saint John's has chosen is the New Revised Standard Version (NRSV) and he has to work closely within the parameters set by the NRSV committee. These are designed solely with printed editions in mind. He said to me, "Some editions of the NRSV are actually anti-aesthetic—it's almost with pride that they are

A book from Saint John's collection illustrates the simple beauty of well-proportioned design. In this fifteenth-century printed Bible, a band of commentary surrounds two columns of scripture. The initial capitals were added by hand with tremendous flair.

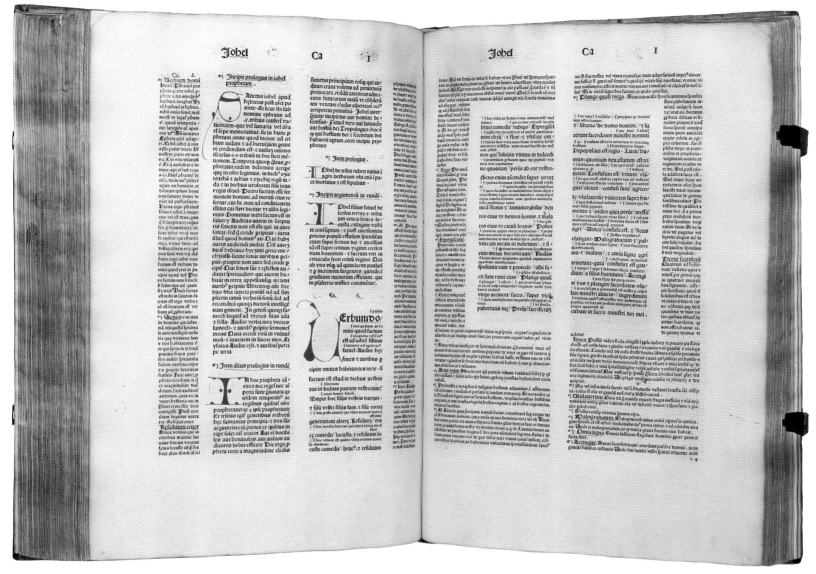

*Strasbourg Bible.*
Bible in Latin (Vulgate) with Glossa ordinaria. Strasbourg: Adolf Rusch for Anton Koberger of Nuremberg, 1481. Kacmarcik Collection of Arca Artium, Saint John's University.

not aesthetic. It's as if they are saying, 'We cannot concern ourselves with the look of the thing.' Contemporary printed Bibles are a kind of spur to me, a validation of the whole enterprise of writing out the Bible by hand. Look at the *self-congratulatory ugliness* of the printed editions." Donald smiled slightly, enjoying the words as he said them. "Compare that with the early printed Bibles—Gutenberg and others. They were printing in gothic type faces and faced the first challenge of mass-producing what had been a written tradition. And they stand on the shoulders of the handmade Bibles which had come before." Modern printed versions rarely live up to Gutenberg. "This is the Word of God: therefore it should be goodly, which is to say, Godly."

A small rectangular title panel marks the beginning of each biblical book. Within the structure of this simple format there is room for improvisation. The smaller Hebrew titles appear above the title panels throughout the Old Testament. They were written by Izzy Pludwinski.

בראשית

שמות

במדבר

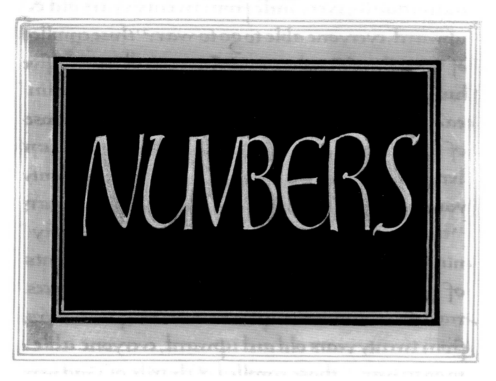

דברים

The initial capitals are written by Donald Jackson with a quill using color and occasionally gold. These are the final page elements to be added to each volume after all the other work has been finished. The lively variety of their shapes is a playful counterpoint to the strong columns of regular text.

* Otto Pacht, *Book Illumination in the Middle Ages.* (London: Harvey Miller Publishers, 1984) pp. 18 & 46.

** Ibid., p. 18.

## The page takes form

WHAT SHAPE would give The Saint John's Bible that goodly form? Donald's quest would send him back to the hand-written tradition to rediscover the sources from which our printed Bibles ultimately derive. There is a variety of manuscripts to choose from. Hand-written Bibles have come down to us in a large range of sizes and shapes. Only a limited number of these manuscripts are valuable as guides to the making of The Saint John's Bible. The oldest manuscripts—the biblical books found amongst the Dead Sea Scrolls, for example—are in a different format. The Saint John's Bible is a codex, the book form most contemporary people would identify as a book. It has pages bound along a spine, sewn together and contained within stout covers. So as beautiful and ancient as the Dead Sea Scrolls may be, they have little to offer as models for this project. Other early manuscripts survive as small fragments written on papyrus. Some, like the Stonyhurst Gospel, which was found in the coffin of St. Cuthbert and dates to the seventh century, are small, portable books designed for private reading. Most biblical manuscripts, in fact, only contain portions of the Bible. Psalters and Gospel books are probably the most common types of these. Some of the most famous books from before the era of printing—such as the Book of Kells or the Lindisfarne Gospels—only contain a small part of the New Testament. Donald was searching out pandects—books which contain all the canonical books of scripture in a single collection. This limited his choice of models.

The British Library is probably the best place in the world to make such a study. Their collection includes some of the earliest pandect Bibles which have survived largely intact. The Codex Sinaiticus and the Codex Alexandrinus, of the fourth and fifth centuries respectively,* give us elegant examples of manuscripts from the early days of the Church after Constantine and are used by biblical scholars as important evidence in establishing the most accurate biblical text. These have a squarish, squat page format, without illuminations or illustrations. Sinaiticus is written in a four-column format, perhaps reflecting the narrow columns of the smaller books from which it may have been copied, or perhaps aping the format of a scroll. The large, square pages create a very wide, horizontal double-page spread with four columns on either side of the center and certainly evoke the horizontality of the scroll. The visual relationship to the scroll may have served to give the Codex Sinaiticus a kind of authority by evoking the older tradition.**

Donald's search took him deeper into the heart of the Middle Ages. He wanted to see books which represented the manuscript tradition in full flower. His idea that The Saint John's Bible should have a kind of monumentality and architectural scale guided him to some of the largest manuscripts in the collection.

Donald said, "On the one hand, books like the Book of Kells are really very dainty in size. Most calligraphic manuscripts are of a scale which is extraordinarily personal: they are books to be held in the hand, or in one's lap. The communion between the reader and the object is private. I think that's a key word. It is a private experience. By contrast, our Bible is public. That's where the monumentality comes in." At the same time the encounter between the reader and the text remains personal. The design problem is to find the right "scale of marks within the overall drama of its size—it's about an intimacy of scale within a larger scale."

The librarians pulled out one large manuscript after another. One of these was the Moutier-Grandval

Bible, a Carolingian book from about 835 AD, copied out at a monastery in Tours in northern France.[*] It is a large book, with pages measuring 19¾ × 14½ inches (50 × 37cm). There are two columns on each page, each composed of fifty lines of text (although in the book of Psalms, a fifty-two line column is used). Much of the manuscript is in a pristine state, the vellum seeming as fresh and clean as the day on which it was written.

Donald looked at the weight and size of the book. It was beautiful, and yet he was disquieted by what he saw: "The vellum is milk white and thin. But the book is just too big: it is a danger to itself. It would be so easy to crease the pages when turning them. I used to go look at it when it was at the British Museum in its case. The skins were so thin and fine but in the dryness of the air, they began to curl. Grandval convinced me that the weight of our vellum had to be heavier, so the book could bear its own weight. It also showed me that the book had to be split into several volumes." He envisaged a book of monumental scale, of an architectural scale, which would suit its setting within the monastic community at Saint John's. He had also imagined it as a work spanning several volumes. The Moutier-Grandval Bible confirmed this instinct. "I saw our book as a collection of seven volumes—it was both a practical and a visual idea. I imagined what it would look like on display, with one volume in the center, flanked by three on each side. The manuscript book, displayed open, is like a peacock opening its tail. But this will be a series of peacocks instead of just one." Later when Donald would present the idea of a many-volume Bible to the community at Saint John's, the committee in charge naturally came up with a seven-volume division of the text. This they did for theological and scriptural reasons and it fit neatly with Donald's practical concerns and his visual concept. So the project began to take form in a way which was beginning to make all the varying ideas converge. The "thing" was beginning to take concrete shape.

## A medieval mentor: the Winchester Bible

DONALD NOW TURNED BACK to the manuscript Bible which seemed best to embody the kind of monumentality he was looking for—the Winchester Bible. "I chose it," he said, "because it was the high point of twelfth-century Bibles."[**] Written in a monastic scriptorium and made for a monastic community, it was an apt choice as a model. It remains today at Winchester Cathedral, in the library attached to the south transept. It seems never to have left the place where it was made, with two brief exceptions—once during the English Civil War and then during World War II when it was removed for safety from bombing raids. Otherwise it has stayed put, surviving the Reformation and the destruction of the monastic community which had once served the Cathedral.

The Winchester Bible is a large manuscript, even larger than Moutier-Grandval, with a page size of 23 × 15¾ inches (58 × 39.5cm). It was written by a single scribe with minor alterations and corrections by a different hand. The writing alone probably took about four years. It is lavishly illustrated in color and in gold. For calligraphers and for art historians it is particularly interesting since its illustrations were left unfinished. Leafing through, one can find examples of every stage of the process of illumination. On some pages only the faint pen-made underdrawing was completed; on others one can see the gesso laid, ready to receive its gold; on others still, fully finished illuminations dazzle with their skill and refinement. Most of the Bible is intact although some initials and pages have been cut out by thieves. One particularly fine page,

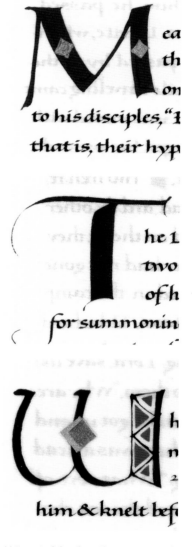

*British Library Additional Ms 10546; reproduced in Stan Knight, *Historical Scripts*, 2nd ed. (New Castle, Delaware: Oak Knoll Press, 1998) p. 6.

** I am indebted to Claire Donovan's excellent short book, *The Winchester Bible*, for the following description of the Winchester Bible and its making. (London and Winchester: The British Library and Winchester Cathedral Enterprises, Ltd., 1993).

A selection of
the initial capitals
written by Donald Jackson.

**A**gain he en
was there
watched
cure him on the sab
him.[3] And he said t
hand, "Come forwa

**N**ow a certa
any, the v
Martha
ed the Lord with per
her hair; her brother
sent a message to le

**B**ut on the first
they came to th
they had prep
rolled away from the to
they did not find the b
plexed about this, sud
clothes stood beside th

mained in the valley

**S**o now, Israel,
ordinances that
so that you m
land that the LORD, th
giving you.[2] You must

publicly to Israel.

2

**I**n those days a decree
Augustus that all the wo
[2] This was the first regi
while Quirinius was gover
to their own towns to be reg

tell you,
taste de
in his ki

**S**

**34**

he LORD spoke to [J]
mand the Israelites, [a]
you enter the land [o]
land that shall fall to you for a
of Canaan, defined by its bou[nd]
sector shall extend from the w[...]

ONOMY

hen
Kin[g]
us, [I]
Edrei.² The LORD s[...]
I have handed him [...]

hen the Lo[rd]
ark, you an[d]
seen that [...]
me in this generatio[n]
of all clean animals
pair of the animals th[...]

in all your settleme[nt]
any blood.

ou are chil[dren]
must not [...]
forelocks [...]
ple holy to the LOR[D]
has chosen out of al[l]
7    [...] maple his treasure

EXODUS

he LORD s[...]
to the peop[le]
sins unin[...]
commandments ab[out]
3    does any one of them

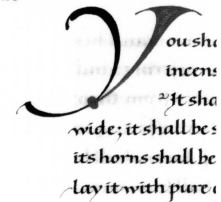

ou sha[ll]
incens[e]
²It sha[ll]
wide; it shall be s[...]
its horns shall be [...]
lay it with pure [...]

Book headings appear at the top of each spread. In the Old Testament they are written in Hebrew and English. In the New Testament only the English headings are used.

Poetry is written in a slightly smaller variant of the main Bible script. This allows a slightly longer word-count per line and avoids broken lines.

Marginalia decorate the edges of many pages. These butterflies, native to Minnesota, were executed in acrylic by Chris Tomlin.

and they sewed fig leaves together and made loincloths for themselves. ❧ They heard the sound of the LORD God walking in the garden at the time of the evening breeze; and the man and his wife hid themselves from the presence of the LORD God among the trees of the garden. 9 But the LORD God called to the man, and said to him, "Where are you?" 10 He said, "I heard the sound of you in the garden, and I was afraid, because I was naked; and I hid myself." 11 He said, "Who told you that you were naked? Have you eaten from the tree of which I commanded you not to eat?" 12 The man said, "The woman whom you gave to be with me, she gave me fruit from the tree, and I ate." 13 Then the LORD God said to the woman, "What is this that you have done?" The woman said, "The serpent tricked me, and I ate." 14 The LORD God said to the serpent,

"Because you have done this,
    cursed are you among all animals
    and among all wild creatures;
upon your belly you shall go,
    and dust you shall eat
    all the days of your life.
15 I will put enmity between you and the woman,
    and between your offspring and hers;
he will strike your head,
    and you will strike his heel."

16 To the woman he said,

"I will greatly increase your pangs in childbearing;
    in pain you shall bring forth children,
yet your desire shall be for your husband,
    and he shall rule over you."

17 And to the man he said,

"Because you have listened to the voice of your wife,
    and have eaten of the tree
    about which I commanded you,
    'You shall not eat of it,'
cursed is the ground because of you;
    in toil you shall eat of it all the days of your life;
18 thorns and thistles it shall bring forth for you;
    and you shall eat the plants of the field.
19 By the sweat of your face
    you shall eat bread
until you return to the ground,
    for out of it you were taken;
you are dust,
    and to dust you shall return."

20 The man named his wife Eve, because she was the mother of all living. 21 And the LORD God made garments of skins for the man and for his wife, and clothed them. ❧ Then the LORD God said, "See, the man has become like one of us, knowing good and evil; and now, he might reach out his hand & take also from the tree of life, and eat, and live for-

ever"— 23 therefore the LORD God sent him forth from the garden of Eden, to till the ground from which he was taken. 24 He drove out the man; and at the east of the garden of Eden he placed the cherubim, and a sword flaming and turning to guard the way to the tree of life.

4

Now the man knew his wife Eve, and she conceived and bore Cain, saying, "I have produced a man with the help of the LORD." 2 Next she bore his brother Abel. Now Abel was a keeper of sheep, and Cain a tiller of the ground. 3 In the course of time Cain brought to the LORD an offering of the fruit of the ground, 4 and Abel for his part brought of the firstlings of his flock, their fat portions. And the LORD had regard for Abel & his offering, 5 but for Cain and his offering he had no regard. So Cain was very angry, and his countenance fell. 6 The LORD said to Cain, "Why are you angry, and why has your countenance fallen? 7 If you do well, will you not be accepted? And if you do not do well, sin is lurking at the door; its desire is for you, but you must master it." ❧ Cain said to his brother Abel, "Let us go out to the field." And when they were in the field, Cain rose up against his brother Abel, and killed him. 9 Then the LORD said to Cain, "Where is your brother Abel?" He said, "I do not know; am I my brother's keeper?" 10 And the LORD said, "What have you done! Listen; your brother's blood is crying out to me from the ground! 11 And now you are cursed from the ground, which has opened its mouth to receive your brother's blood from your hand. 12 When you till the ground, it will no longer yield to you its strength; you will be a fugitive and a wanderer on the earth." 13 Cain said to the LORD, "My punishment is greater than I can bear! 14 Today you have driven me away from the soil, and I shall be hidden from your face; I shall be a fugitive & a wanderer on the earth, and anyone who meets me may kill me." 15 Then the LORD said to him, "Not so! Whoever kills Cain will suffer a sevenfold vengeance." And the LORD put a mark on Cain, so that no one who came upon him would kill him. 16 Then Cain went away from the presence of the LORD, and settled in the land of Nod, east of Eden. ❧ Cain knew his wife, and she conceived and bore Enoch; and he built a city, and named it Enoch after his son Enoch. 18 To Enoch was born Irad; and Irad was the father of Mehujael, and Mehujael the father of Methushael, and Methushael the father of Lamech. 19 Lamech took two wives; the name of the one was Adah, and the name of the other Zil-

Each double-page spread is written by a single scribe to ensure an even texture. Calligraphers define the size of a text by its "x-height": the height of a small letter x. The Bible script has a two-millimeter x-height.

בראשית

lah.²⁰ Adah bore Jabal; he was the ancestor of those who live in tents & have livestock.²¹ His brother's name was Jubal; he was the ancestor of all those who play the lyre and pipe.²² Zillah bore Tubal-cain, who made all kinds of bronze and iron tools.

²³ The sister of Tubal-cain was Naamah. ■ Lamech said to his wives:

"Adah and Zillah, hear my voice;
you wives of Lamech, listen to what I say:
I have killed a man for wounding me,
a young man for striking me.

²⁴ If Cain is avenged sevenfold,
truly Lamech seventy-sevenfold."

²⁵ ■ Adam knew his wife again, and she bore a son & named him Seth, for she said, "God has appointed for me another child instead of Abel, because Cain killed him." ²⁶ To Seth also a son was born, and he named him Enosh. At that time people began to invoke the name of the LORD.

## 5

This is the list of the descendants of Adam. When God created humankind, he made them in the likeness of God.² Male and female he created them, and he blessed them and named them "Humankind" when they were created.

³ ■ When Adam had lived one hundred thirty years, he became the father of a son in his likeness, according to his image, and named him Seth. ⁴ The days of Adam after he became the father of Seth were eight hundred years; and he had other sons and daughters. ⁵ Thus all the days that Adam lived were nine hundred thirty years; and he died. ⁶ ■ When Seth had lived one hundred five years, he became the father of Enosh.⁷ Seth lived after the birth of Enosh eight hundred seven years, and had other sons & daughters.⁸ Thus all the days of Seth were nine hundred twelve years; and he died. ⁹ ■ When Enosh had lived ninety years, he became the father of Kenan.¹⁰ Enosh lived after the birth of Kenan eight hundred fifteen years, and had other sons and daughters.¹¹ Thus all the days of Enosh were nine hundred five years; and he died. ¹² ■ When Kenan had lived seventy years, he became the father of Mahalalel.¹³ Kenan lived after the birth of Mahalalel eight hundred and forty years, and had other sons and daughters. ¹⁴ Thus all the days of Kenan were nine hundred and ten years; and he died. ¹⁵ ■ When Mahalalel had lived sixty-five years, he became the father of Jared.¹⁶ Mahalalel lived after the birth of Jared eight hundred thirty years, and had other sons and daughters.¹⁷ Thus all the days of Mahalalel were eight hundred ninety-five

¹⁸ years; and he died. ■ When Jared had lived one hundred sixty-two years he became the father of Enoch.¹⁹ Jared lived after the birth of Enoch eight hundred years, and had other sons and daughters. ²⁰ Thus all the days of Jared were nine hundred sixty-two years; and he died. ■ ²¹ When Enoch had lived sixty-five years, he became the father of Methuselah.²² Enoch walked with God after the birth of Methuselah three hundred years, and had other sons and daughters. ²³ Thus all the days of Enoch were three hundred sixty-five years.²⁴ Enoch walked with God; then he was no more, because God took him. ²⁵ ■ When Methuselah had lived one hundred eighty-seven years, he became the father of Lamech. ²⁶ Methuselah lived after the birth of Lamech seven hundred eighty-two years, and had other sons and daughters.²⁷ Thus all the days of Methuselah were nine hundred sixty-nine years; and he died. ²⁸ ■ When Lamech had lived one hundred eighty-two years, he became the father of a son;²⁹ he named him Noah, saying, "Out of the ground that the LORD has cursed this one shall bring us relief from our work and from the toil of our hands." ³⁰ Lamech lived after the birth of Noah five hundred ninety-five years, and had other sons and daughters. ³¹ Thus all the days of Lamech were seven hundred seventy-seven years; and he died. ■ ³² After Noah was five hundred years old, Noah became the father of Shem, Ham, and Japheth.

## 6

When people began to multiply on the face of the ground, and daughters were born to them,² the sons of God saw that they were fair; and they took wives for themselves of all that they chose.³ Then the LORD said, "My spirit shall not abide in mortals forever, for they are flesh; their days shall be one hundred twenty years." ⁴ The Nephilim were on the earth in those days—and also afterward—when the sons of God went in to the daughters of humans, who bore children to them. These were the heroes that were of old, warriors of renown. ⁵ ■ The LORD saw that the wickedness of humankind was great in the earth, and that every inclination of the thoughts of their hearts was only evil continually.⁶ And the LORD was sorry that he had made humankind on the earth, and it grieved him to his heart.⁷ So the LORD said, "I will blot out from the earth the human beings I have created—people together with animals & creeping things & birds of the air; for I am sorry that I have made them." ⁸ But Noah found favor in the sight of the LORD. ⁹ ■ These are the descendants

Small pen-made "bullets" written in color mark paragraphs. The verse numbers for paragraphs appear in the margins while the remaining verse numbers appear within the body of text.

Initial capitals in color usually come at the start of each chapter. These are the final page elements added to each volume. Donald Jackson writes them with a quill.

Chapter numbers are written as large numerals separating major portions of the text.

Notes for the New Revised Standard Version appear in the lower margins of each page. The small superscript letters within the text refer to these notes.

Marginalia fill many of the borders and empty spaces within columns. Many of these small paintings depict insects and plants native to the Minnesota woods surrounding Saint John's or to the Welsh countryside near The Hendre. These ground the Bible in a particular place and time.

The butterflies are by Chris Tomlin.

known as the "Morgan Leaf," was detached long ago from the manuscript. It is in the collection of the Pierpont-Morgan Library in New York and represents one of the finest examples of Romanesque illumination. The survival of such a massive work with so few losses is nothing short of remarkable.

The Winchester Bible has been rebound twice. Originally it was a two-volume work. In the nineteenth century, the quires were broken into three volumes and then in 1948 it was bound into its present configuration of four volumes. In its original setting the Winchester Bible would probably have been kept in the chapter room of the monastery attached to the Cathedral where it would serve the community and be read from on a regular basis.

Donald's main reason for turning to the Winchester Bible was what he called its "architectural scale." The writing is dense and dark in a transitional hand, midway between a Carolingian minuscule and a Gothic. Each page is arranged in two columns of fifty-four lines each. The two-column format and the visual strength of the writing create a powerful grid which can act as an armature for a wide variety of illuminations. Because the columns are so strong, they can stand up to the force of full-page illuminations; they also allow illustrations of different shapes and sizes to react to the grid they establish.

The trick was how to translate the strength of the Winchester Bible into a format for the modern Saint John's Bible. In order to do that a whole series of elements had to be brought into the right balance. It is not at all a question of copying the medieval manuscript. Donald's task was to learn from his example and to express what he learned within the very different requirements and limitations of a contemporary book. Copying the format of the Winchester Bible was never an option. In the first place, a straight copy would be nothing more than an antiquarian exercise and not in line with his main aim: to make a book for our own time. His illuminations are much looser and more painterly than the tightly controlled Romanesque illuminations of Winchester.

Secondly, even if he were to copy the format literally, he would never achieve the same texture and balance. The simple act of shifting from the Latin text of the Vulgate, the text used at Winchester, to the English of the NRSV, would immediately alter the look of the book. Latin has fewer ascenders and descenders than does English and it leaves a cleaner channel of white space between each line. The texture of a line of English writing always breaks into this clean channel of white more aggressively. The Winchester copyist also had the luxury of breaking words and abbreviating them as he needed in order to achieve an even right-hand margin. In English word breaks have to be made according to more stringent rules and abbreviations within texts in prose are not possible. Even if he had wanted to, Donald could not have written an English Bible in the same manner as his medieval model and produce the same texture on the page.

The point in any case is not to be a copyist. As Edward Johnston observed, it is legitimate to copy a method but not a style. The modern calligraphy movement has always stressed learning from the workshop methods of the medieval scriptoria in order to understand how things were made by people who were writing with certain tools and materials. They stand as masters because they were imbued with the ethos of making things by hand. We look to them in order to make manuscripts according to methods they developed to such a high degree and we do so to make things by hand for our own generation and our own time. Donald said, "We have a long backward look. We can examine a medieval book, and say to ourselves, 'Here is a codex which functions sweetly and reasonably.' We can benefit from the hundreds of

A sample box of insects was used in Chris Tomlin's research for his marginal illustrations.

A paste-up sketch for the end of Mark's Gospel shows the cumulative process of building up a page. The different page elements—writing, headings, illustration and abstract patterning—are each created by a different artist or scribe. Many hands combine to form a satisfying whole.

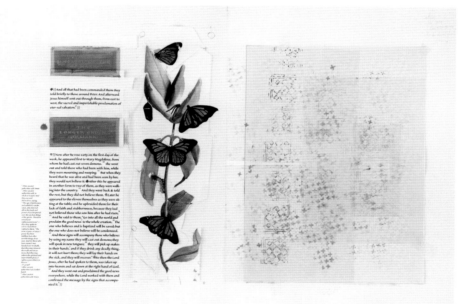

Chris Tomlin, a specialist in botanical and nature illustration, went to Minnesota to research the butterflies and plants which decorate the margins of the Bible.

years of experience represented by these books. The Saint John's Bible is modern precisely because it understands the medieval tradition. It's like a man plastering a wall with a trowel or a man laying bricks. You can do modern things with bricks. It's not a tradition. It's a function." Looking at the Winchester Bible, Donald had found a kind of weight and texture which would suit his needs. He now had the difficult task of rendering this pattern using an English text.

Sally Mae Joseph

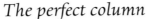

Aidan Hart

* Jan Tshichold, *The Form of the
Book,* trans. Hajo Hadeler. (Point
Roberts, Washington: Hartley &
Marks, 1991) pp. 36–64.

## The perfect column

IN ORDER TO ACHIEVE the best texture of writing, a wide set of variables had to be brought into play. The various elements needed to be subtly shifted in size and weight until they began to hum together in that visual harmonic Donald was searching for. Over and over he returned to this idea of architecture, of the power of his columns of writing. When he talks about the layout of the page and he describes these ideal columns, he reaches out his right hand and inscribes a tall column in the air. All the decisions he took were designed to give these columns the strong character they needed to give structure to his book.

Many visual elements had to be considered as Donald began to create these strong text columns. The page size had to be finalized. The size and proportion of the columns themselves had to be determined. The number of lines per column and the size of the writing needed to be brought into the mix. Once these basic factors had been fixed, all the other graphic elements had to be considered to make sure the whole format worked in harmony.

If listing the elements like this conjures up a pilot doing his pre-flight checklist, then I have failed to describe it properly. Watching Donald at work, it becomes clear that it was more like a composer scoring an orchestral piece: the overarching vision is there but the composer slowly has to bring all the parts into the right relationship. If the horns play too loudly, the violins are drowned out. Even then the piece doesn't come to life until the orchestra plays. Donald knew that a hand-made book is not just a "design" executed by a machine. What he was doing was to lay a foundation on which others—the calligraphic team— would build. As they built, they would subtly influence the shape of the whole. Like a Gothic cathedral, the Bible would change as it passed through various phases; one volume would differ subtly from the one which preceded it. Everything would grow out of a workshop acting together. Knowing this, he still had some decisions to make.

The page size he chose was larger than either Moutier-Grandval or Winchester. He opted for a page 25 x 15⅞ inches. This varied somewhat as the design progressed; the final page size is just a half inch shorter, giving him a page of 24½ x 15⅞ inches (622 x 403mm). "The half inch," Donald explained, "is the measure of reality." The skins available were just that much too small.

The next question was how to position the columns of text on the page and how to break the columns into lines of writing. Sally, Donald's principal assistant, tried designing a format using Jan Tschichold's diagram for determining the size of the text area in relationship to the page.* She told me, "When I began talking that way—" she paused. "Well, it's just not the way Donald thinks." It was too cold and analytical and it didn't produce the tall columns he was aiming at. The squat columns indicated by the diagram would not have had the strength of height he needed; he couldn't break them up with illustrations and still have a strong underlying structure. Donald's approach, as always, relied more on intuition than on theory. Sally remarked, "Designing on the hoof, I think that's what they call it."

The design of the columns had to happen in relation to the developing script as well. For the calligrapher, a long line length is ideal, for this helps the writing hit and maintain its rhythm. Line breaks which come too often only break the flow of writing. At the same time, Donald knew that calligraphy, being a bit less legible to the modern eye than type, required relatively short lines, or the reader would tire quickly. One can't read more than about ten words to a line with ease. Furthermore, in order to get a consistent line length in English requires a certain minimum number of letters per line; the more words on a line,

to be with him, and to be sent out to proclaim the message, ¹⁵and to have authority to cast out demons. ¹⁶So he appointed the twelve: Simon [to whom he gave the name Peter]; ¹⁷James son of Zebedee and John the brother of James [to whom he gave the name Boanerges, that is, Sons of Thunder]; ¹⁸and Andrew, and Philip, and Bartholomew, and Matthew, and Thomas, and James son of Alphaeus, & Thaddaeus, and Simon the Cananaean, ¹⁹and Judas Iscariot, who betrayed him. ■ Then he went home; ²⁰and the crowd came together again, so that they went out to restrain him, for people were saying, "He has gone out of his mind." ²²And the scribes who came down from Jerusalem said, "He has Beelzebul, and by the ruler of the demons he casts out demons." ²³And he called them to him, and spoke to them in parables, "How can Satan cast out Satan? ²⁴If a kingdom is divided against itself, that kingdom cannot stand. ²⁵And if a house is divided against itself, that house will not be able to stand. ²⁶And if Satan has risen up against himself and is divided, he cannot stand, but his end has come. ²⁷But no one can enter a strong man's house & plunder his prop

could not even eat. ²¹When his family heard it, they

Occasional skipped lines are an occupational hazard for the scribes. Sometimes mistakes must be erased by scraping with a knife. When a whole line has been accidentally left out, it is written in the bottom margin with this notation. This sample is reproduced at actual size.

the easier it is to get an even right hand margin. In addition, the interlinear space comes into play. Lines further apart aid legibility as the eye is guided by the broader channel of white between the lines. Move the lines very far apart and the column becomes too light in its overall color, as the balance of black writing and white spaces is thrown out of balance. Move the lines too close together and the column loses its texture composed of distinct lines of writing and becomes a solid grey mass. All these factors had to be borne in mind.

While he played with these delicate balances of visual elements, Donald began to think more and more about the relationship between the texture of writing on the page and textiles. "This is another thread, so to speak, running through the Bible," he said. The texture of the column was meant to be like a subtly woven fabric. The viewer was meant to see the overall shape of the column as a large unit made up of the subtle variation of dense writing and clean interlinear spaces; he didn't want the components to disappear but instead to sit on the page together, rather like a herringbone weave. In the illuminations he has picked up the textile theme by using bits of lace, inked with a roller, to print patterns underneath and through his larger designs. "For me," he said, "textiles are deeply symbolic of interconnectivity. Intertwining threads join to make a wonderful whole." The textile theme also helps him achieve one of the aims of The Saint John's Bible: that of reflecting all the world's societies. "Textiles are, after all, common to almost all the world's cultures."

The computer came into its own in this phase of the design. Using a typeface which approximated the weight and spacing of his hand-written text, he and his computer assistant, Vin Godier, began to produce layouts. Varying the line spacing, they tried out different proportional relationships. They could also see how their decisions would affect the length of each volume. Each layout could be used as a template to "flow in" the text on the computer, giving Donald a very precise measure of how many pages the book would be with a given line spacing and column width.

Eventually the writing and columns began to come together, only taking their final form as the first team of calligraphers arrived to be trained. The computer was put to good use as each and every page could be laid out to the grid. At the last minute, Donald had decided that the right-hand margin should be justified, rather than left ragged. Only a hard right margin gave him the visual strength he needed for his columns. The computer helped him enormously by allowing all the decisions about line breaks to be made in advance.

Donald noted happily that the final design had exactly the same number of lines per column as the Winchester Bible—he had circled around, looking for the right solution and returned to his starting point. The script itself was very far removed from that of his medieval mentor, but the columns had achieved the right balance of weight and texture.

## The elements of the page

Having worked long and hard to find a point of fixed reference within his design, Donald was suddenly free to begin playing with the balance of other elements on the page. The play was restricted, however, by the stringent rules laid down by the NRSV. All editions of the NRSV, including this manuscript version, must abide by established guidelines. This applies not simply to following the text faithfully, but also has important implications for how it sits on the page. Paragraphing and spacing between

A text from Luke 10
by Hazel Dolby.

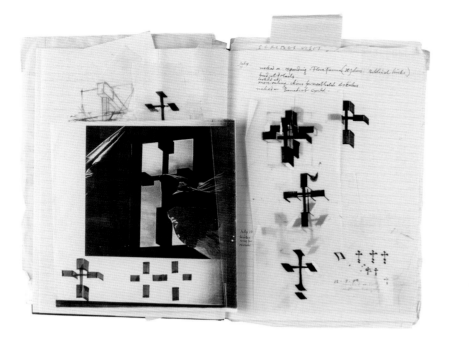

RSB

Acts 4:32
Acts 4:35
Acts 5:1-11

j or child
k or his Christ
l or child
m Gk slaves
n or child
o Gk to men

A small pen-made cross, based on the cross which stands in the bell banner in front of the Abbey church, marks passages which are quoted in the Rule of Saint Benedict. This small visual cue is a reminder of the way in which the Benedictine life has been shaped through the centuries by its encounter with the Bible. Donald Jackson's sketches show the process of abstracting the bell banner cross from a photograph.

paragraphs are all integral parts of the translation. There is even a special dictionary which establishes how words are to be broken. There are rules about the arrangement of poetry passages, as well as guidelines about footnotes. Working with the Committee on Illumination and Text (CIT) as well as with the NRSV guidelines, Donald had quite a few people looking over his shoulder at this stage of the design.

The most important thing was to guard the integrity of the columns. Donald tried breaking paragraphs much as one would in a printed text—but this left large gaps of various lengths in the right-hand margin every time a paragraph ended. He opted instead for a system of small colored bullets within the text block to indicate paragraph breaks. This left the columns solid and uninterrupted. Donald had to negotiate a special permission with the NRSV committee to use these bullets. Most verse numbers are placed within the text, written with a smaller pen, while the verse numbers corresponding to the beginnings of new paragraphs dance in the margins.

The primary divisions in the text break each volume into its constituent books. Each book begins with an illuminated title, fitting largely within the grid of the columns. These are lush and colorful and many have raised and burnished gold letters.

The secondary divisions of the text were made at the chapters. Two or three blank lines between each chapter separate the sections (depending on the length of the "widow," or short line at the end of the preceding paragraph). A large chapter number appears in this space and a three-line drop capital marks the beginning of the new chapter. Every now and again, chapters break in the middle of continuous text or chapters begin right next to illuminations; in these cases the chapter numbers appear in the outer margins.

All the footnotes to the text appear in the outermost margins of each page. The titles of the books appear in "running heads" in the upper left-hand corner of the page; in the Old Testament these are mirrored on the upper right corner by their Hebrew equivalents.

Poetry has to be treated very carefully. The NRSV requires a system of indentations which specifies

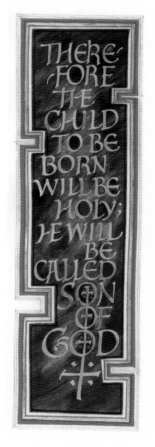

THERE
FORE
THE
CHILD
TO BE
BORN
WILL BE
HOLY;
HE WILL
BE
CALLED
SON
OF
GOD

A text from Luke 1 by Donald Jackson.

Rubber stamps and stencils were used to make the *Tree of Life* carpet page based on an Indian quilt. The stamps were hand cut. Lino ink was rolled out on a glass plate and used to print the pattern. Two mirror-image stamps were cut allowing for the gentle curve of the branches.

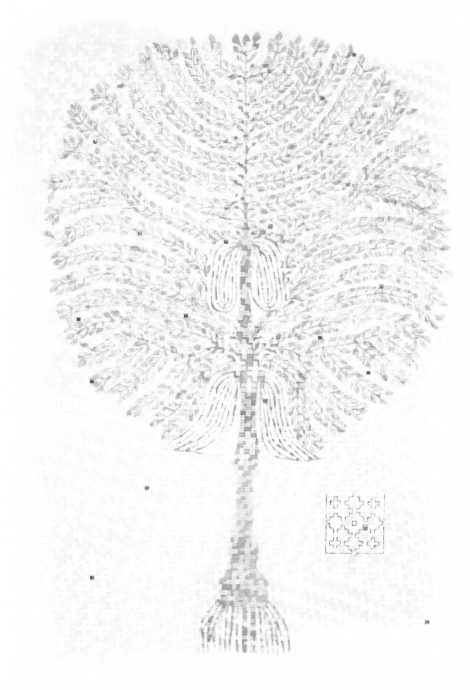

Carpet pages appear at the end of each Gospel, serving two functions: they provide a visual pause between each book and cover the show-through of the full-page illumination on the following page. Sally Mae Joseph created this page with its *Tree of Life* theme.

where each line must begin. There are four different levels of indentation. In order to fit poetry into the format of the column, Donald chose to have it written slightly smaller, which allows many lines to appear in full without having to run into a second line.

The effect of all these carefully orchestrated elements is to enliven the margins and the text with a host of minor themes all carefully balanced to play off the solidity of the great columns of writing.

There are, interestingly, no elaborately illuminated initial letters (in the traditional sense) in The Saint John's Bible. The CIT pointed out that these have relatively little function in an English book. In Latin many of the initial words of sentences are significant, thus illuminating and decorating the first word of a passage often serves as a device to highlight the content of the text. In English where the first word is so often "the" or "a" or "there," these markers lose their significance.

## Carpet pages

THE CARPET PAGES are purely decorative pages appearing at the end of each Gospel. They have a dual function. They create a visual pause between one book and the next. They also veil the back of full-page illuminations. The vellum pages are gently translucent, and show-through can become an unsightly problem to modern eyes when a heavy illustration is placed on the back of a blank page.

There is ample precedent for these illuminations in the medieval tradition. The term "carpet page" is used by contemporary scholars to describe certain full-page illuminations in insular manuscripts like the Lindisfarne Gospels and the Book of Kells. It aptly describes the dense, interwoven texture of crosses and linked animal forms which is the distinguishing feature of these pages. Donald's concept for the carpet pages was inspired by textile patterns of the Middle East, India and Pakistan. His brief to Sally Mae Joseph was to create carpet pages that would incorporate the sense of loosely woven fabric.

Sally began by thinking through how she could achieve the "veiled" background. After many days experimenting, she was having difficulty finding a way. "A friend of mine suggested I experiment with a pattern of interlocking crosses. I made a grid and started coloring in the squares," she said.

These patterns suggested the use of a stencil. "Donald liked that idea, so I made a stencil and using a very dry brush, I covered the whole surface with white Plaka paint. It made a lacy background which was quite neutral."

Sally Mae Joseph then began to create the *Tree of Life* carpet page at the end of Luke's Gospel.

"Donald gave me a photograph of a bedspread his daughter had bought back from India; he wanted me to replicate the design using rubber stamps," she remembered. "I said to him, 'I'm not sure I can.'" Her voice dropped pitch. "'You have to,' he said. And so I did."

She cut two rubber stamps, one for the branches on the right side, the other for those on the left. The difficulty was getting the right amount of curve to enable the subtle shape of the branches to flow "naturally." Rolling out lino ink on a glass plate, she printed the design onto the background she had made. The trunk was added using a hand-cut paper stencil and a very dry brush.

"It was all a very new experience," she reflected. "It was a steep learning curve. Lino ink, rubber stamps, stencils—they were all new to me."

LUKE

**AND MARY SAID,**

46 My soul magnifies the Lord,
and my spirit rejoices in God my Savior,
47 for he has looked with favor
on the lowliness of his servant
Surely, from now on all generations
will call me blessed;
48 for the Mighty One has done
great things for me,
and holy is his name.
49 His mercy is for those who fear him
from generation to generation.
50 He has shown strength with his arm;
he has scattered the proud
in the thoughts of their hearts.
51 He has brought down the
powerful from their thrones,
and lifted up the lowly;
52 he has filled the hungry with good things,
and sent the rich away empty.
53 He has helped his servant Israel
in remembrance of his mercy,
54 according to the promise he
made to our ancestors,
to Abraham & to his descendants forever.

56 And Mary remained with her about three months
57 and then returned to her home. Now the time came for Elizabeth to give birth, and she bore a son.
58 Her neighbors and relatives heard that the Lord had shown his great mercy to her, and they rejoiced with her.
59 On the eighth day they came to circumcise the child, and they were going to name him Zechariah after his father. 60 But his mother said, "No; he is to be called John." 61 They said to her, "None of your relatives has this name." 62 Then they began motioning to his father to find out what name he wanted to give him. 63 He asked for a writing tablet & wrote, "His name is John." And all of them were amazed. 64 Immediately his mouth was opened & his tongue freed, and he began to speak, praising God. 65 Fear came over all their neighbors, and all these things were talked about throughout the entire hill country of Judea. 66 All who heard them pondered them & said, "What then will this child become?" For, indeed, the hand of the Lord was with him. 67 Then his father Zechariah was filled with the Holy Spirit and spoke this prophecy:

Blessed be the Lord God of Israel,
for he has looked favorably
on his people and redeemed them.
He has raised up a mighty savior for us
in the house of his servant David,
as he spoke through the mouth
of his holy prophets from of old,
that we would be saved from our
enemies and from the hand
of all who hate us.
Thus he has shown the mercy
promised to our ancestors,
& has remembered his holy covenant,
the oath that he swore

Three special treatments appear
on a single spread in the Gospel
according to Luke. These were
created by Sally Mae Joseph.
The texts are the *Magnificat*, the
Virgin Mary's canticle of joy, the
*Benedictus*, Zechariah's song, and
the *Gloria in Excelsis*, the song of
the angels in Bethlehem.

to our ancestor Abraham, 74 that we, being rescued from the hands of our enemies, might serve him without fear, 75 in holiness & righteousness before him all our days.

76 And you, child, will be called the prophet of the Most High; for you will go before the Lord to prepare his ways, 77 to give knowledge of salvation to his people by the forgiveness of their sins. 78 By the tender mercy of our God, the dawn from on high will break upon us, 79 to give light to those who sit in darkness & in the shadow of death, to guide our feet into the way of peace."

80 ◼ The child grew and became strong in spirit, and he was in the wilderness until the day he appeared publicly to Israel.

## 2

I n those days a decree went out from Emperor Augustus that all the world should be registered. 2 This was the first registration and was taken while Quirinius was governor of Syria. 3 All went to their own towns to be registered. 4 Joseph also went from the town of Nazareth in Galilee to Judea, to the city of David called Bethlehem, because he

was descended from the house and family of David. 5 He went to be registered with Mary, to whom he was engaged and who was expecting a child. 6 While they were there, the time came for her to deliver her child. 7 And she gave birth to her firstborn son and wrapped him in bands of cloth, and laid him in a manger, because there was no place for them in the inn. 8 ◼ In that region there were shepherds living in the fields, keeping watch over their flock by night. 9 Then an angel of the Lord stood before them, and the glory of the Lord shone around them, and they were terrified. 10 But the angel said to them, "Do not be afraid; for see—I am bringing you good news of great joy for all the people: 11 to you is born this day in the city of David a Savior, who is the Messiah, the Lord. 12 This will be a sign for you: you will find a child wrapped in bands of cloth and lying in a manger." 13 And suddenly there was with the angel a multitude of the heavenly host, praising God & saying,

14 GLORY TO GOD IN THE HIGHEST HEAVEN, & ON EARTH PEACE AMONG THOSE WHOM HE FAVORS!"

15 ◼ When the angels had left them & gone into heaven, the shepherds said to one another, "Let us go now to Bethlehem and see this thing that has taken place, which the Lord has made known to us." 16 So they went with haste and found Mary and Joseph, and the child lying in the manger. 17 When they saw this, they made known what had been told them about this child; 18 and all who heard it were amazed at what the shepherds told them. 19 But Mary treasured all these words and pondered them in her heart. 20 The shepherds returned, glorifying and praising God for all they had heard and seen, as it had been told them. 21 ◼ After eight days had passed, it was time to circumcise the child; and he was called Jesus, the name given by the angel before he was conceived in the womb. 22 ◼ When the time came for their purification according to the law of Moses, they brought him up to Jerusalem to present him to the Lord 23 (as it is written in the law of the Lord, "Every firstborn male shall be designated as holy to the Lord"), 24 and they offered a sacrifice according to what is stated in the law of the Lord, "a pair of turtledoves or two young pigeons." 25 ◼ Now there was a man in Jerusalem whose name was Simeon; this man was righteous and devout, looking forward to the consolation of Israel, and the Holy Spirit

f Other ancient authorities read Elizabeth.
g Gk a horn of salvation
h Other ancient authorities read has broken upon
i Or the Christ
j Gk army
k Other ancient authorities read peace, goodwill among people
l Gk Symeon.

## *Special treatments*

CERTAIN PASSAGES are selected to be handled as "special treatments." These are portions of the text which are written in a larger size and decorated with gold and color. They highlight biblical texts which are used regularly in worship, such as the Lord's Prayer, or key texts within the Judeo-Christian tradition, such as the command to love one's neighbor.

When Donald began the Bible, he intended all these special treatments to be continuous parts of the text and so in the first volume they appear within the body of the writing. He quickly discovered the limitations of this approach. If the special treatments were embedded within the text, their placement on the page was difficult to adjust—they fell randomly on the page. He was also obliged to follow the NRSV strictures for layout. In the first volume he wrestled with these limitations. In later volumes, he opted to treat them as separate illustrations, leaving the text uninterrupted. Special treatments became illuminations in their right, which gave him much greater flexibility in their positioning and allowed him to play with the shapes of the words.

A single opening from the Gospel of Luke illustrates the variety and sumptuousness of these special treatments. Luke's account of the birth of Christ contains a number of key texts which have worked their way into the liturgical life of the Church through the centuries. The *Magnificat*, Mary's song of joy, the *Benedictus*, Zechariah's canticle, and the *Gloria in Excelsis*, the song of the angels to the shepherds of Bethlehem, all stand out from the text in color and gold.

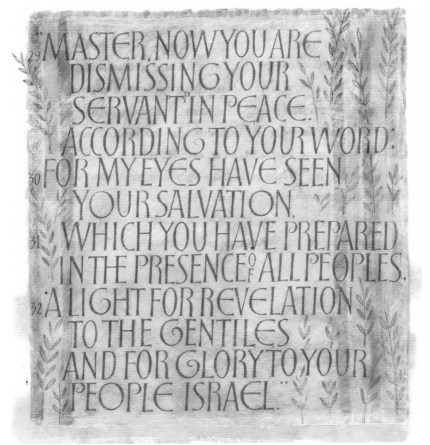

A special treatment by Hazel Dolby. Each artist brings a unique sensibility to the special treatments he or she creates. This text has been treated with great delicacy and refinement in Hazel's signature style.

Sally was responsible for many of these special treatments. She explained, "Donald had done a rough of the text with a gothic script, which had helped him see how much space to reserve at the planning stage when working on layout with Vin Godier. He'd also done a version with a pointed, free italic. I had to use that as my starting point. He liked the free italic and said he wanted gold on a colored background. I had never used a colored background in my work. I spent days with paper and paint doing experiments."

Blue was selected as a background color for the *Magnificat*, a logical choice as blue has always been associated with the Virgin Mary. Sally remarked, "Brown just seemed right for Zechariah. For the *Gloria in Excelsis,* Donald suggested I look at the work of Paul Klee."

The backgrounds were laid with a wide decorator's brush. Rubbed down with sandpaper, they acquired a pleasingly distressed finish. The letters were added in gold—raised and burnished gold on a gesso ground for the *Magnificat* and *Benedictus* and shell gold, a finely ground gold in a gum medium, for the *Gloria in Excelsis.*

"This was the first gilding I did in the studio. I wasn't doing it the way Donald did. In the end I used his method; he was worried that the gesso would dry out too much and not take the gold properly if I did it my way. It was January and we had to keep the heat off so the humidity would stay high in the studio."

The special treatments stand somewhere between text and illumination. The strong architecture of the page is designed to create a powerful armature against which the illustrations and marginalia can dance and play freely. The layout has enough variability in itself to support page after page of continuous text without becoming dull and enough consistency and weight to stand up against the visual demands of the illuminations.

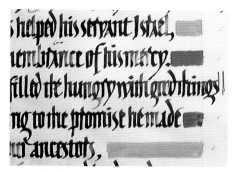

A sketch by Donald Jackson for the *Magnificat* in a vigorous gothic script provided a point of reference for Sally Mae Joseph as she worked on her special treatment of the text.

A full-page illumination of the *Nativity of Christ* appears opposite the opening of Luke's Gospel. Michael Patella, OSB, chair of the Committee on Illumination and Text, commented on this image, "The exciting thing is to see the theological briefs come to life. The Luke page contains everything we said in our brief."

# CHAPTER 6

# THE WORK OF THE C·I·T

I WAS at Saint John's to meet members of the Committee on Illumination and Text (CIT), and I was five minutes behind schedule. When I burst into the room which had been set up for interviews, breathless from running across the campus, Johanna Becker, OSB, was waiting for me.

"I'm sorry I'm late."

"That's all right. You have forty-five minutes. I have another appointment right after this one."

Out came my pad and she launched straight in. Sister Johanna talked with intensity and purpose, barely pausing to take a breath. I wrote furiously, trying to keep up with her stream of thought. Exactly forty-five minutes later, she rose, thanked me and was on her way.

In June 2002, I interviewed four members of the Committee on Illumination and Text, the CIT. These are busy people with impressive academic and career credentials. The chairman of the committee, Michael Patella, OSB, had just left for his sabbatical. Johanna Becker, OSB, Susan Wood, SCL, Alan Reed, OSB, and Nathanael Hauser, OSB, took time to talk with me about the work of the group.

Their different temperaments reflected some of the diversity of the committee. Sister Johanna was as soft-spoken as she was formidable. Sister Susan was quiet, thoughtful, perhaps even guarded. A wry smile sometimes lit her face as she talked. Brother Alan, shifting back and forth to ease his back pain, had an air of world-weariness about him, generous and cynical by turns. Father Nathanael was enthusiastic, leaning forward eagerly in his chair, his eyes dancing as he talked. As they spoke of the work of the committee, they talked with great humility, acknowledging their own limits, giving lots of credit and always wary to criticize others.

The CIT is the key committee on The Saint John's Bible project. Its main work has been to write detailed briefs for each illumination in the Bible. It reviews Donald's sketches and works with him as the illuminations develop. It formally accepts Donald's work. With such a pivotal role, the CIT is a flashpoint for tensions. Its members have a responsibility to the Saint John's community to guide the Bible through its making; they are also responsible to work creatively with Donald. They form a microcosm of community life, working slowly and sometimes painfully to find the best ways of moving the project forward.

Susan said, "This committee's had a rocky history, both internally and with Donald. There have been personality conflicts and ideological differences." There were disagreements about the role of artistic freedom and tensions over deadlines. Susan remarked, "Originally the group was called the Production Committee." This caused problems, suggesting that the committee was responsible for delivering a product on time. With a change of name, the committee's role was more clearly defined as a thoughtful steering group.

Nathanael, who has been on the CIT since its inception, told me, "I was at the first meeting before the committee began. Donald was there. I could see his eyes." Nathanael's own eyes grew wide as he re-imagined the scene. He could see Donald's dawning realization: "These people are going to be directing me."

Susan said, "The CIT is a communal activity. This is a multifaceted project. Did anyone foresee the complexity?"

She continued, "Donald might have thought he could have done the whole thing by himself." Yet clearly he needed direction as he worked. He knew he would need help with the artistic side. "So he assembled an atelier of artisans. That was clear to him from the beginning: he needed to create an artistic community." Similarly he needed a monastic, scholarly community to inform and shape the work.

These intersecting communities, artistic and monastic, reflect the Benedictine setting of The Saint John's Bible. In the Middle Ages many of the great Bibles, like many great cathedrals, were the product of monastic houses. They reflected the shared wisdom of the communities which produced them. The Winchester Bible, which has influenced Donald deeply in his design for The Saint John's Bible, came out of a monastic setting. The whole book was imbued with a collaborative spirit with artists and scholar-monks working side by side. Everything, from the text itself to the illuminations which brought it to life, grew out of a deep contemplation on the Bible and its themes. Scholars labored to provide the best, most correct text and they defined themes and subjects for illumination. The illustrations often made links between passages of the Bible, drawing out the story of redemption in its fullness. The life and prayer of the community shaped the images that were being created. Artists and scribes brought form to these ideas, shaping them to the glory of God. The Saint John's Bible does this for our own time. The CIT was formed to give expression to the communal genesis of the project.

In September 2004, Donald Jackson traveled to Saint John's to deliver Psalms. Here he presents pages from the finished manuscript as Michael Patella, OSB, looks over his shoulder.

Donald Jackson comments on design decisions within the Psalms as Alan Reed, OSB, Nathanael Hauser, OSB, Michael Patella, OSB, and Johanna Becker, OSB, look on.

## Scholars and artists

MOST OF the CIT members are Benedictines. Members of other orders and secular scholars round out the membership. They are highly educated people with impressive lists of multiple higher degrees. And yet, as Susan reminded me, "This isn't a group of highly charged Scripture scholars doing meticulous academic work. It's a diverse group of people: artists, art historians, medieval historians and theologians. Columba Stewart, OSB, represents Monastic Studies, Irene Nowell, OSB, the Old Testament, and Michael, the New Testament."

During the course of the project, committee members have come and gone. While many of them have been on the committee from the beginning, there has been a steady addition of new faces to replace those who have left. At the very start of the project, David Cotter, OSB, and Michael worked together to decide which passages would be illuminated. They produced a document called the "schema" which would guide Donald and the committee. At various times, Jerome Tupa, OSB, was on the committee, as was Rosanne Keller, and Ellen Joyce. Members were chosen to form a balanced group which reflected the broad range of skills needed for a project of this complexity. Their own stories mirror the complexity of monastic life today.

Rebecca Cherry, Donald Jackson's project coordinator since June 2001, accompanied him to Saint John's to deliver the Psalms. Here she chats with Nathanael Hauser, OSB.

Nathanael, who recently celebrated his twenty-fifth year jubilee as a priest, is typical of the group. He teaches art history at the university and has worked at the Hill Monastic Manuscript Library (HMML) and at the prep school.

In the past twenty-five years, "the community has gotten smaller and older," he said. There is a great challenge balancing the spiritual, communal life with a heavy teaching load. With fewer people to do the work, monks have to be careful to defend and nurture their spiritual lives. In some ways this intentionality has deepened their spirituality.

"These days, I have more sense of people talking on a deeper level of spirituality than before. There is a sense of being here for a purpose," he said. "With smaller numbers, we have the same workload. There are some tensions keeping a monastic life. You have to fight for space. Sometimes you have to say, 'This is as far as I can go; I need my time.' We have to take lots of personal responsibility."

The mesh of organizations which makes up Saint John's could easily overwhelm the monastery which is at the heart of the community. "We want to be a monastery which is running a university, not the other way around." As education becomes more complicated, maintaining that equilibrium takes work. At the turn of the century, it was much more straightforward. "Bring a pig, we'll teach your kids—that was the tuition!" Those days are long gone.

Alan was blunt. "I got conscripted onto the committee. I came in the middle of the thing." An artist and designer, as well as curator of the monastery and university art collections, he was quick to point out he had no scriptural qualifications.

"I came to Saint John's as a young man to study architecture," he said. "My vocation to the monastic community was artistic as much as spiritual. I never had a theology course as a young monk. I had one class in Old Testament and one class in New Testament; I don't remember either one. It didn't teach me to love the Old Testament. Working on the committee helped me love the Old Testament."

He wanted to know whom I would interview after him.

"Who's next?" he asked.

"Susan Wood."

"Oooooh. These are such great people."

Susan described herself as coming to the committee both as an insider and an outsider. "I'm not a monastic. I am a Sister of Charity. My community is in Leavenworth, Kansas. Ours is not a monastic but an apostolic, Vincentian spirituality." I asked her to explain the difference.

"It is based on the work of Saint Vincent de Paul," she said. She smiled at the irony of where she has ended up. "Here I am in the rural Midwest. I've been at Saint John's for ten years. I work as the Associate Dean of the School of Theology. I am a systematic theologian, not a Scripture scholar or an artist. I came as an observer of the text."

Johanna also made her disclaimer. "I'm not a biblical scholar. I pray the psalter daily. I'm not a theologian. I am a lifelong artist. Later, in art history, I went in for Asia; I didn't like the Renaissance." She described her contribution to the committee. "I bring visualizations to the CIT. I don't bring a Bible with me. Columba would bring a well-worn Greek Bible, and would translate straight from the text. I want to think what I see: I don't want to have a text in front of me."

There are certain themes which she is eager to see prominently featured in the Bible project. "I'm here to put forward the feminine, artists and non-Christians." Her work with the World Parliament of Religions and the Monastic Interreligious Dialogue reflects her passion for Eastern religion.

"Non-professionally, but personally, I'm interested in how the universe came to be, in cosmology." She noted with a certain pride, "I was the one who sent Donald the NASA URL for the image from the Hubbell Space Telescope," which was included in one of the illuminations.

The committee with all its variety of expertise and opinion, has embarked on a scriptural conversation which has grown and matured over the years. That conversation has guided the making of The Saint John's Bible from its outset.

## Working together

"OUR WORK is sort of like a prayer service with lots of laughter," Alan said. "We're close friends doing communal *lectio divina*."

Nathanael echoed Alan. "We describe it as communal *lectio divina*. We have a good time."

*Lectio divina*—holy reading—is an ancient monastic tradition of careful, prayerful reading. Nathanael explained, "Doing *lectio* is very strongly emphasized in the monastic house. Most people try to get in an hour at least every day."

"Is it a specific technique?" I asked him.

"No. It's not a technique thing. It's more about entering into a psychologically more receptive state: 'This is *lectio* time.'"

*Lectio* time is qualitatively different from ordinary time. It is not a time to study the Scriptures in an academic way. It speaks to a different part of the psyche. "I get into a meditative state," Nathanael said. "The key is to read slowly enough—to be comfortable stopping when a word or phrase catches my attention, and then allowing it to speak throughout my day. It's like a cow chewing the cud."

The practice of *lectio* requires a certain discipline, he said. "At times it takes mental gymnastics to get away from scholarly issues. It's like the way medievals read Scripture. You begin to see underneath the literal word."

Digital artistry reunites the members of the Committee on Illumination and Text for a promotional group portrait taken in 2001. Back row: Johanna Becker, OSB, Michael Patella, OSB, chair, Nathanael Hauser, OSB, Alan Reed, OSB. Front row: Irene Nowell, OSB, Ellen Joyce, Susan Wood, SCL, and Columba Stewart, OSB. The image of Ellen Joyce was electronically imported into the portrait.

Other members of the broader Saint John's community have served at various times on the Committee on Illumination and Text including Rosanne Keller and David Cotter, OSB.

In an early meeting with the Committee on Illumination and Text, Donald Jackson described the vitality he sought for the Bible script. Using the tools he had at hand, he gave an impromptu demonstration.

With the emphasis on *lectio* within the monastic community, there has been a growing appreciation for non-linear, associative reading of Scripture. "The language is starting to come back. It's so different from when I started doing theology," Nathanael remarked.

Communal *lectio divina* clarifies the themes which will inform the making of the book "so Donald is not just drawing on his own resources. He is not an artist working in isolation." His work is drawn into this communal, prayerful exploration of the meanings of the text.

The twice monthly meetings of the committee usually last an hour and a half. In that time the group first looks at images Donald has sent and then turns to a particular illumination.

Before each meeting, Michael sends out a memo describing what the committee will be doing. "So theoretically," Nathanael told me, laughing, "everyone has read what we're going to work on."

Alan described his first meeting. "I was surrounded by people who knew every word of the Bible. I brought my Bible with me, opened it and the spine went crack. It was so humiliating!"

The group humored him—"Oh, you brought your good Bible, not the one you read!"

The committee is almost equally divided between what Nathanael describes as "artistic and theology types." They've worked hard to learn each others' language. He said, "A theologian will give an introductory talk, just to bring us into it. It's like first sitting down and starting to read: it focuses our attention. At the early meetings we had to work through it. People were talking theology—the artist types were nodding off. Now we flow back and forth."

The back-and-forth dialogue has opened up the Bible for many on the committee. Nathanael described the pleasure of listening to "a person with real expertise." It would be exciting if the Bible project spawned other groups who could work creatively with the Scriptures in the way the committee has learned to do.

"My personal vision of the Bible has been deepened by talking about it. It's made my own reading of Scripture more exciting," said Nathanael.

After one of the scholars has talked about the Scripture passage before them, there is an open discussion. Sometimes this begins with a hush. Nathanael described it as a kind of pause; he stared into space for a moment, then snapped his fingers. "Then someone will bring up a topic. People begin bringing up images. It's allowed to be free flowing."

Susan said, "The artists have taught us how to see, to think in images. It hasn't always come naturally. As a systematic theologian, I'm linear and verbal. Johanna's great gift is to sit and imagine. We toss out various possibilities, getting into the text, imagining our way in graphically. Johanna does that best. Alan likes abstract art. He images very differently from Johanna. Johanna does it more concretely. Alan, more abstractly."

"The theologians have good visual insights," Alan said. He gives Sister Irene credit for the way she brought her enthusiasm to their meetings. "I even went out and bought her book—and it doesn't even have pictures in it!"

As they discuss a passage, the group begins to select which images "work" and which ones don't. Nathanael said, "We talk around an image someone has in mind. Then if it becomes clear it's not what we like, it gets edited out." The best images and ideas make it into the briefs.

Susan said, "Most conversation is free association—How does this text relate to other texts?" They might look at particular images, and see what parallels emerge. For instance, a garden image might be in

The members of the Committee on Illumination and Text describe their work as "communal *lectio divina.*" They discuss scholarly aspects of each text and then allow their imaginations free rein to explore new dimensions of meaning.

the text. What does that conjure up? People begin listing passages which occur to them—Creation, Eden, Gethsemane, the Song of Songs.

"We pick up motifs," she continued. "We look for references to Christ and we note passages in the liturgical life of the Church. For example, the Joel passage used on Ash Wednesday. We pull that out of our communal recollection of life. A passage from Sirach came up: 'Spread your fragrance like incense.' I asked, 'Isn't that used on the feast of Saint Benedict?' The others didn't recall."

She added, "The briefs are not academically researched. The footnotes in the Oxford study edition will influence us and *The Collegeville Bible Commentary* of the New American Bible is also available at the meetings." The aim, after all, is not to produce a detailed commentary, but to open a conversation which will inform Donald's working process. It is intentionally open-ended.

Susan said, "We sit until we have nothing left to say."

Johanna remarked, "After one and a half hours, you lose focus. It's so intense." She added, "We have an excellent secretary. She attends the meetings and she makes a tape recording that she can take away." All the spontaneous reactions are typed into briefs under headings. "She gets them concretized. We get the minutes electronically and have input."

The editing of the briefs is an important stage in the process. The committee wants to share their thoughts with Donald, not box him in. Nathanael said it was important to communicate to him that "these were our thoughts. On paper, it sounds like a directive of sorts. So we put it in the subjunctive somehow. Unless we're saying, 'It's theologically important that you do or don't do this,' the rest is suggestion. It stokes the engines, gets them going."

Johanna added, "What are the benefits of CIT? It's non-judgmental: a concrete validation of the importance of free thinking. We're not evaluating—it's a free discussion. We never arrive at an idea by ourselves; there is a creative interplay of concepts with no limits."

The group enjoys these intense discussions. Nathanael said, "It's the only committee where you leave feeling refreshed, excited. Johanna echoed him: "I'm on a lot of committees. I look forward to this one."

## New directions

ON MEMORIAL DAY weekend 2002 the CIT made a breakthrough. Having worked together for several years, they had built a working relationship with each other and with Donald. Michael was about to leave for his sabbatical and so they took themselves away to a retreat center in Chaska, outside Minneapolis. In an intense three-day weekend, they did an entire year's worth of work. The briefs for Psalms, Prophets and Historical Books had to be created. Nathanael told me, "We went through a metamorphosis with Psalms."

Alan said, "At this three-day meeting, there was no minute stuff, no review of images. We just hunkered down with Scripture. 'Bible camp' we called it. It was wonderfully intense. Michael is the most disciplined person I know. Our sessions lasted from eight-thirty in the morning until noon, and two forty-five in the afternoon until six—sitting in a room, hours on end."

The Psalter is at the core of the monastic life. It is also a book of poetry. They decided to throw out earlier ideas and address the psalms from scratch.

Alan said, "The Psalms are easier for me to deal with. The Psalms you know." His face rumpled, and he

The theological briefs created by the Committee on Illumination and Text guide Donald Jackson as he works out visual interpretations of the chosen Bible texts. Freely responding to the ideas in the brief, he begins to work up a sketch. Michael Patella, OSB, remarked, "The illuminations are not illustrations. They are spiritual meditations on a text. It is a very Catholic approach to the Scriptures. It says, 'look at this.' It is rich, decorative, colorful."

The sketch process develops as gold and color begin to define the details. Once a rough has reached a certain point, Donald Jackson sends it via the Internet to the Committee on Illumination and Text for comments.

A rough paste-up demonstrates the relationship of the illumination to the page of writing which it faces. All the essential elements have come into place, balanced around the central gold shaft of divine light. The scale of the drawing has become more refined and delicate, better suited to the scale of the whole.

Photocopies, acetate overlays and painted figures are taped into place as the design is slowly resolved. A vigorous bull based on a Stone Age painting from the cave in Lascaux, France, has taken a prominent place in the composition. Donald Jackson remarked, "The bull expresses the vitality and power of earthly life, as well as the humble circumstances of Christ's birth. It contrasts with the ethereal wonder of the flying angels and heavenly light descending into the world."

added, "That's affected—you can plan your whole day while saying psalms and not miss a word!" But since working on the briefs, "I've started noticing the Psalms."

The committee as a whole was more familiar with the Psalter than with other biblical books. By now it was also more familiar with Donald and his working process. Nathanael described how this affected their work: "With psalms, we now know visually how Donald works. We are veering around to thinking, 'How can we help Donald play to his strengths?' This only came with working through various things. On the psalms, we got almost giddy with what Donald could do with this. That worry—will it work?—has gone away now. At first it was like the New Testament—should every page have something on it? Then we asked ourselves, 'How would Donald feel?'" They imagined him using different styles to express subtle theological ideas. "It's an exciting process—deeply theological—how do we put that on a page? It will all be calligraphically done as far as we can see—a real change from the way we first thought of it."

Nathanael felt that the group had changed. It was "spiritually deepened." He laughed and said, "I think I know what happened. Talking to scholars, the scholastic part of it came to life." He put his hands out in front of him, far apart. "This was the creative side," he said, looking to one hand, "and this was the scholarly." He brought his hands together. "Now, they are integrated much more: I've seen it in the others. For me, I feel that there isn't that kind of break between the scholarly and the creative. It's a kind of prayer experience when you're done."

He added, "I've run study groups: 'we must be serious now.' For us we just go right at it. We make jokes, get angry. It's a whole different experience."

"The Psalms will be the most beautiful book," Alan predicted. "There will be small keys to highlight psalms used in the daily office, or passages quoted by Christ. Maybe it won't have any gold in it!" In an aside, he added, "Gold is like the computer—click a button. 'Oh wow, that's cool!' Gold is like that. When you don't know what else to do, add gold." Gold, to Alan, is "splashy"—not the kindest adjective in his lexicon.

Nathanael is delighted with the gold. "It's a pity that no reproduction will ever stand up to the original. Most people will see reproductions. But they won't have the visceral experience of gold on the page."

Susan said, "The Psalms brief is architectural rather than illustrational." The committee looked at the Psalter and its division into five books. "'Amens' and 'Alleluias' indicate the end of each book." They imagined Donald exploring these textual breaks as a way of building his design. The result is a brief which is much more calligraphic than illustrational. "We didn't want Bambi leaping through the Psalms like a deer. The Psalms are not in narrative form."

Nathanael added. "I can't wait to see what Donald does with the Psalms."

The briefs are just one part of the CIT's work. Reviewing and commenting on Donald's sketches take up a good deal of their time. With this task the artists on the committee naturally come to the fore. As Susan said, "The artists have the language."

Nathanael explained this stage of their working procedure. Sketches are photographed with a digital camera at the Scriptorium and relayed to Saint John's electronically. At first "we tried showing them on the wall—that worked pretty well. Now we print out color copies for everybody; it's easier. These are sent out before our meeting. We go through our own reactions, then process them and come to the

In a last-minute correction, Donald Jackson erases a passage of text from the *Nativity* illumination using a sharp knife. When the finished work was brought to Saint John's, it became clear that the text which had been written over the left side of the image referred not to Christ but to John the Baptist. Donald made the correction on the spot, first erasing the erroneous text and replacing it with free brushwork.

meeting. Now pretty much everybody knows what the others will say. When there are disagreements, they are usually on minor points. There is no huge divergence of opinion."

Susan expressed the difficulty of working long distance. "It's a challenge," she said, "to work across an ocean, meeting with Donald several times a year face-to-face. Communication has gotten better, but Donald is ninety-nine percent visual in his orientation. We are communicating verbally." There is a lot of room for misunderstanding.

If the briefs are open-ended expressions of a process, so are the sketches. Nathanael said, "When Donald sends the images we have to do the same thing: remind ourselves, 'These are just sketches.' It took a while for both sides to become comfortable with that."

The scholars and the artists naturally approached the question differently. Nathanael told me, "On the committee, the theologians were looking at the images and parsing them like a text. The artists were asking themselves, 'What would I do if I were doing it?'"

Johanna said, "Some things I look at and think, 'I wish I'd thought of that.' Like the Bull of Lascaux which appears in the Nativity illumination." The cave at Lascaux in France contains some of the oldest representational paintings in Europe.

"It's hard as an artist not to have a specific image in mind," Alan said, reflecting on the feeling of sending out the briefs. "It's like a teaching assignment. Different stuff comes back and you think, 'These are pretty good.' It's hard not to see colors, patterns, images. For instance, the historical books are full of references to Jerusalem. I'm thinking, 'How do you express the huge sense of a people struggling to discover God in the midst of political and natural disasters?' I start to imagine patterns, contrasting colors."

When the images come back from Donald, there is the shock of another artist's reaction to the brief—"Oh, wow—ooph, I never thought of that."

Alan pulled no punches. "When Donald did one sketch and I didn't see my idea, I thought to myself, 'No, this will never do.'"

It takes a certain distance for an artist to stand back and let another artist work in freedom. Nathanael said, "I remind myself that I am trying to sense *his* vision, not *my* vision. In spirit, bringing Donald in."

The process has changed the briefs as well. Alan said, "It's moved from, 'Here's what we're thinking of' to, 'Here are the issues.'"

Speaking for the scholars on the committee, Susan said, "We all share—we share as individuals, not out of our expertise." This applies to the imagery as well as to the briefs.

Susan said, "The working relationship with Donald has been sensitive. There has been tension between the oversight that comes with patronage versus artistic freedom. Where is Donald free to do his own thing?"

There has been a question about the committee's role: what sort of oversight do they have? Do they have to formally approve each sketch? Susan said, "Donald is delighted when he presents us with something we haven't seen." Johanna told me that sometimes when they review a sketch, "Donald has already moved on." Did this pose a problem, I wondered? "No problem." But it does cause tension.

Even within the committee there is a variety of opinion about the degree of freedom Donald should enjoy as an artist. Some have argued for his complete artistic freedom, while others have wanted the committee to be more directive. Slowly, as they have worked with Donald, they have built a working relationship.

The Committee on Illumination
and Text is not the only con-
stituency which demands Donald
Jackson's time. Here he presents
his work at a media briefing on
May 26, 2004, at the Centro
Russia Ecumenica in the Vatican
City. Dietrich Reinhart, OSB, and
Abbot John Klassen, OSB, sit on
the left while Donald addresses
the crowd.

Johanna said, "Donald is a very interpersonal, sensitive person. I wasn't able to attend the presentation when Donald brought the first pages back to Saint John's. He came up to me twice to say he was sorry I wasn't there. Then he arranged a special showing and went through the whole thing, page by page. My impression is that it's far exceeded our expectations."

She feels the relationship has matured. "It's taken a long time. We were finding out what we were about; at the start, we were very directive. There is a whole bunch of prima donnas on this committee, people used to being in charge."

Sometimes, however, the committee did have to express reservations about sketches. Johanna recounted, "It was painful for both sides when we rejected something Donald did." That led to questions: "What kinds of contribution does the CIT make? How should Donald take the CIT's input?"

Susan said, "We sometimes want to say 'Stop! It's great!' He adds detail. We think he's at his best when he's more abstract, free, suggestive. Sometimes he loses fluidity and freedom and movement."

A growing trust has helped both Donald and the committee. Susan continued, "As he sees the product, he relaxes. He gets better. He has the sensitivity of an artist and a lot of pride." She caught herself, and began to laugh. "How do I say this diplomatically? He needs his independence. The committee can't tell him what he should draw but it takes an outside eye to tell an artist when he achieves the most. It remains delicate, but it's gotten better."

Johanna knows the heart of the artist. "Donald is a great showman, a great demonstrator. We were doing verbal things. He was doing visual. We said to him once, "Leave all your tools behind when we meet next. He brought the briefs which he had highlighted and filled with marginal notes. We saw for the first time how he used the briefs. We saw it was all being used."

Others are less sure how helpful Donald finds the briefs. Susan told me, "The question to ask Donald is, how do you use the briefs? I think he throws up his hands. It's the very fact that Donald envisions the whole process schematically and pictorially." And yet, "He couldn't illuminate what he illuminates without interiorizing the concept: the *Raising of Lazarus* illumination is so gripping. He resonates with the text in a deep way. It does not come out in pious language."

## Controversy and debate

CERTAIN ASPECTS of the project have occasioned deep conversations, even controversy, between Donald and the committee. Aidan Hart's work with its traditional iconographic visual language has sparked a strong debate.

Alan said, "Aidan's work really sticks out."

Nathanael also had concerns. "The Byzantine images. I'm an iconographer myself. I'm still ambivalent about them. I love the tradition. I love making icons. He's a very good iconographer as well. But it's not my vision of how the Bible is going to look."

Some of the concern stemmed from the traditional look of the imagery: did it fit a contemporary Bible? Other concerns had to do with the mixing of different styles and techniques within the volume.

Nathanael felt in the end "different styles are okay, but they have to be throughout the whole book, not willy nilly."

Susan was satisfied that the images had been negotiated successfully. "The whole worked. It will appeal to a variety of tastes. The borders which Sally Mae added around Aidan's illuminations are fluid; the work escapes the border. The borders around the iconography result in a mixed style, less rigid."

Another issue was the use of imagery from other faith traditions. The committee reflected a variety of opinions.

Johanna, who is particularly concerned with interfaith dialogue, argued for the inclusion of images from other traditions. She was also concerned that these not be misinterpreted. She said, "We were very sensitive to not be offensive to the Jewish tradition." The menorah at the opening of Matthew's Gospel went through many versions. "A member of the committee talked to a rabbi, discussing the mixture of images—the menorah, the tree of life, the genealogy of Christ. He gave the okay."

She mentioned other images she had contributed. "I suggested the stamped images from the Koran: lacy medallions in the margins." She was pleased with "some Zen symbols and the Navajo baskets in the *Loaves and Fishes* illumination. They give depth and relationship—the inter-time spanning reality of this phenomenon."

Nathanael expressed his concerns. "There have been objections to the marginalia, both artistic and theological. For example, we discussed the use of Islamic calligraphic imagery. How worldwide do we want to be? How Catholic? It brought up issues for us—what about Buddhist images? This is a Catholic Bible for a Catholic community. The images have to fit that." He was also sensitive to the use of Jewish images. "Some illuminations could be taken as critical of Judaism; a supercessionist interpretation is possible. The Scripture scholars were particularly attuned to this. People looking at certain images could object to them." He felt one of the committee's tasks was to make sure these images were used with sensitivity.

## The fruits of their labor

THEY EACH HAD their favorite illuminations.

Alan said, "I like the special treatments better than the illustrations. They are more inherently part of the writing." He clasped his hands together, fingers intertwined. "It meshes more for me." He was also partial to the *Loaves and Fishes* illumination, running around the edges of the page. It could have been an illustration of "a cute little mountainside, people munching on fish sticks." Instead the illumination exploded into the margins, evoking and not illustrating the scene. "I really, really like this one."

Johanna agreed with him. "I am so pleased with the concept of the loaves and fishes—so much better than pictures of people carrying loads of baskets. And I like the Navajo baskets, spreading through age and time and space symbolically."

Susan thought the *Raising of Lazarus* was stunning. The little figure at the end of a dark tunnel captivated her imagination. "The tunnel is in greater proportion to the figure—the figure is not dominant. The illustration is more about concept of 'raising' than on Lazarus as an individual. I love the enormous contrast between light and dark."

Johanna remembered, "An image we worked with a lot was the *Birth of Christ*. I've never lost the sense of wonder at that. Donald is working with images done for two thousand years, and he's coming up with something fresh. The face of Mary is remarkable in its wonder and tenderness. I'm personally fascinated with the bull from Lascaux—this is getting to the significant meaning of the event rather than doing something which would be illustrative."

Nathanael also recalled working on the *Birth of Christ* which was the first major illumination Donald and the committee worked on together. "I know all the pressures, the various evolutions. It was very frightening for everybody: is this going to work?" He was pleased. It had.

Susan and Alan agreed that the full-page illumination of the *Life of Paul* was successful. Susan said, "Donald is best when he's free. He has an ability to meld abstract form with content. The image of Saint Paul is embedded in a background of overlapping, interlinking churches and buildings." Alan remarked, "Saint Paul: the world and the church, with modern cities in the background, evoking how Paul took the message and spread it. It's a message for the world, against a background of houses and tenements. Donald was not drawing pictures of shipwrecks and jails."

Johanna reflected on the difficulty of creating this kind of imagery today. "There are centuries and centuries of artistic tradition. How do you do this so there's a new door, a new dimension? Every century, the Scriptures take a new dimension as human culture changes and develops." Describing the work Donald and the committee have put in, she said, "Shocking is okay. Errors you want to avoid."

She summed up the role of the committee by saying, "I'm not here to like or dislike. I'm here to perceive, to put the illuminations into context. It relieves Donald of the burden of being everything, knowing everything."

Nathanael expressed the joy of seeing the CIT's labors realized. When he first heard of The Saint John's Bible he thought, "That's serendipity! What a neat thing to do. But I never thought it would happen. There was a big discussion in the community: where does this fit in? What do we do with it afterwards?"

And yet there was "the excitement of doing something which reaches into the Benedictine past. It's deep in the bones. That excited people. And it fits our mission as Benedictines in education. The arts and education are more than vocational tech—it's about more than just getting a job.

"When I saw the first volume, I was excited. I was getting breathless at points." Did he have a favorite illumination? "No. We discuss all of them so much. We feel, 'This is my image.' It's like asking 'Which child is your favorite child?'"

A collection of design studies exploring decorative ideas for marginal illustrations and carpet pages.

# CHAPTER 7

# THE PAGE COMES TO LIFE

L IKE the monastery in Collegeville, the Scriptorium is a community. It has its own rhythms and crises. Its life reflects the passing of seasons and the cycles of the countryside. It is a calm place, but there are also moments of tension and division. Creating the illuminations, in particular, began to put strain on this little community.

## *The end of the beginning*

DONALD AND I walked into the Scriptorium. His working area had changed completely since my previous visit. Before when he had been mostly concerned with the Bible script, his corner had been uncluttered. He needed little more than pen, ink and quill knife.

Now it was different. The desk itself had not changed: it was still the calm eye of the storm, a clean, open space. But now it was surrounded by a tempest of tools and books and scraps of paper and vellum, a cacophony of colors and textures vying for attention. To one side in place of the small chair which had stood to his right hand there was now a large table covered with tubes of paint, burnishers, powdered pigments in small ceramic dishes, brushes, water pots, knives—a whole array of materials at his fingertips. Behind his chair a large flat table stood prepared for gilding and burnishing.

There was a bookshelf to his left under the window. As Donald wandered off to chat with Mark, his studio assistant at the time, I bent down and looked to see what visual sources Donald was using. The bookshelf was crammed to overflowing. Some of these were old. I picked up an exhibition catalog, *An Illustrated Souvenir of the Exhibition of Persian Art:* Burlington House, 1931. It still had a price on its cover: "Five shillings, net." It jostled against books on alchemy, angels and sacred dance. Other volumes included books on Hebrew, Islamic and medieval Christian illumination, Indian textiles, and Palestinian costume. Most of the books were full of little torn slips of paper serving as bookmarks. A glance at the rough drawings on the walls showed that he'd used his books extensively.

Donald joined me at his desk. He was subdued. It was just six weeks since he had made a trip to Saint John's to unveil the first finished pages. He had talked, entertained and politicked. To cap it off, he had walked down the central aisle of the Abbey church with his wife Mabel carrying his *Death of Christ* and *Road to Emmaus* illuminations for a grand ceremony of celebration. For the first time, he had seen his work used liturgically. The assembled crowd had gasped when they saw the page coming down the aisle. For Donald, it was confirmation that all his efforts were coming to fruition: this is why he had wanted to write a Bible. Now it was over. He was physically and emotionally wiped out. Those who see him on stage, in action, know him as a consummate performer, a delightful speaker and a perfect showman. Those who work with him behind scenes know how much he is drained by these performances.

There was more, however, to Donald's fatigue. The ceremony marked a turning point. The opening phase was done. Now the freshness had worn off. From now on it would be a long haul, keeping the pace—keeping it up, page by page, volume by volume.

In purely technical terms, the design problems posed by the Bible had entered a new phase as well. In the opening stages, the most demanding decisions had been essentially about issues of craftsmanship—where to get vellum, how to prepare it, what the script should look like, how to get a team of scribes up and running to produce pages of text. Donald had spent months answering these questions and, with the help of Sally Mae, devising systems for his team to follow. The illuminations he had created during this phase had been relatively few and must have seemed like welcomed breaks after the strain of putting his systems into operation. Now with the text more or less settled, Donald's attention had shifted almost entirely to the illuminations. More than any part of the project, these have challenged Donald to expand his range and to push his abilities. Each illustration is a small design problem of its own. This is the ultimate test because with the major illuminations, the pressure is on Donald the artist. Not the art director, the scribe or the business manager—not even the showman. The artist now came to the fore.

## The artist and his client

WHILE HE PUSHED HIMSELF artistically, Donald was also more directly engaging in a dialogue with his client. The illuminations were the product of negotiation, a back and forth conversation between The Hendre and Collegeville. No wonder Donald looked a bit worn. Sitting in front of his desk, Donald said, "The process of design is different from medieval illuminated manuscripts. It's more of a dialogue; and never forget, I'm being briefed by a committee."

He showed me emails that had gone back and forth between him and Michael. Over one illumination there had been discussions, debates, points of clarification, reactions. Donald was trying to work with a whole body of people looking over his shoulder—committees, finance people, the documentarians who want to record the process and perhaps worst of all, the demons of his own hopes and dreams and expectations for himself.

I asked him to tell me more about how the illuminations were made.

"The illuminations . . . yes," he said softly, wondering where to begin. His mind wanders. You can almost see it working as he tries to think a way in, a way to explain what he's trying to do. He looked at the table: sheaves of emails and computer roughs lay there.

"The thing . . . the thing about the illuminations . . . is that I have to lay out this book perhaps *years* before illuminating it. Look at the steps it has to go through—computer, layout, proofreading, the scribes—all before it comes to me." He paused.

"I've been relatively conservative in my layouts," he said. His eyes hardened somewhat. "You can bet your bottom dollar that the Winchester Bible was a copy of something that already existed. It was a product of generations of continuous tradition."

He picked up a book full of images from the famous manuscript. "Look, look," he said, flipping past pages. "Look at the way this initial fits into a space. They knew what they were doing. They knew what was coming. I'm looking at a computer screen."

If the artist had to come to the front row, he needed to vent his frustrations a bit beforehand. The bril-

One of Donald Jackson's notebooks contains a spontaneous watercolor of a blue heron on the shore of Lake Sagatagan at Saint John's.

Marked and annotated books provide visual stimulus during the design process. Other images are found on the World Wide Web.

Donald Jackson unpeels layers of his sketch for the *Baptism of Christ* to show how the image developed.

liant showman in Donald could handle the client just fine, but the artist wanted space—space to experiment, to be free. He looked at the computer layouts.

"I am designing the book and *guessing* at spaces. I am graphically hindered. The text is largely passive. 'Why isn't he doing exciting things with the layout of the text?'" Donald's over-the-shoulder demons were speaking again. "It's because the pages have to be laid out so long in advance. So the text has got to be a foil. In this book the dialogue between text and illustration is relatively staid."

Pointing to one place where he'd been able to play a bit with the page layouts, he said, "At least the *Raising of Lazarus* breaks the columns." On the whole, however, the layouts do have to be kept fairly simple. Donald has to commit himself very early on to a layout for each page so the scribes can keep churning out their quota of pages. He makes these decisions long before he can embark on the illuminations or even begin sketching out ideas.

His eyes jumped to the rough layout for the Book of Judges. Here he was more positive: "But then in Judges I picked up the idea of the five disparate stories which the CIT gave me. I left five spaces, which will have the five stories, like a ribbon or thread running through the whole book. All this chaos—these stories about God being far from the people, all come together at the end of the book. God is there, but in the spaces in between, in the apparent chaos of these violent stories."

Donald began to describe how he works through CIT's commentary. The sequence of illuminations was defined by a small team at Saint John's at the very beginning of the project. Michael and David

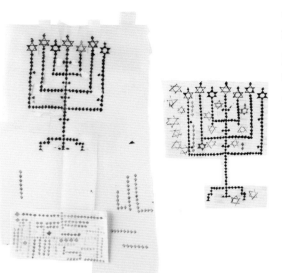

Small pen-made menorah patterns were executed by Sally Mae Joseph as an ornamental counterpoint for the end of the books of Genesis and Deuteronomy.

worked out the schema, a list of passages which would be illuminated. The schema was circulated, refined and presented to Donald with short commentaries. Donald responded, asking for more detail. On one of his copies of the schema he wrote: "By being more expansive you are not tying me down or muddling me: you are feeding me."

The CIT came back to Donald with much more comprehensive theological briefs. In these each illumination is explored at length. The first section of each brief exegetes the passage, which is to say that it explains or comments on it from the perspective of contemporary biblical criticism. The second section contains scriptural cross-references for the passage. The third section, probably the most visually helpful, is a free association in which the committee brainstorms, suggesting a huge variety of images and themes. For some illuminations the schema goes on for several pages. It is not always easy for Donald to take in all this information. "The Nativity scene—twenty-seven different ideas I'm given. I have to please a committee," he said, perhaps forgetting he'd asked to be fed more detail.

Sometimes it is not the quantity of ideas which stymies Donald, but the impenetrability of the prose. The committee sometimes slips into the technical language of its own disciplines, forgetting it is addressing an artist. At times he is utterly perplexed by what he reads: "Here we have a realized eschatology, the 'divine-man,' and yet we must be cautious for this Gospel was indeed redacted to refute Gnosticism." Illuminate that. After you've deciphered it.

Most of the time, however, briefs are more straightforward. Donald ponders the briefs and begins to

A small accordion-fold mock-up of Letters and Revelation helps Donald Jackson visualize the flow of illuminations within the text.

develop his ideas. When he presents his sketches, it is the CIT's turn to interpret what they've been given. Both sides of the negotiation have had to learn how to work together. All the sketches Donald prepares are sent to Saint John's for comment and feedback from the CIT. This has been a sensitive issue. The committee is not always sure how to interpret his sketches or to manage the working schedule. In the early days of the project, when the committee was first formed, they had tried functioning as a group responsible for riding herd on their artist. As Donald describes it, they felt responsible to produce the Bible to schedule. Their brief was refined. The group now saw itself in more of an advisory role. Still, how were they to interpret the drawings and collages they were presented by Donald? And what kind of approvals or comments would they be invited to make? Even now, the relationship was continuing to develop. Each new illumination opened new issues of control and freedom, direction and trust.

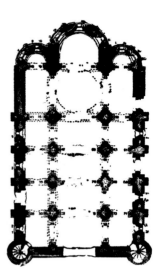

Very early in the process, Donald had produced a half size mock-up using computer type and scanned imagery to suggest the balance of image and text in the book. The imagery itself was drawn from all kinds of sources and included non-Christian religious images. The committee, quite naturally, reacted to the detailed content of the imagery, which, for Donald, was only used to indicate the scale, color and weight of the illustrations he was proposing: their content was largely beside the point. Donald presented his mock-up. The committee looked at it and wanted to know what the Buddha was doing there—a classic example of a visual artist appropriating the visual impact of a selection of images, while the more literal, verbally oriented client reacted to the detailed content of the images.

Later in the process he presented a sketch which incorporated some photocopied images. He had used the photocopier to adjust the size and scale of certain visual elements; because he had photocopied them, they'd ended up in black and white in his presentation sketch. The committee reacted by saying, "We particularly like Donald's use of grey in the image." Once again what they had seen was very different from what Donald had envisaged.

With time, the committee began to see that the images sent from the Scriptorium were rough sketches. They were loose renditions which might shift in tone, scale and color. The task of the committee was to shape and guide the content of the illumination, leaving room for Donald to work visually. Donald and the CIT began to clarify each other's roles.

Despite the CIT's need to see drawings and approve them, Donald knew he needed the flexibility to shift and change his compositions, both for his own artistic integrity, and simply in order to retain some sense of spontaneous joy in the making. In effect he would have to say, "This is a sketch. Now trust me."

With one of the early illuminations Sally Mae recalled, "Donald had done a detailed rough, and then he had to copy it." An almost impossible task especially for an artist like Donald who has always thrived on the spontaneous moment.

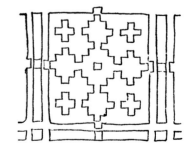

"He wasn't being free and expressive anymore," Sally said. "He did struggle with that."

In all his work, even in very precise legal documents for the Queen's signature, he tries to have some moment on the page when he is able to throw himself in and "wing it." Even in his most formal work there is usually a flourish, a tiny detail, a dab of color, which adds a spark of freshness and vitality to the page. Without it, not only would the page be less vigorous, less lively, but Donald's own interest would be dimmed: he needs to feel that slight sense of danger which comes from every encounter with the page. Plan everything ahead and the result dies. It becomes sterile.

Rubber stamps of designs from many sources are used in illuminations and carpet pages throughout The Saint John's Bible. These small designs are a *leitmotif* which runs through the book.

## Process and product

"SO WHERE DO YOU START with your sketches?" I asked him, pointing at the cluttered collage-like rough on his desk.

"The first question in most of my sketches is: What are the light and dark relationships? Where is there gold?"

Donald sketches with a large brush, using whatever colors are at hand. Dark and light areas are quickly painted in. Great swaths of inexpensive gold paint fill in for the gold leaf. From then on, Donald's sketches become collages. He pastes and tapes things in place. He adds bits and pieces photocopied from his source books; he draws or paints or writes over the emerging composition. Often, he uses acetate overlays to add elements without obliterating what is below. Sometimes he tapes in real plants: a twig, a leaf, a dried frond of plant from outside the Scriptorium door. Frequently, because the page is large, he starts with big, bold figures; these, he quickly realizes, are too large, too crude. The image gets reduced on the photocopier. The scale gets smaller and smaller, more and more precise as he circles into the composition. He picks up smaller brushes and begins adding finer detail.

We looked at the sketch of the *Nativity* page, and Donald talked about his working process. "It's very intuitive. This animal has to have its feet in shit," he said. He works with any materials he finds at hand—anything that will get his ideas down onto the page. The sketches often remain in work for months, changing in only tiny increments.

Donald stands over the work and squints. He moves a small piece of acetate left or right, often only few millimeters. He stares, breathes and moves it back again. Several rough sketches are in process at any one time. And then in a sudden attack, a rough which has hardly changed in weeks will be radically shifted, moved about, changed and come together. The circadian rhythm of the artist doesn't always match the regular meeting pattern of the CIT. There are times when an illustration goes to Collegeville for the committee to look at, only to be transformed the next day by some new intuition on Donald's part. There are times when working directly on the skin on the final illustration he continues to develop his ideas and makes changes. In Collegeville, he had pointed to a "finished" illumination and said to me, "The colors need adjusting in the small panels." He is always looking at ways to improve and develop the work.

I asked him about his sources. The illuminations are quite modern. They feel loose, free and contemporary with their generous brushstrokes, broadly abstracted figures and overlapping, juxtaposed imagery. He surprised me by pulling a book from his bookshelf on Carolingian illumination—a historic style of the ninth and tenth centuries. Turning to a page from the Gospels of Saint Medard, a fine Carolingian manuscript, he pointed to the loose brushwork and freely drawn imagery. Even the color sense echoes his own work; the violets and pinks echoed the colors of his *Road to Emmaus* illumination. He turned to another page: the Vienna Genesis. This uncial manuscript is written gold on purple-stained vellum—an opulent and rich manuscript. The illustrations, unbound by boxes or borders, populate the bottom margins of the manuscript. The relationship of figure to ground in the manuscript is closely related to Donald's free illuminations, always bursting their bounds, exploring and engaging the open space in the margins. It is striking that Donald did not invoke the Winchester Bible for the illuminations—that craftsmanlike manuscript of the Romanesque period had served him well as a model for the craftwork of the page. It could not help him with the free artistry of the illumination. It is also striking

Aidan Hart confers with Donald Jackson. He works as a traditional Orthodox icon painter. In The Saint John's Bible he uses an ancient technique in surprising ways. He and Donald have worked together on several illuminations which blend Orthodox and contemporary modes of expression within the same painting. Donald commented, "People are shocked when they hear I erased and worked over parts of Aidan's image. It's a true collaboration in which we are all working to make something bigger than any of us."

Donald Jackson and Chris Tomlin examine flora and fauna from around Saint John's. In addition to his marginal illustrations, Chris has collaborated with Donald on illuminations such as *Jacob's Ladder* and *the Garden of Eden*.

that Donald could ground his contemporary sensibility in one of the richest parts of the manuscript tradition, exploring an entirely new dimension of these ninth-century paintings.

The transition from rough sketch to final illumination is difficult. Donald, like many artists, prefers to keep his ideas loose even when he begins to attack the final illustration. As he discovered in the *Nativity* scene, if the rough is too tightly resolved the artist is left having to recreate or worse, to copy the rough. In that case the artist feels the working process as a sequence of two distinct campaigns: in the first, he resolves the design, in the second he executes it. Follow it too closely and the final version can simply die

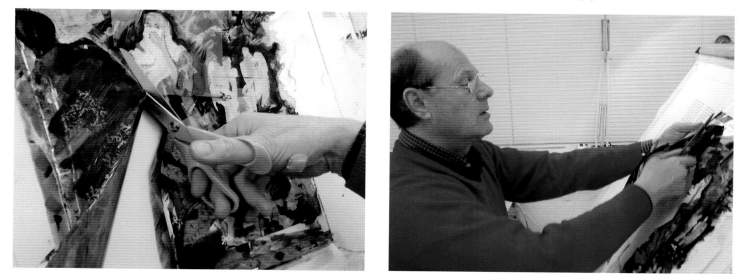

on him, losing all the vitality and spark of the rough. Graced with a clean sheet of white vellum and a fully resolved rough drawing, the artist feels, though he may not say it, that he is done. Why do it again?

The best working process is a seamless progress, not a two-step campaign. The rough sketch does not resolve every artistic question and close every creative door; it simply provides a strong guideline. The artist comes to the moment when he transfers his exploration from sketch to final surface, hopefully not breaking the ongoing feeling of problem-solving and pushing forward. The image continues its unbroken chain of development, but the scene of the battle shifts from rough to finished page.

Certain technical issues make the seamless artistic process hard to achieve. Traditional medieval illumination was usually made in a predictable order. The underdrawing was made in light ink with a pointed pen. Then areas to be gilded would receive their gesso ground. Once this was dry, the gold would be laid and burnished. All other areas of color were then painted in, beginning with large areas and ending with delicate highlights in white or powdered gold paint. The underdrawing was usually extremely precise and it provided distinct boundaries for each color. The illuminator simply colored in the drawing, albeit with great grace and finesse. When the painter departed from the sketch, it was only within certain accepted bounds. Donald's free and loose approach to the illustrations makes this mode of working impossible; his overlapping images and his painterly technique with gold force him to attack the problem differently.

Once his rough sketch is ready to be transferred to the vellum page, the steps are worked out in stages. The vellum skin needs to be prepared for the rough treatment it will receive. Gold is a demanding medium and dictates much of the order in which the components come together.

Donald Jackson takes a scissor to his sketch for the *Resurrection* illumination in John's Gospel. As he works his sketches, layer upon layer of collage begin to evoke his painterly style.

Hazel Dolby talks with Donald Jackson at The Hendre. Hazel is responsible for special treatments and illuminations in several volumes of The Saint John's Bible.

## Making an illumination

THE FIRST HURDLE is the preparation of the vellum skin. Because of its absorbent nature, vellum needs to be readied to receive large coats of wet pigment. It has to be stretched and its edges pinned to a board so that Donald can use as much moisture as he needs. A stretched skin will take this moisture, expand and then contract back into position. An unstretched skin would become more and more distorted in shape as it twisted and contorted itself under successive coats of gesso and paint.

In order to stretch the skin out, the vellum sheet is left in the scrutching shed overnight. The moisture of the damp shed causes the vellum sheet to expand very gently. No extra moisture is added—only the moisture which can be picked up from the atmosphere. The next morning the sheet is pulled flat on a large composite board covered with Formica. It is not pulled too hard, just enough to smooth the wrinkles. It is then stapled to the board along its outermost margin (which will be trimmed off during the binding) and masking tape is applied all around. This tape, too, is applied only to areas which will be cut away. The stretched and mounted vellum sheet is then left in the schoolroom. As it dries it shrinks slowly; the page becomes taut and flat. This procedure may sound rather risky. It is. The skin must not be overstretched. Pulled too tight, the page will go out of square, distorting the regular grid of the book. If there is writing on the sheet, it must not get smudged. It's delicate work.

Even before they are stretched, areas for illumination are treated differently than other parts of the page. Most of the skins are prepared with writing in mind. The final stage of an ordinary skin's preparation involves a final rubbing down with gum sandarac (a substance not unlike the rosin baseball pitchers keep on the pitcher's mound). The liquid-resistant properties of the gum help writing stay clean, crisp and sharp by discouraging the spreading or feathering of the ink. In areas of illumination, where large areas of wet pigment have to be laid onto the page, the water resistance would not be a help but a barrier. On these pages the final sanding of the skin is left out. The skin is therefore left in a slightly smoother, more slick state. Before an illumination can be added to the page, the surface has to be examined: has it been sanded a bit too enthusiastically? If so, it needs to be gently burnished down to flatten it.

Once the skin is stretched and fully dried out, it is ready for Donald to begin working. He makes a tight sketch of the basic elements of his composition, which he transfers to the vellum page. This compositional underdrawing sometimes needs to be transferred to the vellum page repeatedly, as elements disappear under layers of gold and color. He keeps his tracing paper drawing throughout the process. Sometimes Donald uses a kind of white carbon paper sold in the United States for dress pattern making. Donald pulled out two boxes of the transfer paper to show me. Both were a good twenty years old, bought in New York on a trip in the late seventies or eighties. The logo reads "Saral" in a jaunty, old-fashioned commercial script popular in the late fifties.

"Look," he said, holding out the paper for me to look at and to feel. "See how thin and fine that is? The thinner the paper, the better the tracing. This paper is perfectly suited to its task. But then look at this one." He turned around and grabbed the other box. The design of the box had changed slightly; it had been bought a year or two later.

"Feel that—the paper's gotten thicker. The white coating is coarser, too." Indeed it was. I reached forward and felt the two sheets. "They're making this for home dressmakers, and to them it doesn't matter. But it does matter to me. The newer paper is just slightly thicker, slightly coarser. It doesn't transfer the

Thomas Ingmire, one of the illuminators, at work at the Scriptorium.

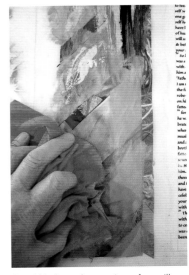

Donald Jackson places a piece of raw silk on top of an illumination in progress. He used the cloth as a model for the dress Mary of Bethany wears in the *Luke Anthology* illumination.

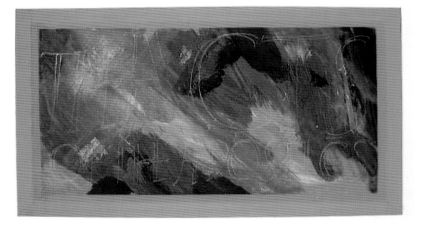

A sketch and its finished version. In the intermediate photograph the background had been laid down; Saral carbon paper, made for dressmakers, has been used to trace down the outlines of the letters, which were then painted in with shell gold using a sable brush.

drawings with as much delicacy and detail. Anything new is problematic." As a craftsman he relies on the properties of his tools and materials. When they change he has to change his practices—and he doesn't like it. So he guards this ancient box of Saral transfer paper, because he knows of nothing like it on the market today.

## The challenge of working in gold

THE BLANK SHEET of vellum stands ready to receive its design. What comes first? As in ancient manuscripts, it is often the gold which determines the order of the work. Now there are three types of gold which are used in The Saint John's Bible. Each of these is made of real gold; fake gold paint is only for roughs. The first kind of gold is powder gold, sometimes called "shell gold" because it was once sold in containers made of discarded mussel shells. This is a fine dust of gold, ground fine. Donald buys this in small tablets in which the grains are pre-mixed with a binding agent. He prefers to add his own binding agent so he soaks the tablets in water, dissolving the gum or glue. Three changes of water are needed to wash out every impurity. He then adds a tiny amount of fish glue—just enough to keep the gold from flaking off. As with other powdered colors, gold becomes dull and lifeless if it is drowning in glue; the master craftsman knows just how much binder is needed to keep the gold or pigment on the page without losing its luster. Powder gold is relatively easy to use: it is painted on with a brush. It is lustrous and rich. It can be rubbed with a burnisher to take on a high sheen, although "Beware," Donald warns. "Too much looks tawdry." The granular nature of the gold makes for a gently rough surface which catches light in a complex way. It never takes on the lucid brightness of gold leaf. Its finish is flatter, darker.

The other two types of gold—acrylic medium and gesso gilding—are technically more demanding. These involve use of gold leaf: sheets of gold which have been hammered out to an incredible thinness. Gold leaf is unbelievably delicate. The least puff of wind sends it flying through the air. Windows must be shut, and even a careless breath on the part of the gilder can send his precious gold sheet scurrying across the room. The tools used for gilding have to be spotlessly clean: the gold leaf sticks to any surface that has even the tiniest residue of grease. And yet it is a stubborn material as well and will not stick evenly to any surface that hasn't been properly prepared. In order to apply gold leaf to the page, a special ground needs to be laid first. Different grounds create different finishes. For a fairly flat, matte effect, Donald uses an acrylic medium diluted with rain water. This is painted on the surface, allowed to dry and then covered with sheets of gold leaf. The inherent stickiness of the material, even when dry, acts as a firm binding agent for the gold.

By far the most demanding—and most spectacular—gilding is the laying of gold leaf on gesso ground. Donald is justly famous for his gesso gilding. He wrote the entry on it in *The Calligrapher's Handbook*.* The gesso recipe varies but it usually includes dental-grade plaster, white lead, sugar, fish glue and a tiny amount of powdered color. Craft calligraphers can debate for hours about the properties of each of these ingredients, about the necessity for the sugar and about acceptable variations and substitutions in the recipe. The gesso must be prepared long in advance; small dried cakes of it made by Sam Somerville, Thomas Ingmire, Donald and Sally Mae are kept at the Scriptorium.

Donald uses the gesso like any cake of watercolor paint, tempering it—that is to say, wetting it—with glair, a liquid drained from beaten egg whites. The gesso, with its plaster and lead ingredients, lies thickly on the page. It adds a third dimension to the gilding and dries both hard and flexible. Donald exploits this third dimension, scratching into the wet gesso before it dries, sculpting the surface. He lays the gesso with a specially cut quill or with a brush; at times, he has been known to use his finger to push the gesso around the page. The laying of the gesso is an exacting craft. The consistency has to be just right or gesso sets poorly. There can be no bubbles or lumps. Once it is dry, it can be sanded or scraped, if needed. Once

Donald Jackson uses a sharp knife to break the outer membrane of the yolk of an egg. A tiny drop of egg yolk added to vermillion both binds the pigment to the page and brightens its tone.

* *The Calligrapher's Handbook*. London: A&C Black, 1985. Ed: Heather Child. Donald's article on gilding appears on pages 176–197.

The gesso letters are written with a quill.

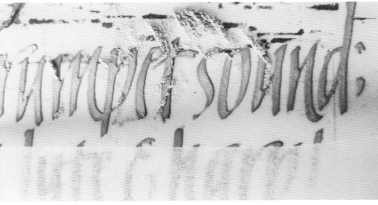

The dry gesso letters are scraped with a sharp knife to produce a smooth cushion to receive the gold.

The shavings here will be vacuumed with a tiny dust buster. Since gesso contains poisonous white lead, extreme caution must be taken not to inhale particles of the fine dust.

The suede gilder's cushion provides a surface on which to position a leaf of 24-carat gold. The leaf is cut into small, manageable pieces. The gilding knife must be kept scrupulously clean; any hint of grease will make the gold stick to the knife.

## A GESSO RECIPE

| | |
|---|---|
| slaked plaster | 16 parts |
| white lead | 6 parts |
| sugar | 2 parts |
| fish glue | 1 part |
| Armenian bole | |
| (enough to color the mixture pink) | |

The ingredients are carefully blended. The liquid mixture is allowed to dry, forming a small cake of gesso.

In order to use the gesso, glair (a liquid made from egg whites) and water are added to the dry cake to create a paint with the consistency of heavy cream.

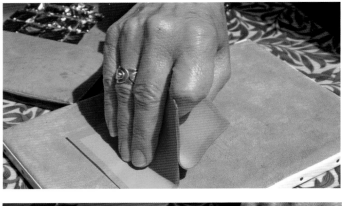

Speed is of the essence when gilding. As Sally Mae Joseph holds the bamboo tube in her mouth, breathing over one tiny section of the piece, she holds a tiny sliver of gold leaf on her left index finger. When the gesso is sufficiently moist, she will gently rest the gold leaf onto the gesso surface. A cloth in her right hand will be used to press the gold down.

Sally Mae Joseph transfers a sheet of gold leaf to the surface of her gilding cushion. The delicate leaves of gold are kept between the pages of a little paper booklet.

Once the gold has been pressed in place, it is burnished onto the surface. Here it has formed a bond with the gesso and has taken on a bright sheen. Although a delicate sense of touch is essential, a surprising amount of pressure can be used when burnishing.

Holding a burnishing tool in her right hand and piece of gold leaf in her left, Sally Mae Joseph breathes gently through a bamboo tube onto the gesso ground. The moisture of her breath activates the glue binding agent in the gesso, until it is sticky enough to bond with the gold leaf.

the gold is laid, every flaw and variation in the surface will show. Donald has been working with gesso for more than forty years, and he handles it with an ease few can match. He knows all its properties intimately, and knows how to push it to achieve a whole range of effects. He produces a crisp, smooth surface which will react well to its metallic golden overcoat.

Once the gesso ground has been prepared to Donald's satisfaction, he lays the gold leaf. Cutting the leaf to size on a small gilder's cushion with his gilder's knife, he picks it up with the tip of his finger. The normal grease of skin attracts the gold like a magnet. His hand hangs in midair, the wispy gold surface dangling gently in the still room. He blows softly on the gesso, warming and moistening it slightly with his breath; this brings the gesso to life. It becomes slightly sticky to the touch. As soon as Donald is satisfied that the gesso is ready to receive gold, then—bam!—down goes the gold. He covers the area with a silk cloth and burnishes the gold hard. This process is repeated until the entire gesso area is covered with gold. A final burnishing is done after the gesso has dried and become perfectly hard again. Sometimes he varies the final effect by pressing a piece of silk into the malleable gesso surface after he has laid the gold. This leaves a gentle fabric imprint which catches the light very differently from cleanly burnished, flat areas of gold.

Gesso gilding results in a thin skin of gold that looks bright and metallic, as though an actual chunk of gold were laid onto the manuscript page. Because the gesso creates a raised surface, its edges curving gently to meet the page, its contours reflect the light in a constantly changing display. Raised and burnished gold captures every tiny bit of available light around it; as the page is turned the highlights flutter across the gold surfaces. Why is it called manuscript "illumination"? Turn a gold-bespecked page in a dim room and you will see. The page will flash to life.

All of this gold is just one stage of the process, of course. Powder gold can be added at any stage in the process of creating a finished illumination; the areas of gold leaf are more demanding. Donald described his working order to me. "The gesso is usually the first to go down; otherwise the gold sticks to paints exactly where you don't want it." The implication of this is that any painted areas need to be added after the gold, so no errant gold flecks stick to adjacent areas of color.

"The traditional method has always been to lay gesso first, then gold, then paint all around," Donald said.

"But is there any way to avoid this?" I asked. "What if your design made it hard to lay the gold first?"

"You can get away, to some extent, with gilding near paint by adding a dusting of French chalk over the places where you don't want the gold to stick, but this is a stopgap and not the ideal way of working."

There are other technical concerns. Donald continued, "Gesso doesn't readily adhere to acrylic." In some illuminations in the Bible, Donald has wanted a figure in raised and burnished gold to sit in the middle of an area of matte gold. "The *Crucifixion*, for example, uses gesso over powder gold." He pointed to the illumination, lying on a table in front of us. His hands inscribed broad arcs across the page. "I used neat glair—undiluted with water—in the gesso. Neat glair is tricky. When it's dry, it becomes almost waterproof which makes it hard to lay the gold leaf." He went quiet, his eyes making wide sweeps across the page. It's always a balancing act, pushing the materials, seeing what he can get away with, trying to make the composition work, both technically and visually.

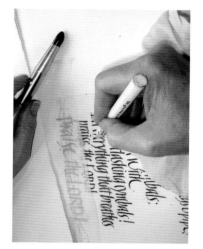

A silk cloth is used to remove excess leaf. In some areas, the gold may stick to the vellum itself. These stubborn patches of gold are removed with an erasing pencil.

Tiny areas where the gold has not bonded properly are touched up.

## Adding color

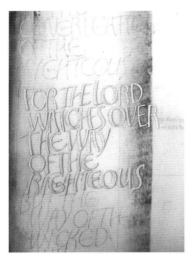

Details from Psalm 1 in various stages of completion. The tracing above was used to transfer the lettering design to the vellum page. Below the gesso has been laid. Its contours are still rough and will require gentle scraping. The image on the facing page shows the gold glistening in light. The three dimensional contours of the letters refract light in every direction.

ONCE THE GOLD is in place then the rest of the painting and drawing can be done. We turned to look at the cluttered table beside his work desk. Tubes of watercolor and gouache were jostling against small pots of casein-based paints. There were pigments in small jars and tubes of acrylic medium. Printmaking rollers, brushes and quills sat side by side.

Donald began to get impatient as I asked him about all these materials. His answers were less forthcoming. They came in short staccato bursts, not in the lush, reflective manner he adopted when talking about the artistic process. Technique seemed to bore him; talking about it seemed frustrating. I wasn't sure whether he was protecting his trade secrets or if he'd simply spent so long with these tools and techniques that they were second nature to him. I tried my best to pump him for information.

"What kind of water do you use?" I ventured.

"I use rainwater for this: it comes off the roof and I ladle it out of the water-barrel by the door," he said.

I picked up a small, beautiful nineteenth century tablet of red color. "Stick vermillion," he said, "mercuric sulphide, bound together with glue. Add egg yolk (just a drop) and water; it glows." The egg yolk helps bind the color to the page. "What you put down should stay on the side of the page where you put it."

"And the roller?"

"The roller is for the water-based printing ink. You can lay the color pretty dry; there's less moisture. That's better for the skin."

"You have a lot of different kinds of paint here," I said.

"Yes, these cost me a lot of money. How much did we spend on the paints? Two hundred, three hundred pounds? I'll ask Mark to check the receipts." Later in the day, Mark would unearth the receipt—£295, or more than $500, for tubes of gouache and watercolor.

"I use casein for its glazing potential," Donald said, explaining that, unlike gouache, the casein would take many layers of paint. "There's no oil paint of course . . . the oils would stain through the vellum. Aidan (the Orthodox icon painter who has painted some of the illuminations) glazes his icons after a year or so." His face brightened. "Apparently they use boiled down beer in Russia. Clearly we can't do that."

"And what about the powdered pigments? How do you use those?"

"Sometimes I add them to gouache. They give more grit." The gritty texture is better to work with.

"Can they be used on their own?" I asked. Donald's brow furrowed. We launched into a conversation about binding agents, pigments and gilding. "Acacia gum as a binding agent will darken the color and become brittle over time. Isinglass, a gelatine of great purity, is made from the flotation bladder of the sturgeon and gives you the purest color. Ordinary fish glue is any old thing: heads, guts, tails. Old sign writers used to use the gelatine pill capsules you could buy through chemists for their glass gilding."

He quickly veered off this topic. The point was something different. It wasn't about the materials, about giving out recipes for using powder pigments. It was about something entirely other, about the feel of the thing. He changed tack: "Arabic calligraphers used particular reeds from a particular place. Marsh Arabs had the best reeds. It is said these improved if they were left in dung for six months. The way of handling materials is different. It's not like the way we talk about technology but about having a feel for their materials."

I was quiet for a moment. As I was about to prod him further about the materials in front of us, he said, "In all the talk about materials, there is a great problem of getting too arcane about everything versus getting it done." Lancashire practicality trumped clever questions about medieval and modern pigments. "It's about feel and integrity. Not about cookery!"

We stood in silence for a time and then began to talk about the rubber stamps he uses in his designs. We chatted about the ways he distresses his paintings with sandpaper, breaking up the colored surfaces. In the middle of our conversation he suddenly said, "Come here, look at this."

He took me outside and pointed up under the Scriptorium eave. There, hanging from an old rusty nail, was a wasp, just beginning to build her paper-thin nest. She had just a few strands in place and patiently, patiently moved back and forth, trying to establish herself and her brood.

"She's been at it since yesterday but isn't showing much progress," he said.

I could see that the place she needed to attach her next paper segment was on the painted rafter into which the rusty nail had been hammered. The paint was too smooth, too new. It didn't give her any purchase and try as she might, she could not get her thin paper walls to stick. We watched her for a while, chatting about the craftsmanship of the wasp, her patience and the danger she faced if she didn't make progress soon. His irritation with the discussion on materials evaporated. As we stood and watched this tiny wasp struggle on with her task, it was as if we were watching ourselves. Her struggle was to make a nest with the materials she had available to her; Donald's is to make a manuscript Bible. The wasp, the Marsh Arabs, the feel of gold under his burnisher—they were all of a piece. It was all about a quality of encounter with the world around us, about living with a kind of sensitivity to the physical realities of life. That's what Donald's Bible illuminations are about. That's what he's about.

Sally Mae once said to me, "Everything he does has to be taken on board, looked at, thought about, touched and smelled." Watching the wasp with Donald, I saw it was so.

Quills and artists' colors lie on a table next to a fragment of illumination from the Gospel according to Matthew. Donald Jackson uses tools and materials of every description in the making of The Saint John's Bible. The red vermillion cakes were made in the 1870s and are used for the red bullets and footnotes throughout the Bible.

# CHAPTER 8

# TOOLS OF THE TRADE

Every tool has its place. Every tool has its purpose. "I use a lot of adhesive tape," Donald said to me. "It keeps the things on my desk from moving around. If I didn't have my heavy metal tape dispenser, I don't know what I'd do. It's cast iron and stays put."

The Saint John's Bible is made with tools as simple and mundane as adhesive tape and with tools as up-to-date and technological as computers. Some of the tools you can buy in any stationery store; others have to be custom-made by hand. Some are precious objects, passed down from scribe to scribe over the years; others are used up and chucked away without a second thought.

The only test of a tool is whether it works.

## Tools for thinking

Perhaps the most surprising tool used in the project is the computer. I asked Donald whether he had taken on the computer gladly, or was it a more grudging acceptance?

"I took to the computer avidly," he said. "I was completely enthusiastic. You know, a number of years ago I was at a conference at Oxford. It was sponsored by the Crafts Council. We were looking at the future of the graphic arts—but there weren't any computers there. Calligrapher Ann Hechle and I both said 'Where are the computers?' I was dying to get my hands on a mouse and see what could be done."

The computer organizes the project in fundamental ways. In Donald's hands it is also an expressive, experimental tool. I asked Vin Godier, the project's graphic designer/typesetter, about the technology.

"In early days doing roughs, the computer was used to create mock-ups for Saint John's. We could create instant visuals. Very early on we produced a whole book of the Gospels, including sample illustrations, to give Saint John's a better feel of what the finished book would be like. If we hadn't had the computer, how many pages would Donald have been able to produce by hand—ten, twelve pages?" The computer gave Donald the freedom to visualize whole books at a time.

It also helped him refine his design more quickly than he could by hand.

"The computer helped Donald decide on the proportions of the text column, the x-height of the letters and the line spacing. It was the very best way of using the computer: Donald could see things very quickly. He had lots of elasticity. He could try anything he fancied. It was almost instant. We used the computer to do all the variations, churning out column after column."

The hardware consists of a PowerMac G3 with an upgraded memory capacity, a Umax PowerLook 3 flatbed scanner, and an Epson Stylus Color 3000 printer.

"The printer is a big beastie. It was the biggest printer we could get," Vin said. "We're printing out sheets of A2"—large sheets in the European A-series of standard paper sizes. "They have even bigger printers now, but it's still large."

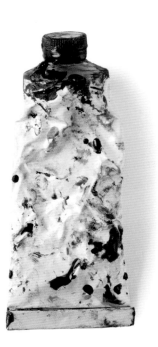

A tube of water-based lino ink bears the marks of frequent use.

A Victorian erasing knife is perfectly shaped for its task. The exquisitely sharp edges of the hollow-ground blade do not need frequent resharpening. The bone handle fits comfortably in the hand.

Rare nineteenth–century Chinese ink comes in solid form. This stick is used to make the dense black ink used throughout the Bible. The thin layer of gold which decorates the outside of the stick does not affect the blackness of the ink when the stick is ground in water.

The software includes QuarkXpress 4.1 and Photoshop 6.

"We've been through several upgrades of Quark Xpress—we must have started with 3.3."

I wondered how it felt to use computer technology on a project like this. Calligraphy is a very intimate thing; it's all about a personal encounter with the writing. The computer seems rather cold by comparison. I asked Vin if there was a personal dimension to working with a computer.

"A personal dimension?" he said. "I suppose the only thing that makes it personal is the way you design your own style sheets; you build the software around you. But then, you can share style sheets so it's not that personal.

"The one thing we did produce which was unique was the font. We created it ourselves, built from Adobe multiple master fonts. The 'font creator' is a kind of mini-program with little flag bars: you slide the bars and it will change the weight and the optical size of the type. It's literally an elastic type."

This special font of type was designed to mimic the weight and spacing of Donald's Bible script.

"Donald wrote a block of text and all the characters in the Bible script. Manipulating a typeface called Sanvito on the computer, I did lots of samples and printed them out. Through trial and error we got it to match Donald's writing."

"How close did it come? When you look at the Sanvito in the printouts, it doesn't really look like Donald's writing," I said.

"It was a case of getting as close as possible. We achieved the best compromise we could using an electronic font."

And indeed it spaces out in a way which is very like the Bible script. Using it, Vin can create a perfect layout; the written Bible will match it line for line. The master layouts are printed in multiples. Originally he printed two copies at the full size (15⅞ x 24½ inches or 403 x 622mm); one for the scribe, one for the proofreader—now only one copy is used for both purposes. Five sets, reduced to standard European letterhead size (A4), are bound as books; two of these stay at the Scriptorium, three go to Saint John's. These are used for day-to-day reference. The last set, reduced even further, is posted on the studio wall in a long strip to serve as a visual diagram for an entire volume. Vin's master layout allows people scattered in sites across two continents to work simultaneously on all the varied processes involved in production, from proofreading to fine writing to illumination. When Vin says, "It's a very useful tool to have," he is understating the case considerably.

Vin takes the raw digital text of the New Revised Standard Version and flows it into the text boxes. Chapter headings, drop caps, and paragraph bullets are added. All the hyphens and em-dashes have to be changed; the default settings of these are wider than the Bible script version. Any blocks of text which are to receive special treatments are marked in color so they stand out. Now the raw columns of text are ready to be justified. This is where things get interesting, because the layout is not a piece of formal typesetting; it is a guide for writing by hand. He breaks all sorts of typographic rules and conventions to produce a master layout for the scribes. The broken rules begin with the type itself.

"We decided on 19.4 point type on 22.572 point leading."

"What a bizarre measurement," I said. "A typesetter would never choose such an odd size."

"It is purely to make it match the Bible script visually—in the end this isn't a computer job. It's replicating calligraphy. That means the job has some strange aspects. I'm not producing neat, clean, tidy typesetting as

An old vial holds a small amount of ground blue artists' pigment which can be mixed with gum, egg yolk or glair.

Donald Jackson uses casein-based paints extensively in the Bible. The lids are color coded for easy recognition.

Rollers can be used to spread a thin film of water-based lino ink on the vellum. The ink's low moisture content allows it to be used to lay down large areas of transparent color. Rollers and lino ink are also used for printing with rubber stamps. A glass sheet provides a perfectly smooth surface for the preparation and mixing of the ink.

you would in a printed book, for example. I'm producing a layout in type which is a guide for the scribes' spacing—it's different from typography.

"For example, I leave no space at all near some punctuation, particularly quotation marks. The proofreaders often mark this as wrong. But most punctuation in calligraphy tucks in tighter. Set electronically, it overhangs far too much."

The result is a computer layout which is incorrect typographically precisely because it is used as a carefully calibrated guide to calligraphic spacing. The automatic settings on the computer would leave holes and gaps in the writing. So Vin spaces out every line by hand, bearing in mind the way the Bible script sits on the page.

Although the columns are justified, with clean, even margins both left and right, Vin instructs the computer to align the text flush left. Through his own hand adjustment, he draws out or squeezes the lines into alignment on the right-hand side. It is extremely labor intensive as he works his way through the text line by line.

"I use tracking to squeeze the words, then I have a coding when the tracking is extremely tight. I color a line green if it's at maximum tracking of –7. That alerts the calligraphers on very tight lines. The text doesn't fall in easily. People think you're using a computer, so it's automatic. It's not. Every single line has to be hand done. The way I approach it the computer is completely serving the calligraphy. On screen it bears no resemblance to good typography."

Once the justification of the text is done, Vin and Donald sit together to decide where the illuminations will sit in the text. This is a creative time.

"When Donald is planning spaces for illustrations, he'll explore various spaces that could be used. He can see what the placement of an illumination does to the chapters which follow on. Sometimes we find it's advantageous to add a few lines to an illustration to avoid awkward breaks. It also lets Donald see different variations from the creative point of view. He can explore the layouts electronically before they're set in stone, if you will. It's given Donald flexibility in creativity; an opportunity to try things out, to have a look."

The marriage between calligrapher and computer is not always smooth. I asked Donald about the computer as a creative tool.

"There is an absolute meeting point," Donald said, "which shows the relationship problem between the scribe and the computer which underlines the limitations of it."

He described to me how he had come to work on the opening passage of the Gospel according to John. This was to be treated as what they are calling an "incipit," a portion of text at the beginning of a biblical book which is given prominence by being written larger and with elements in color and gold. The John incipit poses some delicate design problems. It appears opposite a full page illumination. The name of the book—the Gospel according to John—appears in a box above it. Blocks of text in ordinary Bible script hedge it in at the bottom.

"I sketched that out two years ago," Donald said, "before we had even finalized the choice of translation. It was a rough sketch. I estimated the amount of space I had to do it in. I said to Vin, 'This is how it will look. Let's do a font that imitates my caps.' He flowed it in; it looked reasonable. The line breaks were okay. It looked okay on the computer. The computer is good at organizing text. Then fast forward: it is two years later. All the text is written, the illumination on the opposite full page is progressing, and I come back to the incipit.

Pen in hand, Donald was ready to execute the design. But the computer layout had to be translated into actual pen lettering.

"Now I'm not so sure I like this; it's too squashed." He paused for effect to let this sink in.

"This is where a switch in your head takes place. I start trying to write it. The counter spaces were too big. It was too flimsy. There is too little text and too big a hole."

Fine writing is all about the balance of weight and proportion. In Donald's hands, it is an extremely subtle visual language. The progress of the pen across the page is like a dance, and he was alone on a very large dance floor. The balance was all off.

"There is that subtle point calligraphers look for where the whole thing holds together. You don't want light blasting through the letters from behind. You don't want the line to disintegrate like an old piece of lace."

He went back to Vin; they continued to re-jig the layout on the computer, using what Donald had learned with the pen. Donald's studio assistant had to re-rule the page three times as the layout changed and changed again.

In the end, Donald said, "The computer has to follow the pen: that's a key understanding. It's a tool, not a magic thing."

## Tools for vellum

WHILE THE COMPUTER has become an ordinary part of our post-industrial officescape, the other tools in the Scriptorium are more specialized. The preparation, ruling up and storage of the vellum require a host of tools and skills which are more unusual.

Donald and Sally Mae Joseph established a pattern of preparation for the vellum which has been carried on with minor refinements ever since. Mark L'Argent, who was the studio assistant for two years beginning in June 2000, told me they had discovered that "preparing the vellum in the driest season of the year is best; the skins are more stable. They're easier to prepare, easier to write on. On the flesh side, they aren't so coarse." He paused a moment. "The only thing coarse in the studio is my language."

The raw skins are cut to working size using a wooden template, like a picture frame. After they have been scrutched, they are ready for ruling up. This is done at a large drafting table with an attached parallel motion set-square. The columns are marked with little prick marks. These are made either with a burin or with a pin held in a pencil-shaped device called a pin-vice. The lines on the hair side are ruled first, using a 2H pencil. Measurements permanently attached to the table give the proper alignment for the ruling up.

Ruling the flesh side is more problematic. The skins never entirely forget their original animal contours and never lie quite flat. When the skin is turned over, it will never lie in perfect geometric alignment to the ruling guides. But the lines ruled on the flesh side must register perfectly with those on the hair side.

"You're moving the surface of the skin as you rule up," Mark explained. The three-foot-long metal rule he uses to rule up shifts the skin every time he lays it down. He can see the lines showing through, which give him a guide. The pricked marks for the columns also give him a fixed point.

"I have to do it all by eyeball. There's lots of manipulating the pencil to get the lines to marry-up with the lines on the other side of the page. You have to keep your wits about you, really." Skins get handled

Different brushes serve varied functions. From left to right: a flat sable brush for laying down washes; a coarse, round decorators' bristle brush for gestural, textured marks; a short mixing brush; two stiff brushes for use with casein and gouache; a stenciling brush; and another mixing brush.

A dry brush may be used to loosen excess gold after a gesso design has been gilded.

again and again during the making. Sometimes, inevitably, tiny creases get made in them.

"I use a bone folder for extracting the creases I've made in my haste," Mark said. Bone folders are small tools, usually about five to eight inches long, which look a bit like tongue depressors. Made from real animal bone, they have gentle contours. They are often rounded at one end and gently pointed at the other. Placing a bit of soft card under the crease to act as a cushion, Mark uses the bone folder to gently flatten and push it down.

"Donald takes out creases with his thumbnail," Mark said. It's tricky. "You have to get the tension right."

He demonstrated how Donald would gently pull the skin with one hand, while carefully rubbing the crease out with his thumbnail. The principle is the same: a hard, flattish edge gradually pressing the skin into position—organic tool against organic surface, not too hard, not too rough, coaxing the skin rather than forcing it.

Another tool which is important for the vellum is the hygrometer. Sally Mae explained to me what this tool was for. "The hygrometer measures relative humidity in the atmosphere. We're becoming more aware of humidity and how it affects the skins. We were particularly concerned about some of the skins which had been worked on and which were beginning to show a lot of movement. We had Chris Clarkson, the binder and conservator, come in."

Clarkson is one of the most distinguished book conservators in the world. He has visited the Scriptorium at intervals to give advice about handling vellum and about how the book binding should influence design decisions. Shifts in humidity are a major concern.

"He's discussed with us the idea of getting an air conditioning unit for the studio. Right now, we keep the vellum in the plan chest:* it's a fairly constant fifty percent humidity in there. We were relieved that he wasn't too worried about it."

Sally continued, "I brought in a greenhouse hygrometer. It was really, really basic. I wanted to check the humidity when I was gilding." Gilding requires very moist conditions and works best on really damp days.

"Chris Clarkson was being all technical and asking all sorts of questions like, 'Does your hygrometer have a filament inside?'"

Sally began to laugh as she talked.

"He works in conservancy—it's a very high-tech business, and they're used to these really specialized tools. I was embarrassed by our little greenhouse hygrometer. I brought it out to show him. I mean it doesn't even have measurements on it: it just says 'DAMP' on one side and 'DRY' on the other."

Big laugh. "Clarkson was amused."

Two new high-tech hygrometers now keep watch over the Scriptorium, one in each room of the studio.

Donald told me, "They're quite hypnotic: we rush from one to the other, comparing the readings. This will give us solid information about the ideal humidity for the Bible skins. Because we know how a skin should look, we can tell when it is either too dry or too wet. We'll come up with a definitive ideal humidity for the place where the Bible is eventually kept."

*Sally uses the term *plan chest* to describe what Americans usually call a *flat file*. It is a chest of shallow drawers large enough to accommodate large sheets of paper or vellum without folding or rolling them.

## Tools for writing

THERE WAS A TIME not that long ago when you could walk into a stationers' shop and simply buy a quill.

Donald told me, "We have Victorian price lists. They had seven or eight grades of quills on offer, ranging from pennies to several shillings. I'm still using Victorian quills I was given over thirty years ago."

These days quills are harder to find. The shops no longer stock them and the birds themselves are different. Most people don't even know what to look for.

"I was lucky. I know what a quill should look like. I was around at just the right time. My teacher, M.C. Oliver, didn't have to think about it—he just went into a shop and bought them."

Donald Jackson holds a condor feather in one hand and part of a goose wing in the other as he gives an impromptu lecture on the identification and selection of feathers for quills to a visiting museum curator and designer.

Jars filled with goose and swan feathers await selection and curing.

Donald does have to think about it.

"I'm not interested in the cookery side of calligraphy," he said. But he has had to take an interest in his tools and how they are made because he is one of the few people who have seen, touched and used the old traditional tools. When he set out on his scribal career, there were still little pockets of trade left over from the Victorian era and the tools and materials which were available reflected a different level of craftsmanship. He is not romantic about it; these tools were well made because they had a job to do. And now that there is no significant demand for quills, it is no wonder they are hard to come by. Donald is poised between his teachers' generation, which took good quills for granted, and a younger generation which has never seen or used the real thing. He knows what he is looking for. The trick is finding it.

"Like cooking, the key is in the ingredients," Donald said. "Most geese are produced for the table." The result is a young bird with underdeveloped flight feathers. "I am looking for feathers from mature birds. Any hunter would know this: the gander that leads the skein is completely different from the neophyte who brings up the rear. There's a vast difference—pounds of difference in weight." Their feathers, too, are different.

"I found a swan's wings under a power line. The whole carcass was there. It must have flown into the power line; if a fox had killed it, it would have eaten the feathers. I brought back the wings, which were intact."

I asked if chance encounters with dead birds were the only way to find feathers.

"No, not at all. Last Easter we were given quills by Scott Cleland who collected them in Minnesota.

They were top quality, mature Canada goose flight feathers." He'd picked them up from a field the geese frequented.

The feathers for quill-making come from the leading edge of the wing—the first three flight feathers at the very end of each wing. Ideally, flight feathers from the left wing are used by right handed scribes; the gentle curve of the quill sits comfortably in the hand.

"What kinds of birds provide the best quills?" I asked.

"Turkey, swan and goose."

"Can you describe the different properties of the birds? What is a turkey quill like?"

"Turkey is more rigid than the other two. It can be quite big. The barrel wall of the quill is thicker, not as pliable, not so generous with ink flow. It can be like writing with a stick. So you have to make a larger slit and longer shape to the end of the pen. The 'shoulder' of the cut quill starts further back—but this then adds its own structural problems."

"And swan?"

"Swan and goose are from the same family. They're 'gallinaceous.' The swan is larger than goose. Turkey is from a different family of bird altogether." Donald's impatience began to rise. "The best and most important thing you can say is that a mature bird gives you a strong and not overly pliable quill." It is not about three 'brands' of bird which give you differing quills; it is about knowing how to cut a quill with sensitivity. Donald looks for certain qualities in a pen. He wants a quill which combines strength and suppleness in a very subtle balance. When he cuts the quill, he does not follow a formula. He adjusts the length of the various cuts he makes to the hardness and suppleness of the feather in his hand. He literally feels his way along. He can do that because he knows exactly what the ideal tool feels like in the hand.

Before quills can be cut, however, they have to be prepared. Raw quills are too supple and go soft when kept wet—as, for instance, when subjected to several hours of dipping in wet ink. The curing is a hardening process, like tempering steel. It involves plunging the barrel of the quill in hot sand. Mark does much of the curing.

"We started with ninety-four quills at last curing," Mark told me. "Donald selected, graded and discarded. He got rid of quills with oval-section barrels (quills are best with round barrels). He also rejected soft ones and quills with thin barrel walls. This whittled them down to perhaps fifty. After we cured these, Donald figured about five were just right. Donald calculated his time, Sally's time, my time—it worked out to £45 (or about $75) a quill!"

Donald said to me, "The key problem was this: the ingredients themselves were of poor quality. The goose quills were borderline in the first place because they were from young birds." Perhaps they were lucky to get even five out of the lot.

I asked Mark to take me through the curing process.

"First I cut the end off with quill knife and leave the quills to soak in water for twenty-four hours. The next day I take out the little internal membrane, and warm up the sand in a frying pan on an electric stove."

The traditional method involves quickly filling the empty barrel of the quill with hot sand, and then plunging the barrel into the sand in the skillet.

"We no longer plunge quills in sand; there was no visual control doing it that way. So now, I fill them first, then pour sand over the quill while rotating it. I can watch the color of the barrel change."

Small fragments of lace mounted on cardboard are used to make stamped designs. Their delicate patterns enliven the margins and backgrounds of some of the illuminations.

Well-worn tools reflect the hand
of the craftsman. Donald Jackson
has used many of these burnishers
and knives for decades.
He sharpens his own knives,
carefully honing the edge to
achieve exactly the sharpness
needed. His burnishers are likewise shaped precisely to serve
their intended function.

The hematite burnisher in the foreground was made by Donald Jackson forty years ago. The shape of the tool conforms to a pattern favored by the early twentieth-century master gilder, Graily Hewitt.

"What are you looking for?" I asked.

"I'm waiting for it to go from milky to clear. It gives me real control of what I'm doing. This way I don't leave it too long in the hot sand. It cuts down on quills cracking and going brittle."

The cured quills are stored in a jar. When the time comes for Donald to cut them, Mark cuts the feathery end off. He trims away the long barbs on one side, leaving the shorter barbs from the leading edge of the wing.

I asked Donald if he himself cut all the quills.

"Originally I cut them all so I could determine if they were good quills. So the scribes were provided with hand-cut quills. Now they're so good at cutting and keeping quills in shape, theoretically they could keep the same quill for months and months."

"Doesn't the end get blunt? Don't they have to recut their quills?" I asked.

"The biggest misapprehension is that you would keep changing your quill: you get the hang of one quill and you don't want to change it in any way. You get in a rhythm and relationship to a quill. Each quill has an individual personality—hardness, the way it lies in the hand—the slit needs to run clean and true, but when you know how to take care of your quill, there's very little you need to do to keep it sharp and crisp. First you might take two or three slivers off the underside. Then later you might take a sliver off each side and a shaving off the tip. You only recut them when you have to."

Later, Donald would reflect that he had underestimated the challenge the scribes would face as they tried keeping their quills in good condition. "That 'very little' they have to do," he said, "is like the 'very little' a heart surgeon has to do when making an aortic incision!"

The quill is not the only writing instrument used in The Saint John's Bible. Sally Mae told me about other tools the team uses.

"We have steel nibs for the footnotes," she said. "These are old pointed school nibs. Donald ground them down so they have a slight chisel edge. He gave a pair of these to me, Brian and Sue. There's a smaller one for red footnotes and a larger one for black notes."

These, too, need resharpening from time to time. They get freshened up by being gently rubbed against crocus cloth, a very fine sanding paper.

"They came out of a box in a plan chest in the studio," she said.

I asked Donald how old they were.

"They're just ordinary metal nibs from the 1950s," he told me. "They were making superb pen nibs in Britain well into the 1960s and 70s. Then the school market dried up. And the nibs were too good. Calligraphers were the only ones left buying nibs but they didn't buy enough. So this pattern has been discontinued."

Perhaps the most precious writing implement used on the project is also the most humble: a cut reed. This simple tool has a fine provenance. I'll let Sally tell the story herself. It begins at the house of Heather Child, editor of *The Calligrapher's Handbook,* and one of the most prominent English scribes of her generation.

"I went to visit Heather Child not long before she died. She loved the video I had made on gilding techniques. She sat and watched it through—all two and a half hours of it. Afterwards, she took me across to her studio. She pulled out a box containing about a dozen cut reed pens. She handed me three of

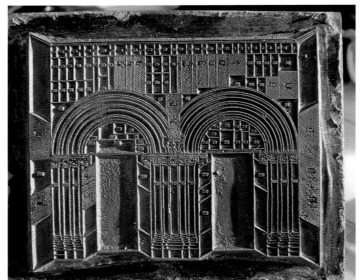

Rubber stamps are a modern addition to the illuminator's tool kit.

them. She said to me, 'These were cut by Edward Johnston.' It was one of those awesome moments. You can't quite believe it's happening. I looked down at them and I thought, 'Blimey. Wow.'"

Edward Johnston founded the twentieth-century British calligraphy movement. His book *Writing & Illuminating & Lettering* is the foundational text of our tradition. Sally was holding his reed pens in her hand. Heather Child was giving them to her.

"It was so moving. I couldn't believe it."

She saved them for something special.

"I used them for the roughs of the *Magnificat* in Luke's Gospel. I wanted the effect of the pen not being completely and utterly sharp. I sanded off the edges slightly. It gave me a different feeling to a quill."

There's a wonderful practicality in that. Yes, these were Johnston's reed pens. But if they needed to be sanded to give the proper effect, then so be it. It is moving to be part of a calligraphic tradition and to use pens cut by our scribal forebears—but the real living tradition is to use the pens without fear and without being precious about them. So Sally sanded them to get the right shape. In a final irony, they weren't used on the actual Bible page.

"It was too bad. But I couldn't use the reed pen on the colored background: it lifted up the paint underneath. So I was going to use it, but in the end I used a slightly blunted quill."

Craftsmanship trumps romanticism every time.

## Tools for cutting and scraping

"OUR QUILL KNIVES come from George Yanagita in America," Mark said to me as he handed me a sharp knife. It was delicately balanced. The wooden handle with its gentle curves sat comfortably in my palm.

"Everybody in the studio gets one. You have to sharpen and take care of them: Donald's and Sally's are well-lived in. Mine is sort of virgin. All of them are numbered." I looked at the number. George keeps a strict accounting of his work; every knife is recorded.

The quill knife is designed specifically for the cutting of quills. The edge of its blade is perfectly straight. One side of the blade is flat; the other is softly curved. In calligraphy circles there's a good deal of mystique surrounding these knives. I asked Donald why that was.

"The quill knife has a very particular shape. You need the curve on one side in order to help you make the curved cuts when shaping a quill. A perfectly straight blade, like a scalpel or X-acto blade, would want to slice in a straight line. In a quill, we're looking for that soft curve."

As Donald described the action, he made a curved motion with his hand, not unlike the motion one might make when peeling a potato with a small paring knife. I could see how the curve on the blade's side echoed the motion of the hand.

This very specialized knife blade is not easy to find. Over the years, Donald has had to teach people to grind and shape commercially available knives to the right shape.

"The nearest I could find was a German brand of wood chipping knife. But these were shaped like an X-acto knife—both sides of the knife were flat. I had to teach people to grind the blade down, to shape it and sharpen it. That was the only way I could provide the right kinds of knives. The curve is crucial; it helps you, it guides you."

George Yanagita now makes knives which, as Donald puts it, "fit the bill." But, like all craftsman's tools, they need to be taken care of.

"You can buy a sharp tool," Donald said. "But if you want to keep it that way you have to take responsibility for doing it. Every time you re-sharpen it, you have to be aware of what you are doing. I strop the blade with a polishing paper jewelers use."

"Is it a problem maintaining the blade?" I asked.

"Mostly stropping the blade is enough to keep it sharp. But when you strop it, you tend to round the flat side. From time to time, you need to grind it and reshape it."

George's knives, as fine as they are, lack one feature which the Victorians used in theirs: the Victorians had hollow-ground blades. Both sides of the Victorian blade were curved. The outer side was convex. The inner side was concave. The edge of the blade, therefore, had an even more acute angle than the edge of George's modern version. The result? The blade didn't blunt as quickly.

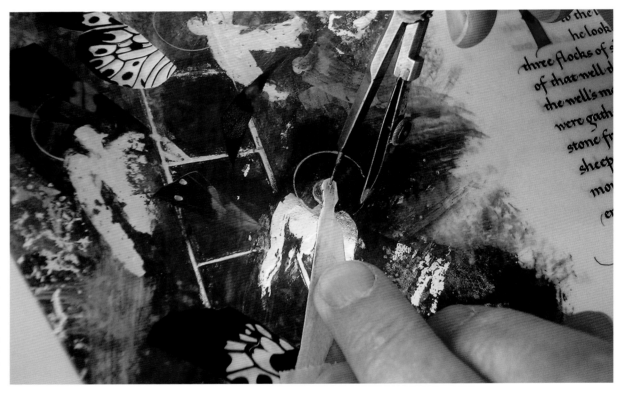

Donald Jackson uses an antique compass to mark a halo around the head of an angel. A small sliver of vellum holds the pointed end, protecting the vellum page underneath from puncture marks. The gold paint he uses is shell gold— pure gold ground to a fine powder and suspended in a gum or fish glue medium.

Nevertheless, George's knives are superbly honed tools. Donald described the absolute sharpness required of a quill knife.

"Cutting a quill, you want almost no burr on the knife. You can tell when a knife is perfectly sharp. It leaves a glassy edge on the quill barrel. Any roughness leaves a chalky edge."

You know you are talking to a craftsman when you reflect that the edge Donald is describing is only hundredths of a millimeter thick.

"When scraping vellum to erase mistakes, you need more tooth. That's why it's best not to erase with a quill knife," he added.

"Sally erases with hers," I countered.

"I know," he said, making no further comment.

Every craftsman has his or her own approach to the craft. I asked Sally to describe how she used the quill knife.

"I use it to cut quills—and to mend small mistakes, mistakes of just one or two letters. The secret to getting out mistakes is having a really sharp quill knife. That may seem obvious, but it's one of the things I had to learn. I didn't understand it until I had a really sharp knife. If you use a slightly dull knife, it leaves a slightly rough, textured surface. You can burnish it down but it's never the same. You have to keep the knife razor sharp."

The ideal tool for erasing is not the quill knife but an erasing knife. Donald has a fine old Victorian knife which he uses. It has a straight handle, terminating in a symmetrical, two-sided blade. The shield shape of the blade provides a perfect curvature for erasing mistakes. Its blade is also larger than that of a quill knife, so it is better suited to erasing large areas. (For large painted surfaces, simple sandpaper is used.)

"Donald has been trying to develop an erasing knife. It's sort of on the back burner," Mark told me. "Donald goes just so far with it, puts it down, then picks it up again."

I looked at the prototype blades at the Scriptorium—seven beautifully shaped samples by George Yanagita. They varied in size and shape. Some of them had blades tilted up from their handles; others were designed flush with their handles. Looking at them reminded me of displays of halberds in medieval armories: a fugue of variations in knife blades.

Donald wasn't so sure about any of these designs. He picked each up, feeling it in his hand. He fretted about how the handle might interfere with seeing the page. He toyed with different ways of holding the blade. I could see his hesitation.

"Then out of the blue," Sally said, "we received these new knives. All of a sudden they landed on the doorstep. They were George's idea."

The new erasing knives were based on a radically different design. Taking the vellum maker's specialist knife, the *lunellum*, as an example, George produced an erasing knife blade positioned like that of a hoe or an old-fashioned safety razor. The blade sits at ninety degrees to its handle.

"We weren't so sure about them at first. They were so different from what we were used to. But I started using mine. I got used to the way it handled. With it you can erase two lines of writing at a time. This knife has a flat area and curved area. You have to be careful using it; you can catch the corner and slice into the vellum. But I've got used to it, and it works rather well."

Donald, too, has begun using Yanagita's scraper and has been taken with it. For a man who claims no interest in "cookery," he gave a pretty good account of George's practices.

"George is using steel. Now when steel is too hard, it snaps. When it is too soft, it doesn't retain its edge. It's the age-old balance of flexibility and strength. In Japan, for example, when they made a traditional chisel, they tempered the first inch but the shank was left untempered. So when you hit it hard, the softer steel absorbed the blow without snapping."

Donald said he was glad to have George working on these knives. "I don't like making tools. George Yanagita adores making tools."

## Tools for rubbing

A WELL-MADE BURNISHER is a beauty to behold. Shaped from agate or hematite, they come in different shapes and sizes suited to different tasks. Donald has a long flat agate burnisher which ends in a straight edge. He has others made of hematite and shaped like lipsticks. Sally has a set of antique agate burnishers which are long, thin and pointed, set into fine handles. Donald has even seen a burnisher made from an actual dog's tooth. Burnishers are used for rubbing the nap of the vellum down, smoothing rough patches of skin. They are used for gilding, pressing gold leaf into a gesso or acrylic medium, rubbing it down so it adheres to every contour of the support. They are used to polish and shape areas of gold, pressing hard on certain areas to make them shine or gently impressing shapes into the gold.

Like quill knives, good burnishers are not easily come by.

"When I was a student at the Central School of Arts and Crafts," Donald said, "I learned about an old gentleman, Victor Hughes, who had been a kind of technical assistant to Graily Hewitt."

Graily Hewitt, one of Edward Johnston's pupils, was particularly famous for his gilding. Through Victor Hughes, Donald was touching one of the great masters of the craft.

"He once made a burnisher for another student in M.C. Oliver's class. When I saw it, I told him I'd like to buy one as well. His response was to say, 'Go and find some hematite.'"

There was wisdom in that. He could have simply given Donald a price and produced a finished tool. Instead, he sent Donald on a quest. "I looked in rock shops. There were all sorts of hematite. I realized I didn't have any idea what I was looking for. When I went back to him, he showed me different unfinished pieces of stone. It gave me an understanding of what I needed for a burnisher. He did me a great favor."

That understanding would benefit Donald years later.

"I was gilding one day in the bathroom (as you do for the high humidity) and I dropped the burnisher in the iron bath. It chipped. But because he had led me through the process, I knew how to reshape it."

Donald has passed that knowledge on to his own students, continuing the transmission of skill and craft from one generation to the next.

"One hematite burnisher I made thirty years ago became a prototype for a lot of what followed. In the States years ago, Louis Strick took a lost-wax cast of my burnisher. He sent the cast to Germany, to a maker for the dental market. They copied it and Louis offered it for sale.

"Lou is an incredibly important part of the last three decades in the story of contemporary calligraphy in the United States. His Pentalic Corporation stocked tools, materials, books, everything. He was a pioneer—he supplied all of America with calligraphers' materials in the seventies and eighties. Back in 1973, I included his address in teaching notes I gave out in California. Someone picked his name up from the notes and he made it into the second *Whole Earth Catalog*."

I pictured Graily Hewitt, the former barrister turned master calligrapher and gilder, working quietly in his rooms in Gray's Inn in London before the First World War. Could he ever have conceived of his work rippling out across the world through a medium as brash as the *Whole Earth Catalog* seventy years later?

## Tools for gold

BESIDES BURNISHERS there are a host of tools used for gilding. Quills and brushes to lay gesso, gilding cushions and knives to cut the gold leaf, pieces of silk through which to press it into position—all the various tools of the gilder's trade have their place. Donald and Sally have both done gilding in the Bible. I asked Sally if they used any unusual tools.

"We use what's called 'Peel-off Magic Rub,'" she said, breaking into a loud laugh. "Sounds quite erotic, that! What does it say on the package? 'Non abrasive, non-smudging vinyl for erasing.' We use it for cleaning off unwanted gold. Sometimes gold adheres in spots where you don't want it. It's especially useful when gilding on watercolor backgrounds. The gold tends to stick to areas of color. It came from America. Mark had to track down someone who sold it; they were in Minneapolis as it turned out."

Donald said, "Diane von Arx Anderson went to a great deal of trouble to go and pick it up and ship it to us. Be sure to mention her."

Sometimes the use of tools has been a bone of contention. I asked Sally to describe how she used the gilders' cushion and knife and stumbled onto a clash of wills.

"At first, I didn't use it. I used scissors to cut the gold leaf, using the little piece of paper which comes interleaved with the gold as a support. This intensely irritated Donald. There were little bits of paper flying all over the studio, and he worried about the length of time it was taking for me to lay the gold."

As she told the story, she started to sputter a bit, hunting for the right words to describe what had happened.

"So I took his advice . . . No, he showed me how . . . No." She began laughing again.

"This grated on him so much. I decided . . . No. He made me . . . I'm struggling here." Now she was laughing hard.

"See, I did learn. I did. The method I was using took a bit longer. I'd never done such large areas of gilding. And time is crucial when you're laying gold. With a whole panel of gold to lay, Donald was worried that the gesso at the bottom was drying out. Cutting on a gilder's cushion, I could get the gold on the gesso faster. He showed me how."

She thought that over. "Of course, I knew how; I was just doing it a different way. But I did learn. I now have a more developed technique of laying gold."

Strong wills battled it out over the gilded *Magnificat*. In the end, Donald's way prevailed.

"I cut the gold on the gilders' cushion and pick it up by the corner with my finger like Donald does." The natural greasiness of the human finger acts like a magnet to gold.

"Immediately after I've breathed on the gesso, to moisten it and activate it, I can place the leaf. I have a silk handkerchief, which I can lay over the gold. I rub the burnisher straight onto the silk. Sometimes you get the silk pattern transferring onto the gold. It makes a beautiful texture. If on the other hand you don't want that, you can take a burnisher and rub it out again."

The tiny remnants of gold leaf left over from gilding are carefully saved. They can be ground into a powder and used in painting.

## A utilitarian miscellany

I ASKED DONALD, Sally and Mark to name all the tools we'd missed—the answers came back fast and furious.

"I like china mixing palettes," Donald said. "And erasers—I prefer green ones. The more plastic ones leave shiny surface. They smear. The old typing eraser is better. It's actual rubber."

Sally mentioned her mortar and pestle. "I grind my own gum sandarac. I prefer a large mortar and pestle; you can see what you're doing. It gives you better control. And then there's the little linen bag to hold the sandarac. I use an old hankie tied up with masking tape." Tapping this little sandarac bag against the vellum dusts the surface with a small, even amount of the rosin-like powder.

"Don't leave out the Optivisor for cutting quills," Sally added, referring to a set of magnifying goggles. "Donald's and my eyes are getting old: we need it to see the detail. Mark thought he could do it without the Optivisor. Now he uses it too. We all need it; we're cutting very fine quills with a slightly oblique cut."

Mark said, "The sharpening stones are important. They're made of artificial diamond in a honeycomb grid. They're so incredibly powerful—you just literally run the blade across once or twice. The surface stays truer than a traditional whetstone."

More tools—rubber rollers, ink stones, scalpels, self-healing cutting mats, sand paper, Frisket for masking areas of color.

Sally Mae brought up the lamps: were they tools, or furniture?

"Lamps with daylight bulbs are crucial as well. They are absolutely essential for fine work, like cutting quills. I always have the lamp on when cutting quills. Donald discourages use of desk lamps when working on vellum, because of the heat they generate."

Donald described brushes of all kinds and shapes. Hog's hair for large areas, sable brushes for finer work. "It's probably libelous to say so, but the quality of sable brushes is not what it used to be. I'm convinced they've changed."

More tools—face masks to protect the scrutchers from vellum particles in the air. Paper towels, scissors and bits of old lace for printing. The photocopier. A little disk, like a slide rule, Donald uses to calculate percentages of reduction and enlargement. This was a gift from a retired Pittsburgh lettering artist. New tools, old tools, rare tools, common tools.

Sometimes tools take on a life of their own.

Sally said, "We make designs for rubber stamps, and send them to a firm in Cardiff where they make them for us. They scan the designs on a computer, make a mould and produce our stamps. Sometimes we cut our own out of Mars plastic erasers using surgical scalpels. I did that for the *Tree of Life* at the end of Luke."

The illuminators who work away from the Scriptorium have taken to the idea.

"We gave Thomas Ingmire one of the geometrical stamps. But then we had a page come back from Suzanne Moore with the same stamp. We spotted it and did a double-take—wasn't that Thomas' stamp?"

"What was going on?" I asked.

"Suzanne saw some of Thomas' work and liked the shape of the stamp. Thomas sent her an impression and she had one made for herself. When she sent her work to us, we recognized the stamp. It feels like they're being cloned all over North America."

"It's Donald's 'spiritual arithmetic' in action, isn't it?" I said. Exponential grace, multiplying across the continents in the form of a simple rubber stamp.

The *Creation* appears opposite the beginning of the book of Genesis.

# CHAPTER 9

# VISIO DIVINA

EACH ILLUMINATION has a story of its own, its own little genesis. Donald and I were standing by a large plan chest, the finished illuminations spread out before us. He waved his hand across a page of bright blues and golds.

"The illumination begins with the marks you make, the unconscious marks. I slap something down. I make big, bold marks from those—it grows." He paused to gather his thoughts.

Sally Mae and Rebecca, the project coordinator, were talking behind us. They were making tea. Donald's eyes flitted back towards the others. He was distracted. Suddenly the door burst open. In came Vin and Mark carrying large, colorful books. Pandemonium. It was a shipment of art books. The group descended on the books, tearing off the plastic wrap, flipping through the pages, commenting on the quality of the pictures. We broke off for a cup of tea; it gave Donald time to decide what he wanted to say. After our tea break, Donald and I sat down in earnest.

"The beginning of the process is Vin and me looking at the computer screen. In each volume we start by manipulating the blocks of text, determining the general location of each illumination," Donald said to me. "Illuminations should be as close as possible to the text they refer to."

Donald then goes back over the volume and tweaks the spaces until he is pleased with the layout. In some ways, he is working blind. At this stage he has not even started to think about the actual design of the illumination; when he does begin his sketches, he is working within parameters established months or even years before.

"Vin reads the theological brief with me and then we discuss it. He's a good listener; it helps me a lot. It helps me sense the shape. A half-page illumination called for in the brief could be split into two quarter pages at opposite corners or it could be one whole column." The different possibilities of arranging the space suggest quite different solutions for the illuminations. The visual choices made at this early stage begin to determine how Donald will work his way into each illumination. He also considers the pacing of images in the book—are the illuminations sprinkled evenly throughout or do they come in groups? Certain illuminations are close to one another; what happens when turning the page from one illumination to the next?

I said, "So once the layout has been decided with Vin, then the pages go into production with the scribes, and you don't return to them for months. Eventually you're ready to begin. What do you do?"

"It's back to the briefs again. I pore over them. I really absorb them. First I look at the exegesis for the main 'angle,' if you like. Then I skip the biblical cross-references and go straight to the free association, then on to the local associations. In the free associations I usually find seeds of a way of dealing with it visually; that's important to me. Even if I don't select a particular idea it gives me a sense of direction. I highlight certain key points from the exegesis."

All of this lays the groundwork.

"Then I get the Bible out. I plough through the passage minutely, looking for my own understanding of it along with the briefs. Then I look up the biblical cross references, too."

Donald's process is not unlike the monastic practice of *lectio divina,* a careful mulling over the text, looking at the details, thinking, meditating, letting it sink in. Donald's sacred reading has a practical aim: to spark visual ideas. Nathanael Hauser of the CIT referred to this work as *"visio divina."* Donald's design process becomes a visual meditation on the text.

"What I'm looking for are core 'action' or 'drama' points." He describes it as a gradual honing in on an idea. "It's a search; it's a bit like a radar scanner." He frowns. "Or a dowser." His face brightens, his hand sweeping left and right, imitating the sensitive movements of a country dowser. "Until I find a definite spring—an image that points me to the essence of what I think they're saying in the brief."

The early stages of design witness the transformation of an idea: from the literary, word-based briefs to a visual, visceral interpretation of the text. Sometimes the briefs suggest a strongly narrative approach to the illumination.

"For instance, it's a very literary thing, an anthology page," Donald says, referring to certain parts of the schema which call for a single illustration to hold a group of stories. "It's a deeply literary concept." He sometimes has to work hard to get beyond the words.

"In the early days, the CIT sometimes specified right down to the toe nails—but they also say 'don't illustrate it.'" The working relationship between Donald and the CIT continues to develop.

"The more they see images from me, the more they realize what I'm doing. They begin to have ideas how it might look. Their approach has become less illustrational, more abstract, symbolic."

We turned to look at specific illuminations. These are listed here in the order in which they appear in the Bible, rather than in the order in which they were made.

## The creation

THE STORY OF THE CREATION in Genesis is told within a framework of counting. As each day of the first week passes, the writer repeats his refrain: "And there was evening and there was morning, the first [or second, or third, or fifth] day." Donald built the structure of his illumination around this ordered counting out of days. Each vertical strip presents a single day and small golden squares are arranged in sequences of the sacred number seven. "I wanted," Donald said, "to symbolize God's presence in nothingness as well as everythingness."

The imagery Donald selected for each day mixes contemporary sources and ancient ones to create a timeless retelling of the ancient story.

"I value those times the CIT and I can talk in person rather than just use the written word," Donald said. "The best ideas come out in discussion. It was their idea to use fractals."

These complex geometric equations create self-perpetuating patterns of ever-greater complexity. "The fractals make patterns which emerge from nothingness." Their fragmented shapes explode from the dark primordial void, expressed verbally at the bottom with the Hebrew words *tohu wabohu*—chaos.

"My assistant Mark collected images of enhanced fractals on the Internet and in books. I got print-

The sketches for each illumination involve many weeks of careful preparation. The elements of the design are built up in collage. Here Donald Jackson uses an acetate overlay to position the large raven which floats over his composition.

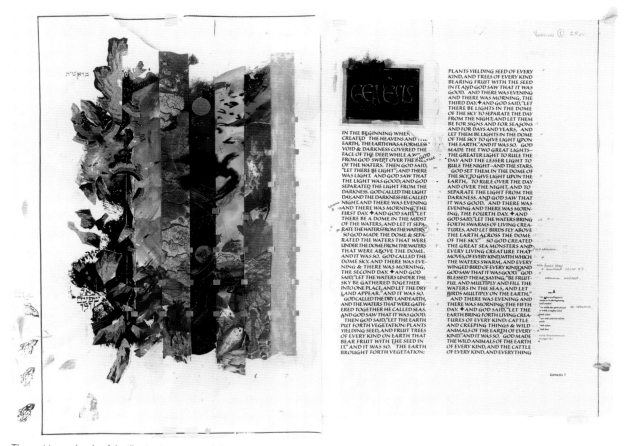

The position and scale of the illuminations are carefully balanced within the two-column design of the text pages. The illustrations break the tight bounds of the grid, engaging the marginal space.

outs and chopped them up. I put them together with the birth of a star—the beginning of space and time. I find that the Genesis story fits a lot of science. It tells us about timelessness."

A long, thin gold line in the midst of the first day marks a moment: "And God said, 'Let there be light.'"

To illustrate the separation of land and sea, a satellite image of the Ganges delta was used. The sun and moon are represented in silver and platinum respectively.

In the fifth day, for the creation of the creatures of the sea, Donald first tried a brightly colored fish. "The CIT said it reminded them of tropical fish in tanks," Donald remembered. "So I made an image of a young, flat fish. It is shown at a stage of its life when it is almost transparent. It has the vulnerability of a newly born fish and at the same time evokes a fossil. Although it is living, it looks like something ancient. I also used the same rubber stamp fish that I had used earlier in the *Loaves and Fishes* illumination."

For the creation of human beings on the sixth day, Donald evoked the most ancient representations of human beings. "I drew images from aboriginal rock paintings in Australia. Above them the huntress appears from an even earlier rock painting in Africa. It represents all of our beginnings."

The background of the sixth day is rendered in earthen tones, suggesting a volcanic landscape.

At the bottom of the sixth day small fragments of a snake imply the danger which awaits in the

Garden of Eden. "Chris Tomlin painted the snake. It has been interesting to watch him modify his technique. He used to work from dark to light; since working with me, he has begun working the opposite way round—from light to dark, letting the vellum speak for itself when it seems right."

*Garden of Eden*

On the golden seventh day, the first sabbath, all is calm and gold and shimmering. "I used gold leaf on a very diluted acrylic base. You burnish on gold; and you can keep adding bits of gold and silver. I tinted the acrylic so it has a slightly sandy color, retaining the earthiness of the creation in the presence of God."

In order to unify the composition, elements from one day overlap and interpenetrate the other days.

"At the end," Donald said, "I took a deep breath and with a coarse brush smudged the raven right on top of the finished illumination. Wisps of paint suggest birds flying across the whole face of creation. Birds are these magical, mobile, extraterrestrial creatures."

The raven is a familiar bird around The Hendre. "I'm surrounded by ravens. Their vocabulary is more extensive than any birds I know. I have learned to recognize many of their calls.

"The raven is a messenger in the Bible. Ravens are dark, powerful, they have that strong wingbeat. Yet they seem to delight in tumbling acrobatics in the air. The raven represents power, continually flying, tireless, endless. It's taking us for a ride across space and time."

## The Garden of Eden and Adam & Eve

Two linked illuminations flank chapter two of Genesis. The first depicts the innocence of the Garden of Eden; the second, Adam and Eve, the parents of humankind.

Donald commented, "There are tiny echoes of the *Creation* scene at the top of the *Garden of Eden* illumination to suggest light and dark, the progression of day and night."

The illumination is full of color; animals surround the humans in the garden. "The whole point was teeming fecundity. There is a feeling of joy with bright colors and that amazing bright face of an ape."

Donald repeated some of the ancient cave painting images from the *Creation* illumination. "The huntress reappears. In a way I suppose she represents work while the family groups in the background dance, make music and play."

Human beings living in harmony, enjoying the innocent companionship of Eden are enveloped in the natural environment. "Surrounding them are poisonous bugs—American—damned exotic! There are little bits of the snake, a parrot and a harlequin shrimp, which is a predator. There is a fraction of it against a background of plankton. At the bottom is the teeming sea."

Donald asked Chris Tomlin to add the animal painting. "I laid in the background and Chris painted the parrot, snake, scarlet-faced monkey, harlequin shrimp and the locusts behind the parrot." Donald then painted in the finishing details. "For the most part, my painting is much more loose, so I pulled it together."

Trying to remember the order in which each element was added, Donald corrected himself. "I think he painted the parrot afterwards. There was a bit of to and fro. I painted the grass over the locust. Chris will always try to make the bugs the most important thing!"

*Adam and Eve*

THAT CREEPS UPON THE GROUND
OF EVERY KIND. AND GOD SAW THAT
IT WAS GOOD. THEN GOD SAID,
26 "LET US MAKE HUMANKIND IN
OUR IMAGE, ACCORDING TO OUR
LIKENESS; AND LET THEM HAVE
DOMINION OVER THE FISH OF THE
SEA, AND OVER THE BIRDS OF THE
AIR, AND OVER THE CATTLE, AND
OVER ALL THE WILD ANIMALS
OF THE EARTH, AND OVER EVERY
CREEPING THING THAT CREEPS
UPON THE EARTH."
27 SO GOD CREATED
    HUMANKIND IN HIS IMAGE,
    IN THE IMAGE OF GOD HE
    CREATED THEM;
    MALE AND FEMALE HE
    CREATED THEM.
28 GOD BLESSED THEM, AND GOD
SAID TO THEM, "BE FRUITFUL &
MULTIPLY, AND FILL THE EARTH
& SUBDUE IT; AND HAVE DOMINION
OVER THE FISH OF THE SEA AND
OVER THE BIRDS OF THE AIR AND
OVER EVERY LIVING THING THAT
MOVES UPON THE EARTH." 29 GOD
SAID, "SEE, I HAVE GIVEN YOU EVERY
PLANT YIELDING SEED THAT IS
UPON THE FACE OF ALL THE EARTH,
AND EVERY TREE WITH SEED IN
ITS FRUIT; YOU SHALL HAVE THEM
FOR FOOD. 30 AND TO EVERY BEAST
OF THE EARTH, AND TO EVERY BIRD
OF THE AIR, AND TO EVERYTHING
THAT CREEPS ON THE EARTH, EV-
ERYTHING THAT HAS THE BREATH
OF LIFE, I HAVE GIVEN EVERY GREEN
PLANT FOR FOOD." AND IT WAS
SO. 31 GOD SAW EVERYTHING THAT
HE HAD MADE, AND INDEED, IT
WAS VERY GOOD. AND THERE WAS
EVENING AND THERE WAS MORN-
ING, THE SIXTH DAY.

FOR
CREATION
WAITS
WITH
EAGER
LONGING
FOR
THE
REVEAL
ING
OF THE
CHILDREN
OF
GOD

## 2

THUS THE HEAVENS & THE EARTH
WERE FINISHED, AND ALL THEIR
MULTITUDE. 2 AND ON THE SEVENTH
DAY GOD FINISHED THE WORK
THAT HE HAD DONE, AND HE REST-
ED ON THE SEVENTH DAY FROM
ALL THE WORK THAT HE HAD DONE.

3 SO GOD BLESSED THE SEVENTH
DAY AND HALLOWED IT. BECAUSE
ON IT GOD RESTED FROM ALL THE
WORK THAT HE HAD DONE IN CRE-
4 ATION. THESE ARE THE GENER-
ATIONS OF THE HEAVENS & THE
EARTH WHEN THEY WERE CREATED.

Using similar colors and repeated motifs, Donald Jackson ties the two illuminations together in his asymmetric composition.

בראשית

4 ⸿ In the day that the LORD God made the earth and
the heavens,⁵ when no plant of the field was yet in
the earth & no herb of the field had yet sprung up~
for the LORD God had not caused it to rain upon the
earth, and there was no one to till the ground : ⁶ but
a stream would rise from the earth, and water the
whole face of the ground~ ⁷ then the LORD God formed
man from the dust of the ground, and breathed into
his nostrils the breath of life; and the man became
a living being. ⁸ And the LORD God planted a garden
in Eden, in the east; and there he put the man whom
he had formed. ⁹ Out of the ground the LORD God
made to grow every tree that is pleasant to the sight,
and good for food, the tree of life also in the midst
of the garden, and the tree of the knowledge of good
10 and evil. ⸿ A river flows out of Eden to water the
garden, and from there it divides and becomes four
branches. ¹¹ The name of the first is Pishon; it is the
one that flows around the whole land of Havilah,
where there is gold;¹² and the gold of that land is good;
bdellium & onyx stone are there.¹³ The name of the
second river is Gihon; it is the one that flows around
the whole land of Cush.¹⁴ The name of the third river
is Tigris, which flows east of Assyria. And the fourth
15 river is the Euphrates. ⸿ The LORD God took the man
and put him in the garden of Eden to till it & keep
it.¹⁶ And the LORD God commanded the man, "You
may freely eat of every tree of the garden ; ¹⁷ but of
the tree of the knowledge of good and evil you shall
not eat, for in the day that you eat of it you shall die."
18 ⸿ Then the LORD God said, "It is not good that the
man should be alone; I will make him a helper as his
partner."¹⁹ So out of the ground the LORD God formed
every animal of the field and every bird of the air,
and brought them to the man to see what he would
call them; and whatever the man called every living
creature, that was its name.²⁰ The man gave names
to all cattle, and to the birds of the air, and to every
animal of the field; but for the man there was not
found a helper as his partner. ²¹ So the LORD God
caused a deep sleep to fall upon the man, and he slept;
then he took one of his ribs and closed up its place
with flesh.²² And the rib that the LORD God had tak
en from the man he made into a woman & brought
her to the man.²³ Then the man said,

"This at last is bone of my bones
    and flesh of my flesh ;
    this one shall be called Woman,
    for out of Man this one was taken."
²⁴ Therefore a man leaves his father and his mother
and clings to his wife, and they become one flesh.
²⁵ And the man and his wife were both naked, and
were not ashamed.

**3**

Now the serpent was more crafty than any
other wild animal that the LORD God
had made. He said to the woman, "Did
God say, 'You shall not eat from any tree in the garden'?
² The woman said to the serpent, "We may eat of
the fruit of the trees in the garden; ³ but God said,
'You shall not eat of the fruit of the tree that is in
the middle of the garden, nor shall you touch it, or
you shall die.'" ⁴ But the serpent said to the woman,
"You will not die; ⁵ for God knows that when you
eat of it your eyes will be opened, and you will be
like God, knowing good and evil." ⁶ So when the
woman saw that the tree was good for food, and
that it was a delight to the eyes, and that the tree
was to be desired to make one wise, she took of its
fruit & ate; and she also gave some to her husband,
who was with her, and he ate. Then the eyes of both
were opened, and they knew that they were naked;

⁵ Or formed a man [Heb
adam] of dust from the
ground. [Heb adamah]
⁶ Or for Adam
⁷ Heb ishshah
⁸ Heb ish
⁹ Or gods

AND ALL
OF US
WITH
UNVEILED
FACES,
SEEING
THE
GLORY
OF
THE
LORD
AS
THOUGH
REFLECTED
IN A
MIRROR,
ARE
BEING
TRANS-
FORMED
INTO
THE
SAME
IMAGE
FROM
ONE
DEGREE
OF
GLORY
TO
ANOTHER;

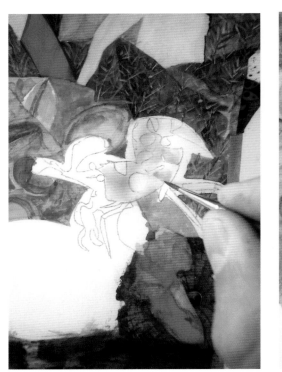

The harlequin shrimp acquires its many-colored coat at the expert hand of Chris Tomlin.

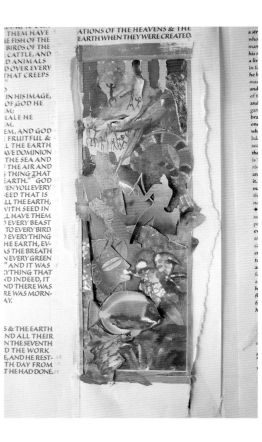

By using collage Donald Jackson can adjust the position and size of the different visual elements. The painting in this initial sketch is crude, roughly approximating the position and color of the finished piece. As the collage progresses the details become ever more refined.

Chris Tomlin paints the detailed, naturalistic animal images in the *Garden of Eden*. Many of the illuminations are the work of many hands, working under Donald Jackson's supervision.

Donald Jackson lifts his tracing paper to check a detail of the collage sketch underneath. The sketch's somber coloring will be considerably brightened in the finished illumination.

Tracing paper is used to transfer portions of the design from the rough sketch to the finished work. Donald Jackson keeps these sheets; as he works, designs sometimes need to be repeatedly transferred.

A small fraction of a mandala arcs into the scene from the left side. "The Buddhist mandala bit is about the birth of intellect. Human beings in the garden are enjoying animal life, but it's not just mindless reveling in life. They are also thinking about what it means. People begin to make patterns."

The second illumination of the pair is a portrait of Adam and Eve.

"The quotation in the margin is from Second Corinthians 3:18. I use that as a kind of caption. Behind Eve is a platinum background, like a mirror, to refer to the quotation. God is within us when we look into the mirror. Eve and Adam are mirrors of us."

The images are based on photographs from Africa. "I was interested in the idea of nakedness. It is both sensual and innocent. There is the joy of nakedness, like the child's freedom at the beach or in the bath. I was looking at African photos, at adult people who rejoice in nakedness.

"I chose her because she was a deliciously mischievous girl, all bedecked with beautiful things. The story is also about the loss of innocence. She's sparky enough, someone you might want to get into trouble for. Adam is inspired by another photograph of a beautiful man looking pensive."

Adam and Eve have painted their bodies. "The first clothing was to paint oneself. On the right I added a pattern from a Peruvian cape of feathers. It is clothing of a kind, but it is also about status. The horizontal stripes are details of Middle Eastern textiles. There's a progression from painted skin, to 'primitive' stuff, to woven textiles. In our loss of innocence, we are one."

The coral snake is deadly poisonous. "The disturbing presence of the snake, fragmented, separates Adam and Eve. Once again, Chris painted the snakes with life-like detail."

GENESIS

shall be blessed in you & in your offspring." Know that I am with you and will keep you wherever you go, and will bring you back to this land; for I will not leave you until I have done what I have promised you." ¹⁶ Then Jacob woke from his sleep and said, "Surely the LORD is in this place — and I did not know it!" ¹⁷ And he was afraid, and said, "How awesome is this place! This is none other than the house of God, and this is the gate of heaven." ¹⁸ So Jacob rose early in the morning, and he took the stone that he had put under his head and set it up for a pillar and poured oil on the top of it. ¹⁹ He called that place Bethel; but the name of the city was Luz at the first. ²⁰ Then Jacob made a vow, saying, "If God will be with me, and will keep me in this way that I go, and will give me bread to eat & clothing to wear, ²¹ so that I come again to my father's house in peace, then the LORD shall be my God, ²² and this stone, which I have set up for a pillar, shall be God's house; and of all that you give me I will surely give one-tenth to you."

## 29

Then Jacob went on his journey, and came to the land of the people of the east. ² As he looked, he saw a well in the field and three flocks of sheep lying there beside it; for out of that well the flocks were watered. The stone on the well's mouth was large, ³ and when all the flocks were gathered there, the shepherds would roll the stone from the mouth of the well, and water the sheep, and put the stone back in its place on the mouth of the well. ⁴ Jacob said to them, "My brothers, where do you come from?" They said, "We are from Haran." ⁵ He said to them, "Do you know Laban son of Nahor?" They said, "We do." ⁶ He said to them, "Is it well with him?" "Yes," they replied, "and here is his daughter Rachel, coming with the sheep." ⁷ He said, "Look, it is still broad daylight; it is not time for the animals to be gathered together. Water the sheep, and go, pasture them." ⁸ But they said, "We cannot until all the flocks are gathered together, and the stone is rolled from the mouth of the well; then we water the sheep." ⁹ While he was still speaking with them, Rachel came with her father's sheep; for she kept them. ¹⁰ Now when Jacob saw Rachel, the daughter of his mother's brother Laban, and the sheep of his mother's brother Laban, Jacob went up and rolled the stone from the well's mouth, and watered the flock of his mother's brother

AND HE WAS AFRAID, AND SAID, "HOW AWESOME IS THIS PLACE!"

Jacob's vision of angels descending and ascending a heavenly ladder spills out from a single column opposite Genesis 28.

## Jacob's Ladder

"THIS STORY really moved me," Donald said. "I was familiar with it from childhood. I became powerfully affected by the sheer enormity of this vision—suddenly you are thrust into the midst of this incredibly awesome event. I wanted it to be surreal, shining things and light, with dawn about to break."

His original sketch caused some controversy when it was first seen by the CIT. Sally Mae recalled, "Oh, on that one, Donald really dug his heels in."

Donald agreed with her. "I'll show you the correspondence. It was complicated."

In the brief, the CIT had mentioned in passing a common monastic image from the Middle Ages—the *Ladder of Perfection,* depicting monks mounting upwards toward their heavenly goal as some fall to their doom. They compared this admonitory image to the Jacob story. In Donald's words, this inadvertently created a "red herring," a distraction from Jacob's vision.

The schema had also called for Jacob's vision to be tied to the story of Jacob wrestling with an angel. These two stories needed to be separated. Donald remarks, "I had to break free from my original instructions." He created a place on another page for a small picture of the wrestling Jacob.

More discussion ensued about the angels in the piece. Were some fallen angels and others angels of light? And what, the CIT wanted to know, were the butterfly wings? Were they some other class of angel?

Donald stuck to his guns about the butterflies. His conversation with the CIT clarified the awesome simplicity of the story. This was not about sorting the good from the bad; this was a moment when heaven and earth were momentarily joined and Jacob received his new name—Israel.

"I suppose I had a bee in my bonnet. I wanted to use butterflies as an analogy for angels," he said. "Ask yourself how you feel about a butterfly. Their enormous rarity! They are beautiful, full of grace, fragile and very mysterious in a funny kind of way. There is a subtext, too. You bat your eyelid and the butterfly

Layers of paint go down only to be scraped away. Using an erasing knife Donald Jackson removes one butterfly wing. Sometimes the knife or sandpaper are used to distress the surface, creating subtle gradations in contrast to areas of solid color.

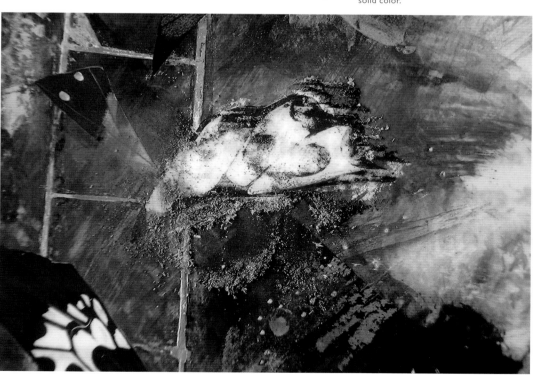

Donald Jackson carefully peels away a layer of frisket masking film. Spaces for butterfly wings were masked out while Donald used free vigorous brush-strokes to fill the background.

is gone. Now it's there, now it isn't." It was the perfect metaphor for the fleeting wonder of Jacob's vision.

"They have such a life-will," he continued. Their incredible fragility contrasts with the thousands of miles they travel on their yearly migrations. "I was determined to use super-realistic bits of butterfly wings. They appear against a lacy pattern of gold, a gossamer presence. The pattern is a textile print. I applied acrylic medium to a crocheted material."

Making the finished illumination carried its own challenges. "I thought this was relatively straightforward. I painted the background, masking off spaces with frisket for Chris to paint in the butterfly wings. He really went to town, working in exquisite detail with immense care. That's the danger of distance collaboration. If he'd been here while he was painting them, I would have realized there were one too many wings. As it was, I ended up having to scrape off some of his lovely work to regain the color balance of the whole."

## The Ten Commandments

DONALD INVITED Thomas Ingmire to create several major illuminations for The Saint John's Bible, including this image from Exodus. Thomas was rather quiet as I interviewed him by phone. He thought carefully before answering questions and weighed his words before speaking.

"I said to Donald, 'I've always avoided illustrative things.' Donald has selected pieces for me to do which have lettering as their major feature. I had no direct contact with CIT; everything went through Donald.

"I do two or three really very sketchy sketches. Donald and I talk about it conceptually, we discuss a direction, then I do a detailed sketch. I also write an explanation of my ideas to Donald. They rewrite what I say and they submit it to the committee. So far the CIT has been really positive to my things. They liked this one right from the beginning."

In the brief, five different passages from Exodus were to be incorporated into a single illumination. Thomas said, "My first thought was, 'How do I make this into one image?' Any one of these stories could be the most important."

שמות

In the *Ten Commandments* illumination, a collage of scenes from Exodus is presented in a highly abstract form immediately before Exodus 20.

An early sketch by Thomas Ingmire sets out the bones of the design. Working in colored pencil he works out areas of light and dark and begins to bring his composition together.

A later sketch opts for dark tones. The final design would be much brighter.

The brief suggested that the story of the giving of the Ten Commandments represented a new creation, the gift of law bringing order to the chaos of human affairs. Thomas chose this as the principal image around which he grouped the others.

"The other passages were all miracles—evidence of God or God's power. Seeing them as miracles gave me one way to think of these four as one unit."

The four stories along the top of the composition are: the burning bush, the first Passover, the parting of the Red Sea, and Israel at Mount Sinai. Across these four stories Thomas has arrayed the voice of God speaking in gold letters.

"In so far as the structure of the page goes, the only gilding is within the top of the page where the miracles take place."

The bottom of the page contains the commandments themselves, overlapping and dissolving the colored background behind them. Thomas used typography for the letters.

"The CIT made reference to the Ten Commandments etched in tablets of stone. They described God's hand etching the tablets. I didn't feel the text could be written by hand; for me to write them calligraphically didn't seem right. I used the typeface Stone Sans. Was it semi-bold? I forget.

"That solved a lot of technical problems, too. It was an awkward skin. It had a surface like glass, and it was slimy. So the decision to use type solved a lot of problems.

"Another reason I thought of the possibility of using type was that I was in Bruges visiting Brody Neuenschwander. We were going around town looking at things he had done. He'd made a piece on the wall of a hotel lobby. He'd done the thing in Photoshop and it was all executed in stencil." Thomas liked the stencil idea, so he used it.

"It's a complicated process. I discovered many ways to make mistakes. All the letters are pre-cut but there is a sheet of release paper. You roll out this paper and lay the stencil down and peel away the paper.

My first mistake: I didn't get the release paper flat, so there was a wrinkle. I had to start again. On the second try I positioned it wrong."

Eventually he mastered his technique. "It's a very precise, fine stencil. You get beautiful sharp lines with a stencil brush."

Conceptually Thomas found the text very engaging. "I was reading a book called *The Alphabet versus the Goddess,* by Leonard Shlain. He has a whole section on the Ten Commandments. He saw the commandments as the transforming of culture with the invention of the alphabet. It represented the first time the alphabet as we know it emerged. Before then we had pictograms. This new kind of writing must have seemed like wizardry or magic and was tied to a God who forbade graven images. So the background shows Egyptian motifs, gods, goddesses, society before the giving of the commandments. It is a kind of chaos, active in color contrasts. The alphabet comes over the top of it."

Thomas' other work often involves looking at the alphabet and thinking about the implications of this social construct of writing. He reflected, "It's interesting that this is an extension of things I've been developing in my own work. It's very hard to make that kind of connection."

Others have offered their own interpretations of his illumination. Thomas recalled, "Donald told me a rabbi saw it and had a whole different interpretation from mine. The illuminations have a life of their own."

Thomas also commented, "It's really a bit brighter than I'd like. Vellum gives everything this unbelievable richness and density. Paper absorbs more; it's more muted. On vellum it pops!"

## The Genealogy of Christ

THE *Genealogy of Christ* stands at the beginning in more ways than one. This is the page which launched the entire project. It is the frontispiece to Matthew's Gospel and therefore stands at the beginning of the first volume Donald made. The *Genealogy of Christ* was also shown at the launching ceremonies for *The Saint John's Bible* at The Minneapolis Institute of Arts and the New York Public Library.

It has crossed the Atlantic several times. It has been displayed at meetings of donors. It has been under the hot lights of television studios. It has even made the cover of the *Smithsonian Magazine.* The fact it has survived all of this hustle and bustle says something about the quality of its craftsmanship; radical changes in temperature and humidity are invitations for gold to pop off and paint to fleck or smear. It is still pristine.

The genealogy page was made before many decisions were finalized in the project. The script had not been fully developed. Even the page size was not entirely fixed.

"It came straight from the schema," Donald says. "There was no brief, just a five line description, beginning, 'The genealogy contains the whole sweep of Jewish history . . . Abraham, David, Tamar, Bathsheba and Ruth should be highlighted.'"

The first chapter of Matthew's Gospel traces the lineage of Jesus back through David to Abraham. The schema highlights this chapter as a sign of continuity, rooting the Gospel in the traditions of the Old Testament. In Donald's illumination, the names of Christ's ancestors appear in Hebrew letters sprinkled across the page.

"I was on my own—I had to work it out. My idea was to suggest a bridge between the Old Testament and the New. So I used the menorah to acknowledge Christianity's Jewish roots."

This sketch closely resembles the finished illumination. The tightly drawn menorah on the upper left would later become much more abstract and the piece would become more layered. The basic elements of the design have, however, been resolved.

The *Genealogy of Christ* appears as the frontispiece to Matthew's Gospel. This was the first illumination made for The Saint John's Bible.

It was a delicate thing to use the religious symbol of another tradition. "I was asked to temper it, to make it more like a tree with leaves, to tone down the statement. Although the text is an incantation if you like—a plea for the authenticity of Christ's claim—for me it is an invocation of the idea of a family of all people including your family and mine. Hence the connection with the idea of the DNA symbol pushing that connectedness."

The menorah stands as an armature through which different shapes swirl. Small DNA double helixes made with a little rubber stamp dance in the spaces between its branches.

"The menorah becomes the tree of life. And it has a springing point, a circle: the core from which all life comes." The imagery comes from sources from across the world.

The illumination "implies a kinship with other spiritual teachers—that's why I introduced Islamic style candles, light devices and cosmic mandala fragments from the Buddhist visual tradition. A tiny word written in Arabic quietly emphasizes Hagar, Ishmael's mother." This makes a subtle and quiet visual link to the third great Abrahamic faith, Islam.

Donald's ultimate aim was to suggest the "connectedness of all seekers of enlightenment. All paths lead to God."

## The Loaves and Fishes

THIS ILLUMINATION includes two different stories—the feeding of the five thousand and the feeding of the four thousand—in a single image. The theological briefs suggested that these were variants of a single story and so Donald concentrated on the image of the multiplication of the loaves and fishes, the element common to both versions.

It was meant to be a rather small illumination. As Donald worked on it, however, it exploded into the margins, filling the edges of a whole spread.

"This isn't two halves," Donald said. "You have two stories, one is hot, the other is cold." But they are unified into a single unified composition. "It just grew. I worked with overlays and collage. The CIT had some visual suggestions—the fish, for instance. Michael sent me a postcard of a mosaic from Tabgha on the Sea of Galilee where the miracle was said to have taken place."

On the left he placed two fish and five loaves from one version of the story; on the right there are three fish and seven loaves.

"What elements have you got?" he asked out loud. "Bits of loaves, fragments which start to float. Baskets to take up and pass on the remnants."

The basket designs are based on Native American patterns. "I'd been looking for baskets. I found some Native American baskets and I said to myself, 'This is sacred geometry!' Basketmakers in some North American traditions sing sacred songs as they make their baskets. I wanted them in there because they are American. But they were also like the abstract intellectual constructs of sacred geometry."

With these elements—baskets, fish, bread, two sides of the Sea of Galilee—the design began to lay itself out. "It speaks for itself. I did this organically." The images began to multiply across the margins of the page.

"This is all about love," he said. "These few fish and few loaves were given out, symbolically shared with the many. It was an act of giving, of loving. The basket shapes started to spin, a dizzy feeling. The baskets themselves have a geometrical shape. The arithmetic of love is exponential. One act of love begets another."

The use of rubber stamps allows patterns to repeat and multiply across the page. The fish are based on a Byzantine mosaic from Tabgha in Galilee identified by tradition as the site of one of the miraculous feedings. The spiral pattern of the Native American basket suggests the exponential multiplication of loaves and fishes.

# 6

He left that place and came to his home town, and his disciples followed him. On the sabbath he began to teach in the synagogue, & many who heard him were astounded. They said, "Where did this man get all this? What is this wisdom that has been given to him? What deeds of power are being done by his hands! Is not this the carpenter, the son of Mary & brother of James and Joses & Judas & Simon, and are not his sisters here with us?" And they took offense at him. Then Jesus said to them, "Prophets are not without honor, except in their hometown, and among their own kin, and in their own house." And he could do no deed of power there, except that he laid his hands on a few sick people and cured them. And he was amazed at their unbelief.

Then he went about among the villages teaching. He called the twelve and began to send them out two by two, and gave them authority over the unclean spirits. He ordered them to take nothing for their journey except a staff; no bread, no bag, no money in their belts; but to wear sandals and not to put on two tunics. He said to them, "Wherever you enter a house, stay there until you leave the place. If any place will not welcome you and they refuse to hear you, as you leave, shake off the dust that is on your feet as a testimony against them." So they went out and proclaimed that all should repent. They cast out many demons, & anointed with oil many who were sick and cured them. King Herod heard of it, for Jesus' name had become known. Some were saying, "John the baptizer has been raised from the dead; and for this reason these powers are at work in him." But others said, "It is Elijah." And others said, "It is a prophet, like one of the prophets of old." But when Herod heard of it, he said, "John, whom I beheaded, has been raised." For Herod himself had sent men who arrested John, bound him, and put him in prison on account of Herodias, his brother Philip's wife, because Herod had married her. For John had been telling Herod, "It is not lawful for you to have your brother's wife." And Herodias had a grudge against him, and wanted to kill him. But she could not, for Herod feared John, knowing that he was a righteous and holy man, and he protected him. When he heard him, he was greatly perplexed; and yet he liked to listen to him. But an opportunity came when Herod on his birthday gave a banquet for his courtiers and officers & for the leaders of Galilee. When his daughter Herodias came in & danced, she pleased Herod & his guests; and the king said to the girl, "Ask me for whatever you wish, and I will give it." And he solemnly swore to her, "Whatever you ask me, I will give you, even half of my kingdom." She went out and said to her mother, "What should I ask for?" She replied, "The head of John the baptizer." Immediately she rushed back to the king and requested, "I want you to give me at once the head of John the Baptist on a platter." The king was deeply grieved; yet out of regard for his oaths and for the guests, he did not want to refuse her. Immediately the king sent a soldier of the guard with orders to bring John's head. He went and beheaded him in the prison, brought his head on a platter, and gave it to the girl. Then the girl gave it to her mother. When his disciples heard about it, they came and took his body, and laid it in a tomb.

The apostles gathered around Jesus, and told him all that they had done and taught. He said to them, "Come away to a deserted place all by yourselves and rest a while." For many were coming and going, and they had no leisure even to eat. And they went away in the boat to a deserted place by themselves. Now many saw them going and recognised them, and they hurried there on foot from all the towns and arrived ahead of them. As he went ashore, he saw a great crowd; and he had compassion for them, because they were like sheep without a shepherd; and he began to teach them many

other ancient authorities read *son of the carpenter and of Mary*

Or *stumbled*

Gk *his*

other ancient authorities read *he was*

Gk *he*

other ancient authorities read *he did many things*

Other ancient authorities read *the daughter of Herodias herself*

Gk *his*

The miracle of the multiplication of loaves and fishes explodes into the margins of Mark 6 and 7.

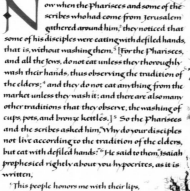

things.³⁵ When it grew late, his disciples came to him & said," This is a deserted place, and the hour is now very late; ³⁶ send them away so that they may go into the surrounding country and villages and buy something for themselves to eat."³⁷ But he answered them," You give them something to eat." They said to him," Are we to go and buy two hundred denarii worth of bread, and give it to them to eat?" ³⁸ And he said to them," How many loaves have you? Go and see." When they had found out, they said, "Five, and two fish." ³⁹ Then he ordered them to get all the people to sit down in groups on the green grass.⁴⁰ So they sat down in groups of hundreds and of fifties.⁴¹ Taking the five loaves and the two fish, he looked up to heaven, and blessed & broke the loaves, and gave them to his disciples to set before the people; and he divided the two fish among them all.⁴² And all ate and were filled; ⁴³ and they took up twelve baskets full of broken pieces and of the fish.⁴⁴ Those who had eaten the loaves numbered five thousand men. ■ Immediately he made his disciples get into the boat & go on ahead to the other side, to Bethsaida, while he dismissed the crowd. ⁴⁶ After saying farewell to them, he went up on the mountain to pray. ■ When evening came, the boat was out on the sea, and he was alone on the land. ⁴⁸ When he saw that they were straining at the oars against an adverse wind, he came towards them early in the morning, walking on the sea. He intended to pass them by. ⁴⁹ But when they saw him walking on the sea, they thought it was a ghost and cried out; ⁵⁰ for they all saw him and were terrified. But immediately he spoke to them & said," Take heart, it is I; do not be afraid." ⁵¹ Then he got into the boat with them & the wind ceased. And they were utterly astounded, ⁵² for they did not understand about the loaves, but their hearts were hardened. ■ When they had crossed over, they came to land at Gennesaret and moored the boat.⁵⁴ When they got out of the boat, people at once recognized him, ⁵⁵ and rushed about that whole region and began to bring the sick on mats to wherever they heard he was.⁵⁶ And wherever he went, into villages or cities or farms, they laid the sick in the marketplaces, and begged him that they might touch even the fringe of his cloak; and all who touched it were healed.

7

Now when the Pharisees and some of the scribes who had come from Jerusalem gathered around him, ² they noticed that some of his disciples were eating with defiled hands, that is, without washing them. ³ [For the Pharisees, and all the Jews, do not eat unless they thoroughly wash their hands, thus observing the tradition of the elders; ⁴ and they do not eat anything from the market unless they wash it; and there are also many other traditions that they observe, the washing of cups, pots, and bronze kettles.] ⁵ So the Pharisees and the scribes asked him," Why do your disciples not live according to the tradition of the elders, but eat with defiled hands?" ⁶ He said to them," Isaiah prophesied rightly about you hypocrites, as it is written,

⁷ 'This people honors me with their lips,
    but their hearts are far from me;

⁷     in vain do they worship me,
        teaching human precepts as doctrines.'

⁸ You abandon the commandment of God & hold to human tradition." ■ Then he said to them," You have a fine way of rejecting the commandment of God in order to keep your tradition! ¹⁰ For Moses said,' Honor your father & your mother'; and,' Whoever speaks evil of father or mother must surely die.' ¹¹ But you say that if anyone tells father or mother,' Whatever support you might have had from me is Corban' [that is, an offering to God] – ¹² then you no longer permit doing anything for a father or mother, ¹³ thus making void the word of God through your tradition that you have handed on. And you do many things like this." ■ Then he called the crowd again and said to them," Listen to me, all of you, and understand: ¹⁵ there is nothing outside a person

קרבן

The denarius was the usual day's wage for a laborer
Meaning of Gk uncertain
Other ancient authorities read and when they come from the marketplace, they do not eat unless they purify themselves
Other ancient authorities add and beds
Gk walk
Gk korban to God

All the basic elements are in
place in the rough sketch. The
design does not, however, tie in
to the text. In the final version
text and image overlap and
become a subtly
integrated whole.

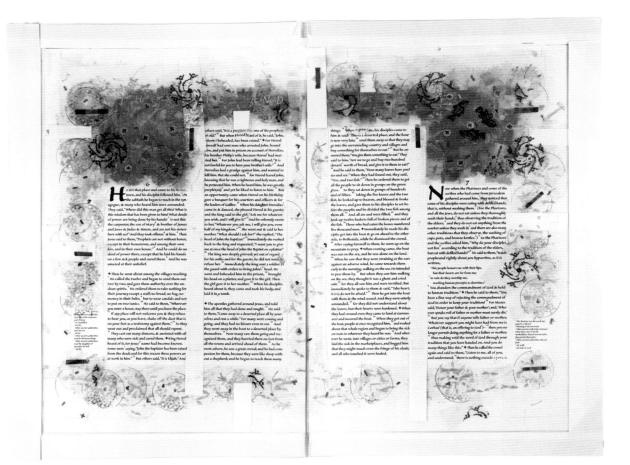

A fifteenth-century Book of Hours from
northern Europe shows a late medieval
tradition of marginal illumination. Tiny vines
and flecks of burnished gold spill out around
the text. The *Loaves and Fishes* illumination
is a modern echo of this ancient tradition.
Gavin Hill Book of Hours. Gavin MS 2. Hill
Monastic Manuscript Library, Saint John's
University.

A design issue then led to the addition of the blue batons which interrupt the composition. "As these shapes are flowing around the page, it could be mushy. I needed something staccato to give the design fixed points. Dark blue batons which are placed at intervals represent obstacles to the flow. In a design sense, they create little eddies and in a moral sense they represent sins of commission, moments when our actions interrupt the flow of love. I also left blank spaces, representing times when we should act with love but don't; these would be sins of omission."

When he stepped back from the work, he realized he'd made something with a medieval precedent. "Then I thought, this is fifteenth century illumination—little bits of gold in the margins with that three-pronged leaf pattern. It's a cracking solution. They got it right. But I wasn't recreating an ancient thing. It could very easily have become a re-creation. I did this illumination in this way because of the logic of it." Almost by accident he had stumbled on a graphic solution which was centuries old and made it his own.

## The Luke Anthology

THE *Luke Anthology* incorporates five parables and a story from the life of Jesus. The five parables—the lost coin, the lost sheep, the prodigal son, the good Samaritan, and Dives and Lazarus—appear on the left hand page while Jesus appears on the right with Mary and Martha. Donald worked hard to blend all these tales into a single image.

"It was truly an anthology," Donald recounted. "How do you sum up Luke's Gospel? The brief alone ran to three pages of dense text—and I had to boil that down to a single page."

Donald also knew he would have to visually separate the parables from the narrative of Jesus with the two sisters. "Five parables, then a story about Jesus. They're quite different. It's a gear change." He solved that dilemma by separating parable and narrative onto two different pages. The whole composition is unified with strong diagonal lines. As he explained, "There is a lot going on and the onlooker has to hunt." It is an illumination which repays careful examination.

The themes of love and forgiveness run through all the parables. "These stories are about the power of God's love beyond human comprehension and what happens out of sheer love between human beings."

In the story of the prodigal son, in the lower left, the father carries the finest, brightest coat out to his penitent son. His gesture points upwards toward a golden image of the World Trade Center. The diagonal band holding these images leads the viewer's eye straight up to the gilded face of Christ.

"This parable is all about forgiveness. You're really challenged to overcome your anger. It's got to be really difficult to forgive." Donald used the image of the Twin Towers as a modern expression of the challenge of forgiving evil. It is an example, he said, "representing the difficulty of achieving pure, unreasonable love."

The figures of father and son in the parable were painted by Aidan Hart in his traditional icon-painter's style. Donald reworked Aidan's image a bit, explaining, "The paint surface was a bit too coarse in finish. But I wanted that period look. It contrasts well with the Twin Towers. I wanted to express a sense of then-and-now, showing the relevance of these old stories in our contemporary world."

The finished illumination begins to take shape next to the complex sketch. The stages of making the final work are carefully considered as layer upon layer is added to the composition. Here the diagonal bands are hard and crisp. They will later be overpainted and interrupted. In the final version they recede into the background, creating a subtle armature within which the stories are placed.

A series of parables is tied to the story of Mary and Martha in the *Luke Anthology* opposite Luke 15.

younger of them said to his father, 'Father, give me
the share of the property that will belong to me .'
So he divided his property between them. ¹³ A few
days later the younger son gathered all he had & 
traveled to a distant country, and there he squan
dered his property in dissolute living. ¹⁴ When he
had spent everything, a severe famine took place
throughout that country, and he began to be in need.
¹⁵ So he went and hired himself out to one of the
citizens of that country, who sent him to his fields
to feed the pigs. ¹⁶ He would gladly have filled him
self with the pods that the pigs were eating; and no
one gave him anything. ¹⁷ But when he came to him
self he said, 'How many of my father's hired hands
have bread enough & to spare, but here I am dying
of hunger! ¹⁸ I will get up and go to my father, and
I will say to him, "Father, I have sinned against heaven
& before you; ¹⁹ I am no longer worthy to be called
your son; treat me like one of your hired hands."'
²⁰ So he set off and went to his father. But while he
was still far off, his father saw him and was filled
with compassion; he ran and put his arms around
him and kissed him. ²¹ Then the son said to him,
'Father, I have sinned against heaven & before you;
I am no longer worthy to be called your son.' ²² But
the father said to his slaves, 'Quickly, bring out a
robe – the best one – and put it on him; put a ring
on his finger and sandals on his feet. ²³ And get the
fatted calf and kill it, and let us eat and celebrate;
²⁴ for this son of mine was dead and is alive again;
he was lost and is found!' And they began to cele
brate. ❡ ²⁵ "Now his elder son was in the field; and
when he came & approached the house, he heard
music and dancing. ²⁶ He called one of the slaves
and asked what was going on. ²⁷ He replied, 'Your
brother has come, and your father has killed the
fatted calf, because he has got him back safe and
sound.' ²⁸ Then he became angry and refused to go
in. His father came out and began to plead with
him. ²⁹ But he answered his father, 'Listen! For all
these years I have been working like a slave for you,
and I have never disobeyed your command; yet you
have never given me even a young goat so that I might
celebrate with my friends. ³⁰ But when this son of
yours came back, who has devoured your property
with prostitutes, you killed the fatted calf for him!'
³¹ Then the father said to him, 'Son, you are always
with me, and all that is mine is yours. ³² But we had
to celebrate & rejoice, because this brother of yours
was dead and has come to life; he was lost and has
been found.' "

ʲ Other ancient authorities
read *filled his stomach
with*

ᵏ Other ancient authorities
add *Treat me like one of
your hired servants*

ˡ Gk *he*

Donald painted in the prodigal son's pigs "after an image out of a children's pictorial encyclopedia I grew up with."

Sally Mae added some fragments of the recurring mandala motif which had appeared in the *Genealogy of Christ*. Donald explained, "The cosmic mandala fragments here on the right and the left do not signify Buddhism per se. They stand for the working of people's minds, trying to make sense of their experience." These motifs provide a thread which runs through the Bible, unifying the whole.

Martha and Mary, who stand on the right at the bottom, complete the composition and were finished by Donald while he was at Saint John's. Christ's words to Martha appear in gold above their heads. Donald said, "It's the punchline quote: 'There is need of only one thing.' For me, it is the love of God, the need to reach out to God."

The diagonal bands pick up the cosmic mandala theme which runs through a number of the illuminations.

The inscriptions in small capitals are added late in the process of making a finished illumination. Loosely indicated in white, they are written with great freedom.

The *Crucifixion* illumination slowly takes form in a series of variations. The photocopied reference of a late tenth-century crucifix is transformed into a splash of gold in the final drawing. Sketches like these were sent over the Internet from Wales to Minnesota for the comments of the Committee on Illumination and Text.

## The Crucifixion

THE DEATH OF JESUS is rendered with great directness. The crucified figure in raised and burnished gold is central to the composition. The cross is set at an angle, heightening the drama of the scene. To one side fragments of purple seem torn by the bright glory of the gold.

"The brief tells us that the curtain of the Temple was covered with astrological symbols," Donald said. The text in Luke says the Temple curtain was torn in two at the moment Jesus died. Here it tears into fragments. Above the cross a patch of sky suggests the "blue of enlightenment and the new order" breaking in. The crucifixion marks a transition from an old, hierarchical ritual order to a liberating freedom.

"I used a coarse bristly brush for the blue, applying direct, dry dabs of paint right onto something that's taken me weeks. That's just a need—I have to do it. You do a coarse brush stroke with brute energy, and this then calls forth a delicate counterpoint. There is the energy of attack with the delicate supporting of embellishment."

Surrounding the vibrant scene is a cool grey/blue border. This has medieval precedents: often a heavy Romanesque illustration will have a transitional, softer edge. Hard color gives way to softer color; it helps tie the illustration to the page on which it lies. In this case there was a practical reason for it as well.

"The writing on the page behind was disturbing the delicacy of anything I could add, so I needed to obliterate it. That's why I added the grey border. I broke that down by printing on it with *Broderie Anglaise:* English lace. It also brought in the recurring theme of textiles. I am always looking for links, visual metaphors linking each illumination to the others. For the torn curtain, I inked a piece of silk and printed it."

*The Crucifixion* is depicted opposite Luke 24.

## The Life of Paul

THE *Life of Paul* began as another anthology page, illustrating a series of scenes from the Acts of the Apostles. As it took shape, it became a unified image. The details of specific events dropped out—Donald didn't want to make what he calls "a comic strip" with seven little illustrations. Instead he opted for a broader treatment.

Paul's role as the Apostle to the Gentiles led him to found churches across the Mediterranean world and Donald chose to express this through the collage of urban images, both ancient and modern, which surround his portrait. A ship in the background evokes Paul's many preaching journeys. The text above his head, in gold, refers to his dramatic conversion to Christianity in a light-filled vision. The text under his feet describes his missionary calling to the far ends of the known world.

The first sketch was almost completely executed by Aidan Hart. The CIT balked. Donald recalled, "They threw up their hands at all this Greek Orthodox stuff. This threw us into a tailspin. They want to know, 'How much is Donald going to do in the book?' At that point, I had been struggling with ideas for the *Resurrection* scene and they hadn't seen much work from me for a while. So I revised Aidan's sketch a bit and put a gold background to it—I didn't want to offend Aidan. They still said no. So I did the whole thing myself."

The initial sketch by Aidan Hart envisioned a very literal rendition of Paul's life drawn in a traditional iconographic style. Based closely on the theological brief, the design was rejected on stylistic grounds.

Aidan Hart's work is based on a strong sense of line. Clearly delineated figures contrast with solid backgrounds. Donald Jackson's work by contrast is informed by bold brushwork and a fluid relationship between figure and ground.

In a later version the narrative vignettes have been replaced with a more evocative rendering of cityscapes both ancient and modern. The story of Paul is told in a symbolic rather than literal fashion. Aidan Hart's precise painting is integrated into Donald Jackson's broader, more painterly style.

The final illumination was a collaboration between Aidan Hart and Donald Jackson. Here Aidan paints in the figure of Saint Paul.

The design went through three versions. "Aidan first, then I," said Donald, "Then Aidan and I together." Some of the earlier versions literally lie in layers under the paint of the sketch.

The buildings to Paul's left and right are apartment buildings which line Fifth Avenue in New York City. Above them, to the right, the jewel-like Stella Maris chapel, which overlooks Lake Sagatagan in Collegeville, makes a reference to Saint John's. Below these, black line drawings evoke the thousands of churches built through Christian history. Paul holds a little model of a church in his arms. He is wrapped in a Jewish prayer shawl, evoking his youth as a devout Pharisee.

Old and new combine once again to form a unified whole.

## Illumination

THE ILLUMINATIONS bring texts to life and give them visual form. They are not simply illustrations but come out of a long process of living with the text. Some of them are exercises in pure painting; others are more densely theological in their visual logic. All of them do more than translate the text from words into images—they resonate with the text.

"The process begins with the intellectual," Donald remarked. "There is a selection. I look coldly at the text: what is the essential message? The several foci? Then there is Bible reading: what the text 'says.' But finally, it is emotional: how does it *feel?*"

And ultimately, if he can make us feel the text as well as simply understand it then he has done his job.

*The Life of Paul* appears opposite Acts of the Apostles 15.

All the major visual themes for Psalms appear in the frontispiece. Broad, vigorous brushstrokes are contained within long vertical shapes which evoke open books. The skittish lines in gold, blue and black which pass across the page are the visual representation of chants sung by the monks of Saint John's. The vertical patterns represent sacred music from other world traditions interweaving with the Christian voices. Donald Jackson incorporated the text of Psalm 1 into the design of the frontispiece.

# CHAPTER 10
# THE BOOK OF PSALMS

*My tongue is like the pen of a ready scribe.*
PSALM 45:1 (NRSV)

EMAIL is cold and quick. For two years digital messages passed back and forth between the Scriptorium in Wales and the CIT in Minnesota. Sketches were made and photographed; they whizzed over the wires and by satellite across the Atlantic with terse messages of explanation. Comments bounced back in icy, pixellated prose.

Donald is not cold. He is warm. He wants to read the nuances in your face as you talk. As the first two volumes were coming to completion, he wanted to reinvigorate his relationship with the committee.

"I insisted on a face-to-face meeting with the CIT," Donald remarked. "For the chemistry of it."

Through the making of the first two volumes, the relationship between artist and committee had sometimes been stormy but over time it had matured. The members of the CIT grew to understand Donald and his work; he learned how to digest and make use of the dense theological briefs. They all learned the limitations of long-distance communication. A single remark in the briefs could take on an importance it never would have had in a face-to-face conversation. It was hard to judge which ideas were crucial and which were simply suggestions.

Donald was given the briefs for the third volume, Psalms, in June 2002. The members of the committee were very proud of their work. By the time they wrote the brief, they had worked with Donald for several years. They knew his quirks and his strengths. They could see how his mind worked and what had sparked his imagination. And they could picture the kinds of solutions which might arise from their theological reflections.

The Psalms are not like the rest of the Bible. The Psalter is pure poetry, composed to be sung. The recitation of Psalms forms the core of the Benedictine hours of prayer. These were texts that every member of the monastic community knew intimately.

The CIT took the opportunity to devise a different kind of brief. The Psalms don't lend themselves to illustration; they are not narrative. So the members of the CIT decided to treat the book as a set of texts which would receive a more purely calligraphic treatment. Whatever illuminations might appear would be more abstract, tied to broad themes and they would serve to divide the text into sections. They felt sure that this text-based approach would please Donald and play to his strengths.

## A meeting of minds

DONALD RECEIVED the brief for Psalms and began to work his way through it. There was a good deal of detail and one theme overlapped another. He wasn't sure how he could include all these ideas into his manuscript.

"There were so many different ideas. For instance, some of the psalms are written as acrostics; the first

Donald Jackson examines sketches for the book of Psalms.

letter of each verse is a letter of the Hebrew alphabet. They thought I could do something with that.

"Then, every psalm is in a particular genre. Some psalms were half in one genre, half in another. Irene, who is a scholar of the Psalms, was big on genres. Other scholars would like this, she thought. Perhaps there was a way of differentiating each genre graphically.

"Then they wanted to highlight the penitential psalms. They also felt it was important to divide the text into five parts: the whole book of Psalms is broken into five books. They thought each of the five books should have a different tone," said Donald.

He wasn't sure how he could pull it off. Their wish list was too long. And he began to worry that it would throw the whole project out of schedule. Donald asked Sally Mae to work out how long it would take. She did; it was more time than they had.

"We worked out how long it would take to do all these things, and it simply didn't fit the schedule or the budget. Had I not insisted on meeting with them in person, we would have been driven mad."

The book of Psalms evokes a long tradition of musical manuscripts. The square notes of this medieval Processional find a contemporary, abstracted echo in the gold squares which dance across each page of Saint John's Psalms. The manuscript shown here was made in Spain in 1541.

Processional. Dominican Rite.
*Processionariu[m] secu[n]du[m] ordinem predicatoru[m].*
Spain, 1541. Manuscript on vellum.
Black leather binding over boards.
Kacmarcik Collection of Arca Artium,
Saint John's University.

Using a computer program, sounds of sacred music from many cultures are transformed into oscillating patterns on the screen. These trembling lines were rendered as rubber stamps to be used in the illuminations.

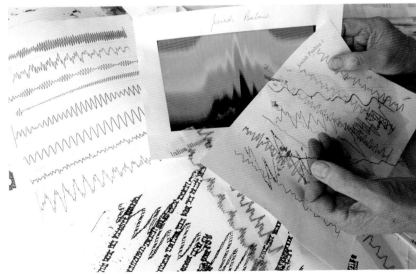

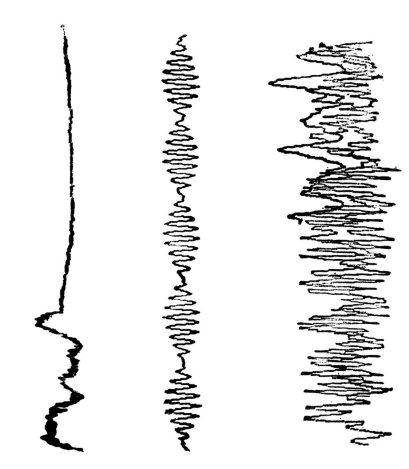

*Graphic renditions of sacred song from across the world provide a motif which appears on the frontispiece and book divisions of the Psalms.*

Native American

Taoist

The *Adhan*, the Muslim call to prayer.

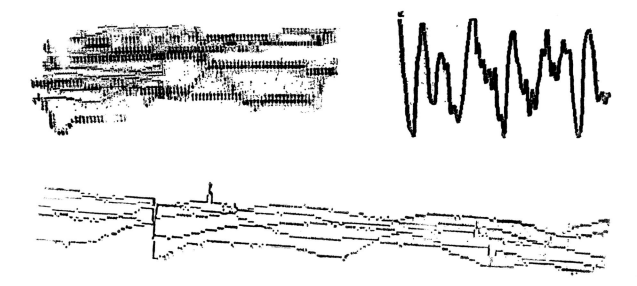

The monks at Saint John's.

The Wicked are not so but are like chaff that the wind blows away therefore the wicked will not stand in the judgement

Nor sinners II in the congregation of the righteous

For the Lord watches over the way of the righteous but the way of the wicked will perish

Donald Jackson describes the Psalms as poems full of controlled passion. In his rough sketches for the frontispiece, his raw, exuberant brush strokes grew into an ordered composition of upright shapes. The free brushwork is safely contained within the bounds of vertical strips evoking open books.

Donald and the CIT sat down in September 2003 at Saint John's and began to go through the brief. Donald's fears were misplaced.

He recounted, "Nathanael said to me, 'I can see how this bothers you. You're reading this wish list as a to-do list in order of preference.' They weren't asking for anything like as much."

Back in the studio, Donald decided that the first and last psalms would receive special treatment but the rest of the text would remain relatively simple. The five book divisions were crucial but the different genres could be marked with small notations. Each book would be written in a slightly different hand, by a different scribe. A changing color scheme for the psalm numbers could also distinguish book from book.

The genres would be noted with small roman numerals, I–IX, and a key would be added to the marginal notes.

What had seemed daunting in a long, detailed brief was now much simpler. "We boiled it back down," Donald said. Face-to-face he knew what was really important to the committee and what could be relegated to secondary significance and what could be dropped altogether.

5 Their ways prosper at all times;
   your judgments are on high,
   out of their sight;
   as for their foes, they scoff at them.
6 They think in their heart, "We shall
      not be moved;
   throughout all generations we shall
      not meet adversity."

7 Their mouths are filled with cursing and
      deceit and oppression;
   under their tongues are mischief
      and iniquity.
8 They sit in ambush in the villages;
   in hiding places they murder the innocent.

   Their eyes stealthily watch for the helpless;
9   they lurk in secret like a lion in its covert;
   they lurk that they may seize the poor;
   they seize the poor and drag them
      off in their net.

10 They stoop, they crouch,
   and the helpless fall by their might.
11 They think in their heart, "God has forgotten,
   he has hidden his face, he will never see it."

12 Rise up, O LORD; O God, lift up your hand;
   do not forget the oppressed.
13 Why do the wicked renounce God,
   and say in their hearts, "You will not
      call us to account"?

14 But you do see! Indeed you note
      trouble and grief,
   that you may take it into your hands;
   the helpless commit themselves to you;
   you have been the helper of the orphan.

15 Break the arm of the wicked and evildoers;
   seek out their wickedness until
      you find none.
16 The LORD is king forever and ever;
   the nations shall perish from his land.

17 O LORD, you will hear the desire of the meek;
   you will strengthen their heart,
      you will incline your ear
18 to do justice for the orphan and the oppressed,
   so that those from earth may strike
      terror no more.

Meaning of Heb uncertain
Gk Syr Jerome Tg: Heb flee
to your mountain, O bird

IV Confidence
I Lament

## Psalm 11

To the leader. Of David.

In the LORD I take refuge; how can
      you say to me,
   "Flee like a bird to the mountains;
2 for look, the wicked bend the bow,
   they have fitted their arrow to the string,
   to shoot in the dark at the upright in heart.
3 If the foundations are destroyed,
   what can the righteous do?"

4 The LORD is in his holy temple;
   the LORD's throne is in heaven.
   His eyes behold, his gaze examines
      humankind.
5 The LORD tests the righteous and the wicked,
   and his soul hates the lover of violence.
6 On the wicked he will rain coals
      of fire and sulfur;
   a scorching wind shall be the
      portion of their cup.
7 For the LORD is righteous;
   he loves righteous deeds;
   the upright shall behold his face.

## Psalm 12

To the leader: according to The Sheminith.
A Psalm of David.

Help, O LORD, for there is no longer
      anyone who is godly;
   the faithful have disappeared
      from humankind.
2 They utter lies to each other;
   with flattering lips and a double
      heart they speak.

3 May the LORD cut off all flattering lips,
   the tongue that makes great boasts,
4 those who say, "With our tongues
      we will prevail;
   our lips are our own – who is our master?"

5 "Because the poor are despoiled, because
      the needy groan,
   I will now rise up," says the LORD;
   "I will place them in the safety for
      which they long."
6 The promises of the LORD are promises
      that are pure,
   silver refined in a furnace on the ground,
   purified seven times.

The volume of Psalms is divided into five component books, each written in a distinctive script. Book I (Psalms 1–41) was written by Brian Simpson in a variant of the poetry script used in the Prophets and Wisdom volumes of the Bible.

¹⁰ You water its furrows abundantly,
  settling its ridges,
  softening it with showers,
  and blessing its growth.
¹¹ You crown the year with your bounty;
  your wagon tracks overflow with richness.
¹² The pastures of the wilderness overflow,
  the hills gird themselves with joy,
¹³ the meadows clothe themselves with flocks,
  the valleys deck themselves with grain,
  they shout and sing together for joy.

# Psalm 66

*To the leader. A Song. A Psalm.*

Make a joyful noise to God, all the earth;
² sing the glory of his name;
  give to him glorious praise.
³ Say to God, "How awesome are your deeds!
  Because of your great power, your enemies
    cringe before you.
⁴ All the earth worships you;
  they sing praises to you.
  sing praises to your name."                    Selah

⁵ Come and see what God has done:
  he is awesome in his deeds among mortals.
⁶ He turned the sea into dry land;
  they passed through the river on foot.
  There we rejoiced in him,
⁷   who rules by his might forever,
  whose eyes keep watch on the nations —
    let the rebellious not exalt themselves. Selah

⁸ Bless our God, O peoples,
  let the sound of his praise be heard,
⁹ who has kept us among the living,
  and has not let our feet slip.
¹⁰ For you, O God, have tested us;
  you have tried us as silver is tried.
¹¹ You brought us into the net;
  you laid burdens on our backs;
¹² you let people ride over our heads;
  we went through fire and through water;
  yet you have brought us out to
    a spacious place.

¹³ I will come into your house with
    burnt offerings;
  I will pay you my vows,
¹⁴ those that my lips uttered
  and my mouth promised when
    I was in trouble.

ᵃ Cn Compare Gk Syr
Jerome Tg: Heb *to a*
*saturation*

II Hymn [Psalm 66 v. 1–12]
III Thanksgiving [Psalm 66 v. 13–20]
VI Liturgy

¹⁵ I will offer to you burnt offerings of fatlings,
  with the smoke of the sacrifice of rams;
  I will make an offering of bulls and goats.
                                          Selah

¹⁶ Come and hear, all you who fear God,
  and I will tell what he has done for me.
¹⁷ I cried aloud to him,
  and he was extolled with my tongue.
¹⁸ If I had cherished iniquity in my heart,
  the Lord would not have listened.
¹⁹ But truly God has listened;
  he has given heed to the words of my prayer.

²⁰ Blessed be God,
  because he has not rejected my prayer
  or removed his steadfast love from me.

# Psalm 67

*To the leader: with stringed instruments.*
*A Psalm. A Song.*

May God be gracious to us and bless us
  and make his face to shine upon us,    Selah
² that your way may be known upon earth,
  your saving power among all nations.
³ Let the peoples praise you, O God;
  let all the peoples praise you.

⁴ Let the nations be glad and sing for joy,
  for you judge the peoples with equity
  and guide the nations upon earth.       Selah
⁵ Let the peoples praise you, O God;
  let all the peoples praise you.

⁶ The earth has yielded its increase;
  God, our God, has blessed us.
⁷ May God continue to bless us;
  let all the ends of the earth revere him.

# Psalm 68

*To the leader. Of David. A Psalm. A Song.*

Let God rise up, let his enemies be scattered;
  let those who hate him flee before him.
² As smoke is driven away, so drive them away;
  as wax melts before the fire,
  let the wicked perish before God.
³ But let the righteous be joyful;
  let them exult before God;
  let them be jubilant with joy.

Book II (Psalms 42–72) was written by Sally Mae Joseph in an elegant script inspired by the work of the Renaissance scribe Palatino.

listen to my cry of supplication.
7 In the day of my trouble I call on you,
for you will answer me.

8 There is none like you among the gods, O Lord,
nor are there any works like yours.
9 All the nations you have made shall come
and bow down before you, O Lord,
and shall glorify your name.
10 For you are great and do wondrous things;
you alone are God.
11 Teach me your way, O LORD,
that I may walk in your truth;
give me an undivided heart to
revere your name.
12 I give thanks to you, O Lord my God,
with my whole heart,
and I will glorify your name forever.
13 For great is your steadfast love toward me;
you have delivered my soul from
the depths of Sheol.

14 O God, the insolent rise up against me;
a band of ruffians seeks my life,
and they do not set you before them.
15 But you, O Lord, are a God
merciful and gracious,
slow to anger and abounding in steadfast
love and faithfulness.
16 Turn to me and be gracious to me;
give your strength to your servant;
save the child of your serving girl.
17 Show me a sign of your favor,
so that those who hate me may see it
and be put to shame,
because you, LORD, have helped me
and comforted me.

## Psalm 87

Of the Korahites. A Psalm. A Song.

On the holy mount stands the city he founded;
2 the LORD loves the gates of Zion
more than all the dwellings of Jacob.
3 Glorious things are spoken of you,
O city of God.    selah

4 Among those who know me I mention
Rahab and Babylon;
Philistia too, and Tyre, with Ethiopia —
"This one was born there," they say.

5 And of Zion it shall be said,
"This one and that one were born in it";
for the Most High himself will establish it.
6 The LORD records, as he registers the peoples,
"This one was born there."    selah

7 Singers and dancers alike say,
"All my springs are in you."

## Psalm 88

A Song. A Psalm of the Korahites. To the leader:
according to Mahalath Leannoth. A Maskil of
Heman the Ezrahite.

O LORD, God of my salvation,
when, at night, I cry out in your presence,
2 let my prayer come before you;
incline your ear to my cry.

3 For my soul is full of troubles,
and my life draws near to Sheol.
4 I am counted among those who go
down to the Pit;
I am like those who have no help,
5 like those forsaken among the dead,
like the slain that lie in the grave,
like those whom you remember no more,
for they are cut off from your hand.
6 You have put me in the depths of the Pit,
in the regions dark and deep.
7 Your wrath lies heavy upon me,
and you overwhelm me with
all your waves.    selah

8 You have caused my companions to shun me;
you have made me a thing of horror to them.
I am shut in so that I cannot escape;
9 my eye grows dim through sorrow.
Every day I call on you, O LORD;
I spread out my hands to you.
10 Do you work wonders for the dead?
Do the shades rise up to praise you?    selah
11 Is your steadfast love declared in the grave,
or your faithfulness in Abaddon?
12 Are your wonders known in the darkness,
or your saving help in the land
of forgetfulness?

13 But I, O LORD, cry out to you;
in the morning my prayer comes before you.
14 O LORD, why do you cast me off?
Why do you hide your face from me?
15 Wretched and close to death
from my youth up,

RSB
Psalm 88:15

7 Or Nubia; Heb Cush

VIII Zion Songs
1 Lament

Book III (Psalms 73–89) was written by Donald Jackson in his formal italic hand.

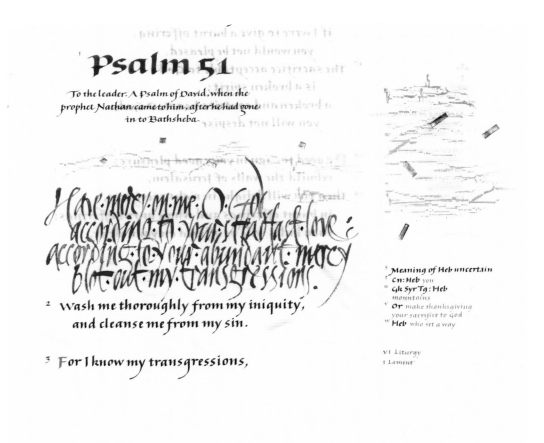

# Psalm 51

*To the leader. A Psalm of David, when the
prophet Nathan came to him, after he had gone
in to Bathsheba.*

Have mercy on me, O God,
according to your steadfast love;
according to your abundant mercy
blot out my transgressions.

2 Wash me thoroughly from my iniquity,
and cleanse me from my sin.

3 For I know my transgressions,

s Meaning of Heb uncertain
t Cn: Heb *you*
u Gk Syr Tg: Heb
  *mountains*
v Or *make thanksgiving
  your sacrifice to God*
w Heb *who set a way*

VI Liturgy
1 Lament

Psalm 51, one of the seven Penitential Psalms, opens with large, vigorous letters which break the bounds of the column.

## Working

DONALD CHOSE Sally Mae and Brian to write one book each. He would write a third. He engaged another calligrapher, not previously connected with the project, to write out a fourth. Where would the fifth scribe come from? There was no one available with the requisite skills and there was no time to train anyone. The writing of the psalms had to begin right away, so Donald decided to write two of the books. Then after the other scribes had begun writing, the extra scribe pulled out—he had too many work commitments. Sally Mae stepped into the breach and agreed to write the remaining book in addition to the one she'd already begun.

The books were divided up. Brian would write Book I (Psalms 1–41). Sally Mae would write Book II (Psalms 42–72) and Book V (Psalms 107–150). Donald would write Book III (Psalms 73–89) and Book IV (Psalms 90–106). Donald would do the illuminations at the beginning of each book, as well as the special treatment of Psalm 1. Sally would do the special treatment of Psalm 150.

Sally, Brian and Donald each devised special scripts for the books they would write out. They agreed certain details would remain constant throughout the book, including psalm headings, the genre notations and the Amens.

Sally remembers, "I did Book V first, my first allocation. It was special to me. I had to develop a script different from the standard poetry hand which I'd been using for the prophets. So I played around. I gave a slope to it and gave it a distinctive feel."

Book V is full of psalms of praise. They are joyous and celebratory. They matched Sally's mood as she wrote in a script of her own devising. "I had the enjoyment of writing a script that was more natural to

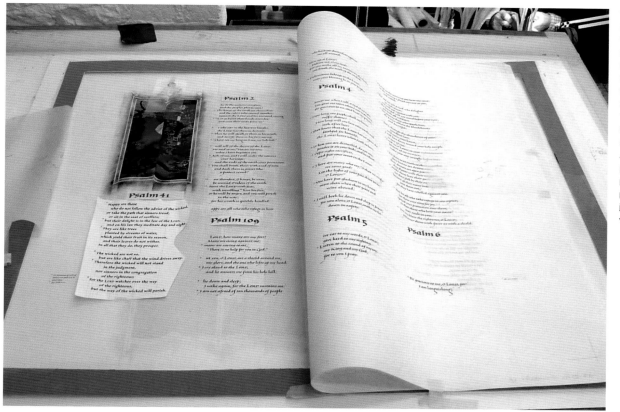

The vellum pages pass through many hands as they are brought to completion. Sometimes the scribes are asked to write on the back of pages which have already received an illumination. Here the first page of the text of Psalms has been stretched on a board. The frontispiece which has already been completed can be seen showing through the vellum. A printout of Psalm 1 has been placed on the page. The facing page has been gently rolled into position to help Brian Simpson judge the weight of the script he will write on the stretched sheet.

me," she said, "rather than emulating Donald's hand. I just loved writing the Psalms. I would go home elated. They are full of human feelings—they run the gamut. I would go home and read the Psalms after writing them all day."

Once Book V was complete, she turned her attention to Book II. Here she wanted to try another style of writing. "In Book II, I tried a very formal hand, a kind of angular Renaissance italic. I liked it, so I decided to use it. I did try some other variations, including one that was closer to the standard Bible hand, but I decided to base it on the Renaissance script in the end because it contrasted with Brian's and Donald's more fluid styles in the books which were on either side of it."

This script had its own character, with a very precise rhythm. She recalled, "It's all down to spacing between the letters, keeping the right pen angle and keeping the letters upright like soldiers marching across the page. It took a bit of getting used to but you haven't got weeks and months. You are actually practicing on the real thing. You can't live your life on a scrap of vellum. It's just like life: you have to live it to do it. You are learning as you write. Changes and variations happen. That's why I always start in the middle of the book, then go back to the beginning."

Brian and Donald, too, devised their new scripts. Brian's was close to the standard Bible poetry hand. Donald used a classic oval-based letterform in Book III. His script for Book IV had rounder shapes and more measured spacing between the letters and words. There is a family resemblance between their work, reflecting, perhaps, the fact that both of them trained with Irene Wellington at the Central School in London.

## Sacred song

IN THE MEANTIME, Donald began to work out the illuminations. A large frontispiece would appear at the beginning of the whole volume and then smaller variations would mark the division between the other books.

Donald explained, "I walked away from the CIT meeting with the idea of using sound as a visual image. To that theme, I added the idea of using sacred music from different traditions."

The theme was perfect for a book of sacred song. "Johanna said to me that sound never stops. Once uttered, it reverberates through the universe forever. When you think about sacred music sounding out through the ages—that's something."

He continued, "There are no interpretations in the brief, so I had a great deal of freedom to define my theme. I wanted to use many chanting voices—Jewish, Buddhist, Native American, along with the sheer singing energy and power of the Psalms themselves. In my design the voices of many traditions interweave with the Christian voice, which runs throughout the volume. The Saint John's Bible includes and respects those voices."

How was he to find a graphic means of expressing this idea? Donald began to explore computer programs which could translate sound into visual images. "By using two programs, we were able to obtain representations of the sound—you play a disk and it comes out as oscillations on the screen. I think they're called oscillographs."

Rebecca loaded CDs with different chants into the computer. Sarah, the studio assistant, sat in front of the screen with a digital camera. "We couldn't print out the moving images, so we had to sit and shoot away until we got an interesting pattern."

Sally Mae Joseph applies gesso over a frisket stencil in preparation for the gilding of the small squares and rectangles which appear throughout the book of Psalms. Once the gesso has dried and the gold has been laid and burnished, the frisket is pulled away, leaving perfectly sharp edges. This new technique gives Sally tremendous control gilding the geometric shapes.

They played with different kinds of oscillations until they had a working set of images. Fragments of these wavy patterns of song were made into rubber stamps. The voices of monks at Saint John's provided the most important stamp. Running horizontally through the middle of every page, it became the unifying Christian voice which tied the volume together. On the frontispiece and at the opening of each book, the patterns of non-Christian voices were used. Placed vertically, they create a counterpoint to the Christian voices.

The key illumination in the volume was the two-page spread at the beginning of the book. All the rest of the book divisions would be constructed of details from this principal image.

"I did a sketch," he said. "It became five open books. They grew and I started to divide them up. Motifs like the menorah from Matthew's Gospel just crept back in."

The large opening spread was then sliced up. "Book II began with two sections, Book III with three sections and so on. It is a simple idea, but it works."

Throughout the volume rubber stamps and small golden squares and bars create a rising and falling rhythm, a counterpoint to the lines of writing, a visual *leitmotif* which ties the volume together visually.

## Providence is the word you're looking for

THERE IS NEVER an uncluttered moment in the making of this Bible; even as Donald was buried in preparations for the Psalms, he continued to supervise scribes writing out the fourth and fifth volumes. His research, too, is ongoing. And in the process little accidents happen which move the project along.

Donald recounted, "I was at the British Museum looking at the whole period of art before Christ, the period of the growth of the Israelite nationhood. I especially wanted to look at Assyrian and Babylonian art. I was photographing chariot wheels and thinking about Ezekiel's visions of wheels within wheels." Although the vision described the wheels as "covered with eyes" Donald noted how sturdy and practical the Assyrian wheels were: no eyes, certainly.

A week later, he found himself at a wedding in France. "I met a man there. He was a professor of exegesis from Belgium. Suddenly there we were, in the middle of the French countryside, hammer and tongs into the design of Assyrian cartwheels. I told him my thoughts about the Assyrian and Babylonian sources for some of the biblical stories. I had a gut feeling that those visions were rooted in that sort of multicultural exposure.

"He said the description of chariot wheels with eyes in them was a mistranslation for 'brass studs' or 'brass nails.' When I thought about the photographs I'd taken, the wheels in them were covered with these little studs. Hearing him speak, I felt that little light bulb go off.

"Things just fall into place with this project. We don't even roll our eyes anymore. Like meeting an exegete who likes to talk about Assyrian chariot wheels."

Donald tried to characterize these odd coincidences once in a press conference. He was in Rome with a delegation from Saint John's to present the Pope with a facsimile of the first volume of the Bible. In front of the reporters, he struggled to find the right word to describe these unusual coincidences. Cardinal Pio Laghi, who was listening, smiled indulgently and said, "I think the word 'Providence' is what you're looking for."

Donald Jackson experiments with the frontispiece of Psalms. On his desk acetate overlays of the oscillographs stand ready to be placed in the sketch.

⁵ Your decrees are very sure;
 holiness befits your house,
 O LORD, forevermore.

## Psalm 94

O LORD, you God of vengeance,
 you God of vengeance, shine forth !
² Rise up, O judge of the earth;
 give to the proud what they deserve !
³ O LORD, how long shall the wicked,
 how long shall the wicked exult ?

⁴ They pour out their arrogant words;
 all the evildoers boast.
⁵ They crush your people, O LORD,
 and afflict your heritage.
⁶ They kill the widow and the stranger,
 they murder the orphan,
⁷ and they say, "The LORD does not see;
 the God of Jacob does not perceive."

⁸ Understand, O dullest of the people;
 fools, when will you be wise ?
⁹ He who planted the ear, does he not hear ?
 He who formed the eye, does he not see ?
¹⁰ He who disciplines the nations,
 he who teaches knowledge to humankind,
 does he not chastise ?
¹¹ The LORD knows our thoughts,
 that they are but an empty breath.

¹² Happy are those whom you discipline, O LORD,
 and whom you teach out of your law,
¹³ giving them respite from days of trouble,
 until a pit is dug for the wicked.
¹⁴ For the LORD will not forsake his people;
 he will not abandon his heritage;
¹⁵ for justice will return to the righteous,
 and all the upright in heart will follow it.

¹⁶ Who rises up for me against the wicked ?
 Who stands up for me against evildoers ?
¹⁷ If the LORD had not been my help,
 my soul would soon have lived
 in the land of silence.
¹⁸ When I thought, "My foot is slipping,"
 your steadfast love, O LORD, held me up.
¹⁹ When the cares of my heart are many,
 your consolations cheer my soul.
²⁰ Can wicked rulers be allied with you,
 those who contrive mischief by statute ?
²¹ They band together against the

life of the righteous,
 and condemn the innocent to death.
²² But the LORD has become my stronghold,
 and my God the rock of my refuge.
²³ He will repay them for their iniquity
 and wipe them out for their wickedness;
 the LORD our God will wipe them out.

## Psalm 95

O come, let us sing to the LORD;
 let us make a joyful noise to the
 rock of our salvation !
² Let us come into his presence with
 thanksgiving;
 let us make a joyful noise to him
 with songs of praise !
³ For the LORD is a great God,
 and a great King above all gods.
⁴ In his hand are the depths of the earth;
 the heights of the mountains are his also.
⁵ The sea is his, for he made it,
 and the dry land, which his
 hands have formed.

⁶ O come, let us worship and bow down,
 let us kneel before the LORD, our Maker!
⁷ For he is our God,
 and we are the people of his pasture,
 and the sheep of his hand.

O that today you would listen to his voice !
⁸ Do not harden your hearts, as at Meribah,
 as on the day at Massah in the wilderness,
⁹ when your ancestors tested me,
 and put me to the proof, though
 they had seen my work.
¹⁰ For forty years I loathed that generation
 and said, "They are a people whose
 hearts go astray,
 and they do not regard my ways."
¹¹ Therefore in my anger I swore,
 "They shall not enter my rest."

## Psalm 96

O sing to the LORD a new song;
 sing to the LORD, all the earth.
² Sing to the LORD, bless his name;
 tell of his salvation from day to day.
³ Declare his glory among the nations,
 his marvelous works among all the peoples.

RSB
Psalm 95:7-8

ⁿ Heb the thoughts of
humankind.

I Lament
II Hymn

For Book IV (Psalms 90–106), Donald Jackson chose to write in a rounded roman hand.

The LORD will keep you from all evil;
he will keep your life.

8 The LORD will keep
your going out and your coming in
from this time on and forevermore.

## VIII Psalm 122

A Song of Ascents. Of David.

I was glad when they said to me,
"Let us go to the house of the LORD!"
2 Our feet are standing
within your gates, O Jerusalem.

3 Jerusalem – built as a city
that is bound firmly together.
4 To it the tribes go up,
the tribes of the LORD,
as was decreed for Israel,
to give thanks to the name of the LORD.
5 For there the thrones for judgment
were set up,
the thrones of the house of David.

6 Pray for the peace of Jerusalem:
"May they prosper who love you.
7 Peace be within your walls,
and security within your towers."
8 For the sake of my relatives and friends
I will say, "Peace be within you."
9 For the sake of the house of the LORD our God,
I will seek your good.

## Psalm 123

A Song of Ascents.

To you I lift up my eyes,
O you who are enthroned in the heavens!
2 As the eyes of servants
look to the hand of their master,
as the eyes of a maid
to the hand of her mistress,
so our eyes look to the LORD our God,
until he has mercy upon us.

5 Have mercy upon us, O LORD,
have mercy upon us,
for we have had more than
enough of contempt.
4 Our soul has had more than its fill
of the scorn of those who are at ease,
of the contempt of the proud.

VIII Zion Songs
I Lament
III Thanksgiving
IV Confidence

## III Psalm 124

A Song of Ascents. Of David.

If it had not been the LORD who
was on our side
– let Israel now say –
2 if it had not been the LORD who
was on our side,
when our enemies attacked us,
3 then they would have swallowed us up alive,
when their anger was kindled against us;
4 then the flood would have swept us away,
the torrent would have gone over us;
5 then over us would have gone
the raging waters.

6 Blessed be the LORD,
who has not given us
as prey to their teeth.
7 We have escaped like a bird
from the snare of the fowlers;
the snare is broken,
and we have escaped.

8 Our help is in the name of the LORD,
who made heaven and earth.

## IV Psalm 125

A Song of Ascents.

Those who trust in the LORD are like
Mount Zion,
which cannot be moved, but abides forever.
2 As the mountains surround Jerusalem,
so the LORD surrounds his people,
from this time on and forevermore.
3 For the scepter of wickedness shall not rest
on the land allotted to the righteous,
so that the righteous might not stretch out
their hands to do wrong.
4 Do good, O LORD, to those who are good,
and to those who are upright in their hearts.
5 But those who turn aside to their
own crooked ways
the LORD will lead away with evildoers.
Peace be upon Israel!

Book V (Psalms 107–150) was written by Sally Mae Joseph in a script developed from the poetry script used in the Prophets and Wisdom volumes of the Bible.

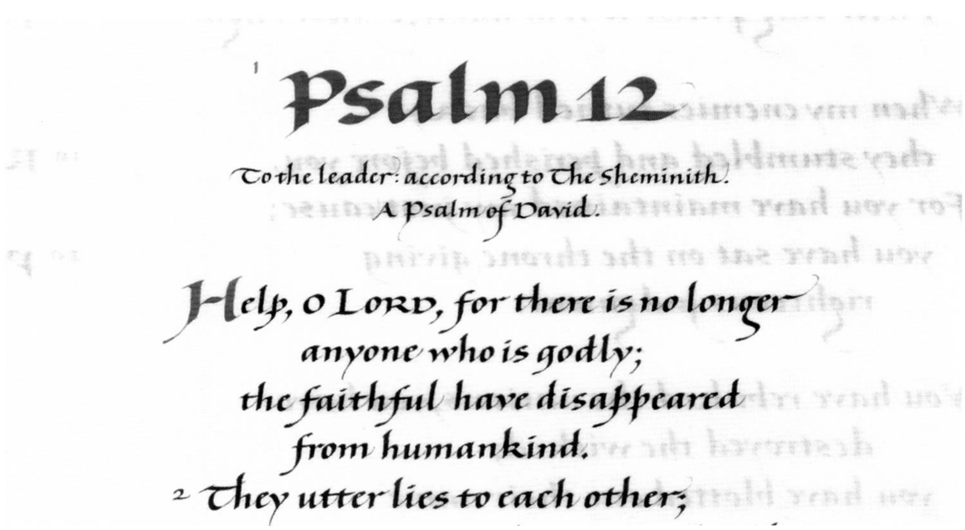
1 Psalm 12

To the leader: according to The Sheminith.
A Psalm of David.

Help, O LORD, for there is no longer
anyone who is godly;
the faithful have disappeared
from humankind.
2 They utter lies to each other;

Book I
Brian Simpson

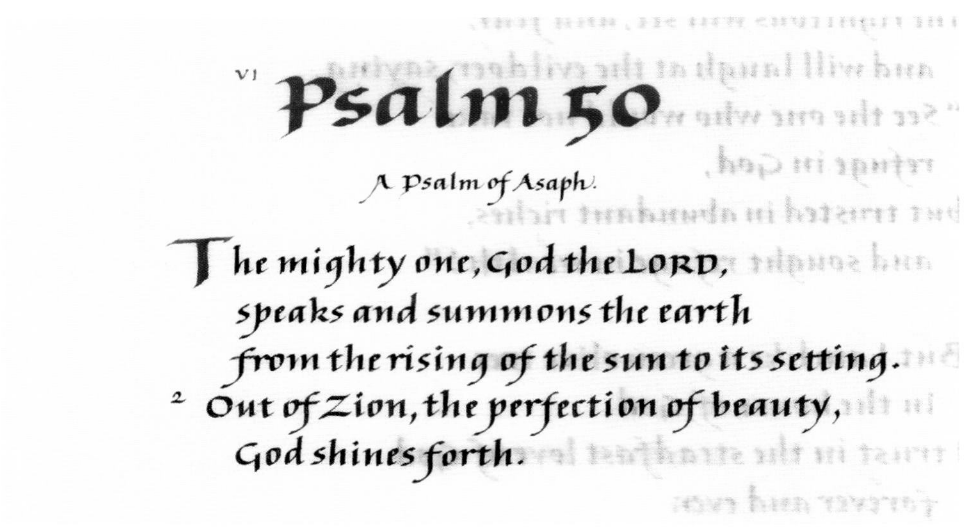
VI Psalm 50

A Psalm of Asaph.

The mighty one, God the LORD,
speaks and summons the earth
from the rising of the sun to its setting.
2 Out of Zion, the perfection of beauty,
God shines forth.

Book II
Sally Mae Joseph

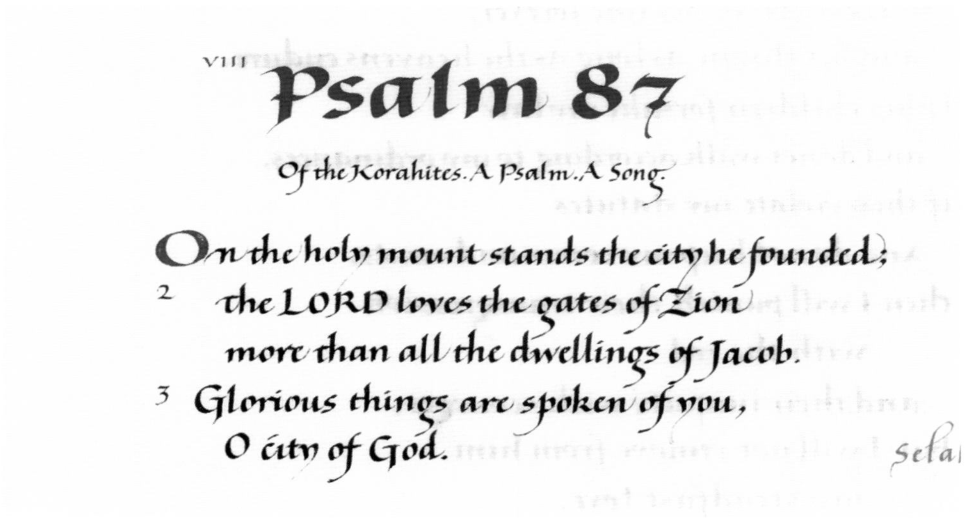
VIII Psalm 87

Of the Korahites. A Psalm. A Song.

On the holy mount stands the city he founded;
2 the LORD loves the gates of Zion
more than all the dwellings of Jacob.
3 Glorious things are spoken of you,
O city of God. Sela

Book III
Donald Jackson

Book IV
Donald Jackson

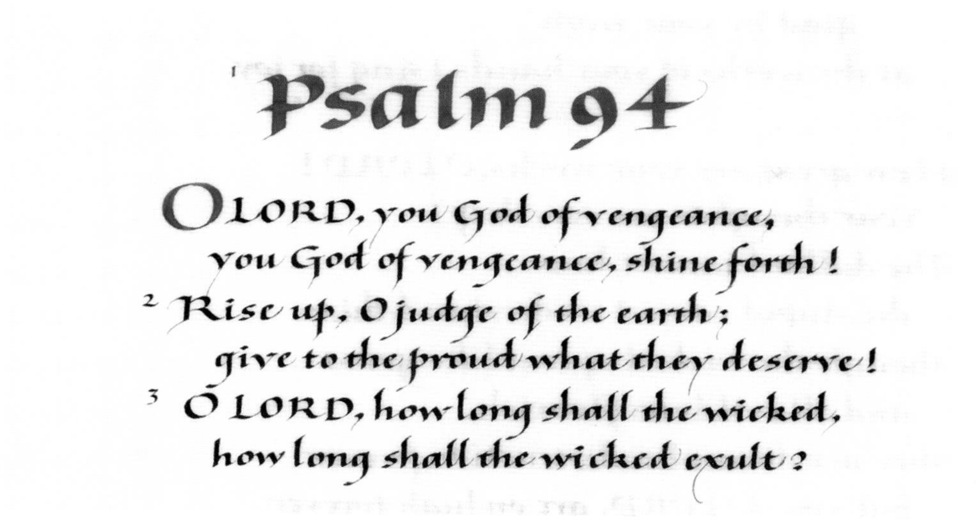

# Psalm 94

O LORD, you God of vengeance,
you God of vengeance, shine forth!
² Rise up, O judge of the earth;
give to the proud what they deserve!
³ O LORD, how long shall the wicked,
how long shall the wicked exult?

Book V
Sally Mae Joseph

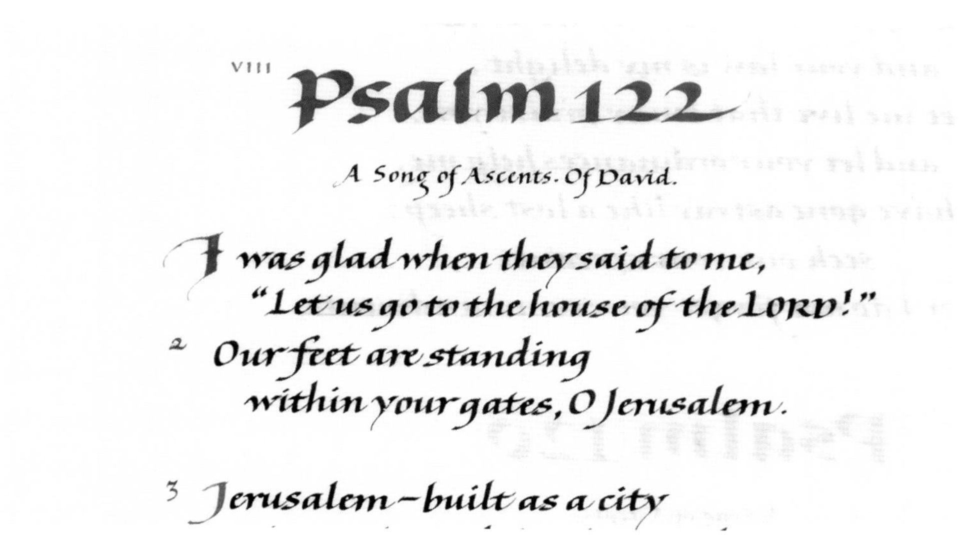

VIII

# Psalm 122

*A Song of Ascents. Of David.*

I was glad when they said to me,
"Let us go to the house of the LORD!"
² Our feet are standing
within your gates, O Jerusalem.

³ Jerusalem – built as a city

A selection of passages from the Psalms, showing the work of different scribes.
The headings for all the psalms were written by Brian Simpson. A different color is used for each book.

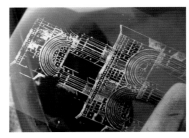

A rubber stamp of a church door evokes sacred buildings which are filled with the sound of chant and sacred song. The stamp has been used here to make an acetate overlay which will be used as part of a sketch. As in the other volumes rubber stamps were used extensively in Psalms. The technical, mechanical lines of the stamps contrast with fluid marks made by pen and brush.

A study for the frontispiece to Book V of the Psalms.

## *Special treatments and happy accidents*

The volume opens and closes with two special treatments in gold. Sally Mae tackled hers first.

"Donald saw Psalm 150 as being like the *Magnificat* from Luke," she said. "He wanted me to use that lettering. He saw it in gold. I thought about colored backgrounds again and played around with a few ideas. Nothing seemed to work. The Psalms pages had a voice of their own. So gold lettering on plain vellum was what the page needed."

She ended up with quite a calm composition. "But within that calmness there's a lot of movement, like tai-chi."

The large quantities of gesso she was using began to worry Donald. One of the ingredients of the mixture is white lead, a deadly poison which can be all too easily breathed in. Lead poisoning is a serious hazard any craft gilder must be attentive to.

"Mabel bought a dust buster, so I had to use it. My own little gesso hoover—it feels so bizarre hoovering the vellum!"

It is a wise precaution, nonetheless.

Donald turned to his special treatment for Psalm 1 and immediately ran into his own problem.

"We hit a major snag. I'm not sure how it happened. For some reason—it was probably my own fault—Vin had printed out all the psalm layouts starting on the wrong page. Instead of having a whole page to work with, I ended up with no place to put the special treatment of Psalm 1."

The writing had long been under way; there was no question of rearranging the layouts now. Donald would have to work with the space he had available.

"It left only half a column. Suddenly, I had to redesign the frontispiece to include the whole of Psalm 1."

Remarkably he was able to fit the whole of his text into the existing design. It was a beautiful solution to an ugly problem. But he wasn't out of trouble yet.

"Sara started to check it," he remembered. "Then she goes quiet. 'You've left out a full verse on the first psalm.'"

Of all the places to make a mistake, this was about the worst Donald could imagine. Days of illumination could have gone down the tube.

He continued, "We're talking and she says, 'Wait, there's a space here.' And suddenly I see the text is missing where I've actually left a space. So I sketched out the missing verse in caps and then laid it over the gap. Sally had already gilded the small gold rectangles that spangle the frontispiece, so I had those shapes to contend with as well. Not only did the new tracing fit, but each space between the words corresponded exactly to where the small squares of gold had already been laid. There was only one little gold square in the way which I'd have to scrape off."

Grateful for his uncanny good fortune, he bent down to scrape off the single errant gold square.

"Sally had used a new technique we'd devised, using frisket to mask the areas of gilding. She had started to gild this rectangle, but she'd neglected to remove the frisket—so it just popped off when I touched it with my knife!"

Talk about good fortune. Or providence.

# Psalm 150

Praise the LORD!
Praise God in his sanctuary;
praise him in his
    mighty firmament!
2 Praise him for his mighty deeds;
praise him according to
    his surpassing greatness!

3 Praise him with trumpet sound;
    praise him with lute & harp!
4 Praise him with
    tambourine and dance;
    praise him with strings & pipe!
5 Praise him with
    clanging cymbals;
praise him with
    loud clashing cymbals!
6 Let everything that breathes
    praise the LORD!
Praise the LORD!

*Praise the LORD!*

*Praise the LORD!*

*Praise the LORD!*

Psalm 150, the
final psalm in the
book, received
special treatment
rendered in gold
by Sally Mae
Joseph.

ILLUMINATING
THE WORD

—————

*201*

## Too soon

DONALD GREW WISTFUL as he spoke of the Psalms. "It's hard for me to talk about them. The cooking time was so long on it, then it was taken away from me so fast."

The process of writing this volume had been grueling, unforgiving.

"It was preceded by four or five months of being tired. I got back from delivering the Pentateuch in September 2003. I was burned out from that trip—people, people, people. I didn't have energy and couldn't psych myself up. I needed to have time to recharge."

He was grateful for the support of his family and staff. "Oh, the brilliance of people—Sally, Mabel, Rebecca and Sarah. They all knew I would do it. I had to write two full books. It gave me so much respect for the calligraphy scribes. The people around me never wavered in their belief that I'd come up with the goods and deliver it on time."

After Christmas 2003, Donald worked seven days a week, every week until April 2004.

"That's how it got back on track. It was physically and emotionally demanding on top of everything."

And yet despite the tight schedule, he could still say, "To write the Psalms was just a beautiful experience because of the words themselves."

The bright casein colors used for Psalms reflect the emotional intensity of the text.

A small dash of gold evoking a candle flame is added to the opening of each book. The rough edges of the gold demonstrate the painterly possibilities of this enormously flexible material.

The *Raising of Lazarus* appears next to John II.

kill and destroy. I came that they may have life, and have it abundantly. ■ "I am the good shepherd. The good shepherd lays down his life for the sheep. ¹² The hired hand, who is not the shepherd and does not own the sheep, sees the wolf coming and leaves the sheep and runs away — and the wolf snatches them and scatters them. ¹³ The hired hand runs away because a hired hand does not care for the sheep. ¹⁴ I am the good shepherd. I know my own & my own know me, ¹⁵ just as the Father knows me & I know the Father. And I lay down my life for the sheep. ¹⁶ I have other sheep that do not belong to this fold. I must bring them also, and they will listen to my voice. So there will be one flock, one shepherd. ¹⁷ For this reason the Father loves me, because I lay down my life in order to take it up again. ¹⁸ No one takes it from me, but I lay it down of my own accord. I have power to lay it down, and I have power to take it up again. I have received this command from my Father." ■ ¹⁹ Again the Jews were divided because of these words. ²⁰ Many of them were saying, "He has a demon & is out of his mind. Why listen to him?" ²¹ Others were saying, "These are not the words of one who has a demon. Can a demon open the eyes of the blind?" ■ ²² At that time the festival of the Dedication took place in Jerusalem. It was winter, ²³ and Jesus was walking in the temple, in the portico of Solomon. ²⁴ So the Jews gathered around him and said to him, "How long will you keep us in suspense? If you are the Messiah, tell us plainly." ²⁵ Jesus answered, "I have told you, and you do not believe. The works that I do in my Father's name testify to me; ²⁶ but you do not believe, because you do not belong to my sheep. ²⁷ My sheep hear my voice. I know them, and they follow me. ²⁸ I give them eternal life, and they will never perish. No one will snatch them out of my hand. ²⁹ What my Father has given me is greater than all else, and no one can snatch it out of the Father's hand. ³⁰ The Father and I are one." ³¹ ■ The Jews took up stones again to stone him. ³² Jesus replied, "I have shown you many good works from the Father. For which of these are you going to stone me?" ³³ The Jews answered, "It is not for a good work

that we are going to stone you, but for blasphemy because you, though only a human being, are making yourself God." ³⁴ Jesus answered, "Is it not written in your law, 'I said, you are gods'? ³⁵ If those to whom the word of God came were called 'gods' — and the scripture cannot be annulled — ³⁶ can you say that the one whom the Father has sanctified & sent into the world is blaspheming because I said, 'I am God's Son'? ³⁷ If I am not doing the works of my Father, then do not believe me. ³⁸ But if I do them, even though you do not believe me, believe the works, so that you may know and understand that the Father is in me & I am in the Father." ³⁹ Then they tried to arrest him again, but he escaped from their hands. ■ ⁴⁰ He went away again across the Jordan to the place where John had been baptizing earlier, and he remained there. ⁴¹ Many came to him, and they were saying, "John performed no sign, but everything that John said about this man was true." ⁴² And many believed in him there.

# 11

Now a certain man was ill, Lazarus of Bethany, the village of Mary and her sister Martha. ² Mary was the one who anointed the Lord with perfume and wiped his feet with her hair; her brother Lazarus was ill. ³ So the sisters sent a message to Jesus, "Lord, he whom you love is ill." ⁴ But when Jesus heard it, he said, "This illness does not lead to death; rather it is for God's glory, so that the Son of God may be glorified through

I AM THE RESURRECTION AND THE LIFE

# EPILOGUE

A WOMAN WALKS into the Hill Monastic Manuscript Library and asks where she can see The Saint John's Bible. She is taken to a small display room where five openings are on display. As she looks intently at the manuscript, a guide comes in to give a tour. She sidles up to him and poses many questions.

At the end of the tour she says, "I'm from California. I had to fly to New York and suddenly I realized I would be flying right over The Saint John's Bible. I changed my plans so I could make a stopover in Minnesota and see it. Thank you!"

As I write these last few paragraphs, the project remains in production. Donald Jackson and his team continue to write, gild and illuminate the last four volumes. The finished pages, however, have begun to take on a life of their own. Preparations are underway for an exhibition of the first three volumes at The Minneapolis Institute of Arts in the spring of 2005. A printed trade edition of Gospels and Acts is in the last stages of preparation.

I have tried to provide a series of snapshots of the making of the The Saint John's Bible, little glimpses into the world of Donald Jackson and the people who work with him. Once the project is completed in 2007, there will be many more stories to tell. Every illumination in the Bible deserves its own commentary and eventually the work of the CIT will be edited to serve as a study guide. When the volumes are complete, the pages will be trimmed, folded and bound between stout oak boards.

Johanna said to me once, "I think The Saint John's Bible is radically countercultural. It is an object of worth, made painstakingly by hand on real vellum. It reestablishes the value of the human element in expression. It is elaborate, extensive, big. In the age of paperbacks, we have *this?*"

The monastic community at Saint John's has always planned for the long term. The buildings they build are meant to last; the forests and fields which surround them are managed sustainably; the university and libraries and institutes are handed from one generation of students and scholars to the next. As one of the monks remarked to me, "Benedictines by nature always look into the future."

When the Bible is finished, bound and installed at the Abbey, the story will not be over. Like the great manuscripts of the past, The Saint John's Bible is meant to speak to generations to come, igniting the imagination, encouraging a rich engagement with the Scriptures and inviting people to explore a living tradition of art, spirituality and theology through the written and illuminated word.

# SCRIBES AND ILLUMINATORS

*Donald Jackson, as artistic director, gathered a group of artist-calligraphers and illuminators from around the world. He worked together with them to produce the very best in calligraphy and illumination. They each brought their own skills and perspectives. Their expertise and affection for the art and for The Saint John's Bible contributed to this project in countless ways.*

## HAZEL DOLBY (Illuminator — Hampshire, England)

Trained at Camberwell Art College, London, and later at the Roehampton Institute with Ann Camp. Fellow of the Society of Scribes and Illuminators (FSSI). Lecturer at University of Roehampton, teaching art and drawn and painted lettering. Teaches workshops in Europe and the United States. Her work is in various collections including the Poole Museum and The Crafts Study Centre, London.

## AIDAN HART (Iconographer — Shropshire, Wales)

Studied in New Zealand, the United Kingdom, and Greece. He was a full-time sculptor in New Zealand before returning to the United Kingdom in 1983. Since then he has worked as a full-time iconographer. A member of the Orthodox Church, his work is primarily panel icons but also includes church frescoes, illuminations on vellum and carved work in stone and wood. His work is in collections in the United Kingdom and Europe, including Litchfield and Hereford Cathedrals. He has contributed to numerous publications. Tutor at The Prince's School of Traditional Arts, London.

## SUE HUFTON (Scribe — London, England)

Trained at the Roehampton Institute, London, studying calligraphy and bookbinding. Fellow of the Society of Scribes and Illuminators (FSSI). Lecturer at the University of Roehampton, teaching calligraphy and bookbinding. Teaches in Europe, Canada and Australia, and has lead calligraphic retreats to Holy Island (Lindisfarne), United Kingdom. Author of *Step-by-Step Calligraphy,* Sue is editor of the SSI Journal *The Scribe* and has contributed articles to other publications.

## THOMAS INGMIRE (Illuminator — San Francisco, California)

Trained as a landscape architect at Ohio State University and University of California, Berkeley, before beginning the study of calligraphy and medieval painting techniques in the early seventies. He is the first foreign member to be elected Fellow of the Society of Scribes and Illuminators (FSSI) (1977). Thomas teaches throughout United States, Canada, Australia, Europe, Japan and Hong Kong. He has exhibited widely in United States. His work is in many public and private collections throughout the world including San Francisco Public Library's Special Collections, The Newberry Library, Chicago, and the Victoria and Albert Museum, London.

## DONALD JACKSON (Artistic Director — Monmouthshire, Wales)

Donald Jackson is one of the world's leading calligraphers and the artistic director and illuminator of The Saint John's Bible. He is a Senior Illuminator to the Queen of England's Crown Office. Past chairman of the Society of Scribes and Illuminators. His thirty-year retrospective exhibition, *Painting with Words,* premiered at The Minneapolis Institute of Arts in Minneapolis, Minnesota, in August 1988, and traveled to thirteen museums and galleries in the United States, Europe and China. A new exhibition, *Illuminating the Word: The Saint John's Bible,* premieres at The Minneapolis Institute of Arts in April 2005.

ANDREW JAMIESON (Illuminator — Somerset, England)

Trained at Reigate School of Art and Design, specializing in heraldry and calligraphy and manuscript illumination. He works as a heraldic artist and illustrator. Andrew's work is in public and private collections in Europe and the United States.

SALLY MAE JOSEPH (Scribe / Illuminator and Senior Artistic Consultant — Monmouthshire, Wales)

Sally Mae Joseph studied illumination, calligraphy and heraldry at Reigate School of Art and Design and calligraphy, applied lettering and bookbinding at the Roehampton Institute, London. Fellow of the Society of Scribes and Illuminators (FSSI). She has exhibited and lectured in Europe and the United States. Sally Mae has contributed articles to numerous publications. She was a lecturer at Roehampton Institute between 1991 and 1993. She is the author and presenter of the teaching video "Gilding for Calligraphers" and presenter of the information video "Making a Manuscript Page" in the Living Workshop area of the British Library, London. Her work is in many public and private collections.

SUSAN LEIPER (Scribe — Edinburgh, Scotland)

Born and brought up in Glasgow, Scotland. She studied French at the University of St. Andrews and History of Art at the Courtauld Institute of Art in London. After calligraphy classes in Hong Kong and in Edinburgh, Susan completed the Society of Scribes and Illuminators Advanced Training Scheme in 2000. Has undertaken commissions from major institutions including the British Museum, The National Museums of Scotland and the BBC. She contributed to the *Great Book of Gaelic*. She also edits books on Chinese art which is the major source of inspiration for her own work. Susan lives in Edinburgh with her husband and four children.

SUZANNE MOORE (Illuminator — Cleveland, Ohio)

Suzanne Moore earned a BFA in Printmaking and Drawing at the University of Wisconsin, Eau Claire. She began creating manuscript books in the early 1980s and has taught book design in the United States, Europe and Asia. She art directs the Lettering Design Group at American Greetings. Her current work combines contemporary vision and painting with traditional scribal techniques in manuscript books. Her books are in major public and private collections in the United States and Europe, including the Library of Congress, Washington, DC, the Pierpont Morgan Library, New York, and the Houghton Library, Harvard University.

IZZY PLUDWINSKI (Hebrew Scribe — Jerusalem, Israel)

Izzy Pludwinski has been working as a professional calligrapher since 1980, starting out as a certified religious scribe (*Sofer* STaM) and then branching out into calligraphy and design. He studied at the Roehampton Institute where he completed the certificate in Calligraphy and Design in 1989. He has also taught for many years, in both London and Israel. Born in Brooklyn, New York, in 1954, he lives in Jerusalem with his wife and two wonderful daughters.

BRIAN SIMPSON (Scribe — Leicestershire, England)

Brian Simpson studied calligraphy and heraldry (he was a fellow student of Donald Jackson) at Central School of Arts and Crafts, London, with Irene Wellington and Mervyn Oliver. He worked as a lettering artist and graphic designer for forty-nine years. Now concentrates on calligraphy and heraldic art.

ANGELA SWAN (Scribe — Abergavenny, Wales)

Angela Swan studied calligraphy and bookbinding at the Roehampton Institute from 1985 to 1988. She was an assistant to Donald Jackson in Monmouth, Wales, for three years (1988–1991). Works as a freelance calligrapher, and teaches and exhibits in the United Kingdom. She has contributed to various books and publications.

CHRIS TOMLIN (Natural History Illustrator — London, England)

Chris Tomlin trained at the Royal College of Art, London, studying natural history illustration. He has worked for Oxford University Press and the National Trust, as well as other publishers. He also studies flora and fauna in the field on expeditions in countries as far away as the United States (Minnesota) and Madagascar, where he worked in the rainforests recording endangered species.

OTHER MEMBERS OF THE SCRIPTORIUM TEAM: Mabel Jackson (partner), Rebecca Cherry (project assistant/coordinator), Sarah Harris (studio assistant), Olivia Edwards (project manager: 1999–2001), Vin Godier (computer graphics), Mark L'Argent (studio assistant: 2000–2002) and Sally Sargeant (proofreader).

# COMMITTEE ON ILLUMINATION AND TEXT

## MICHAEL PATELLA, OSB

Michael Patella, OSB, is the chair of The Saint John's Bible Committee on Illumination and Text. He is an Associate Professor of New Testament and teaches in both the Theology Department and the School of Theology at Saint John's University. He also serves as the Director of the School of Theology's Early Christian World Program. He is the author of *The Death of Jesus* and the *Gospel of Luke* for the *New Collegeville Bible Commentary*. Other writings include the *Seers' Corner* for *The Bible Today* and writings published in the area of Luke-Acts. He earned a License in Sacred Scripture from Rome's Pontifical Biblical Institute and a Doctorate in Sacred Scripture from the École Biblique et Archéologique Française in Jerusalem.

## SUSAN WOOD, SCL

Susan Wood, SCL, is a professor of Theology in both the Theology Department at Saint John's University and the School of Theology. She earned her Bachelor's degree at Saint Mary College in Leavenworth, Kansas, and her Master's degree at Middlebury College, Middlebury, Vermont. She earned her Doctorate at Marquette University, Milwaukee, Wisconsin.

## COLUMBA STEWART, OSB

Columba Stewart, OSB, is the executive director of the Hill Monastic Manuscript Library. Having served on the CIT and as curator of special collections, he is often asked to speak on how and where The Saint John's Bible fits into Saint John's University's vision for the book arts and religious culture. Father Columba is a Professor in the Theology Department at Saint John's University and the School of Theology. He is also the former chair of the Theology Department. He received a Bachelor's degree from Harvard College and his Master's degree from Yale University. He studied at the University of Oxford where he received his Doctorate in Philosophy. Columba also studied for one year at the Dominican Studium in Oxford.

## IRENE NOWELL, OSB

Irene Nowell, OSB, is a visiting associate professor of Theology for the School of Theology's Summer Sessions at Saint John's University. She is a Professor at Benedictine College in Atchison, Kansas. Sister Irene received her Bachelor's degree from Mt. St. Scholastica College in Kansas, her Master's degrees from The Catholic University of America and Saint John's University. She received her Doctorate from The Catholic University of America.

## JOHANNA BECKER, OSB

A Benedictine potter, teacher, art historian and Orientalist, Johanna Becker, OSB, combines these in the different facets of her work. As a teacher in the art department of the College of Saint Benedict and Saint John's University, she taught both studio classes (primarily ceramics) and art history focusing for the past several years on the arts of Asia. As a specialist in Asian ceramics, particularly those of seventeenth-century Japan, she has done connoisseurship for public and private museums, published a book, *Karatsu Ware* and written and lectured worldwide. Her art history classes benefit from the years she lived in Japan and her time spent in the majority of Asian countries as an art researcher. She holds a Bachelor of Fine Arts degree from the University of Colorado, a Master of Fine Arts degree in studio art from Ohio State University and a Doctorate in art history from the University of Michigan. Although retired, she continues to teach Asian art history classes. She is a member of the Monastery of Saint Benedict, St. Joseph, Minnesota.

## NATHANAEL HAUSER, OSB

Nathanael Hauser, OSB, is an assistant professor of Art History at Saint John's University. He has taught calligraphy extensively at universities and at workshops. Father Nathanael has undertaken commissions for churches, monastic communities and private collections creating icons, crosses, books and reliquaries. His work and papers have been exhibited and presented in the United States and Rome, Italy. Father Nathanael received his Bachelor's degree in Philosophy from St. John's Seminary College in Camarillo, California. He received his Sacra Theologia Baccalaureato from the Pontificio Ateneo di Sant'Anselmo, Rome, and his Doctorate in Classical and Medieval Art and History from the University of Minnesota. Other studies include Orthodox and Russian iconography, enamel work and mosaic techniques.

## ALAN REED, OSB

Alan Reed, OSB, is the curator of Art and Artifacts for Saint John's Abbey and University. Under the auspices of the Hill Monastic Microfilm Library, he is the curator of the *Arca Artium* collection of rare books and art, and liaison to faculty interested in using all these collections. Previously Brother Alan taught design and drawing in the joint Art Department of Saint John's University and the College of St. Benedict for twenty-five years and toward the end of that time was chair of the department for six years. He holds a Bachelor's degree from Saint John's University in studio art, a Masters of Art Education from the Rhode Island School of Design and a Masters of Fine Art from the University of Chicago in studio art and art theory.

Other members of the broader Saint John's community have served at various times on the Committee on Illumination and Text including Susan Brix, David Cotter, OSB, and Rosanne Keller.

# GOSPELS AND ACTS

*Interpretive illuminations, incipits and special treatments in this volume are the work of Donald Jackson, except:*

| CHAPTER | ILLUSTRATION | ARTIST | NOTES |
|---|---|---|---|
| **MATTHEW** | | | |
| 1 | *Decoration facing Frontispiece* | Donald Jackson (DJ) | With contributions from SMJ |
| 5 | *Sermon on the Mount* | Thomas Ingmire | |
| 9 | *The Calming of the Storm* | Suzanne Moore | |
| 14 | *Middle-Eastern Arabesque* | Andrew Jamieson (AJ) | |
| 22 | *"You shall love the Lord"* | Hazel Dolby | |
| 24 | *Last Judgement* | Suzanne Moore | |
| 28 | *Carpet Page* | Sally Mae Joseph (SMJ) | |
| **MARK** | | | |
| 1 | *Decoration* | Aidan Hart (AH) | |
| 3 | *Sower and the Seed* | Aidan Hart | With contributions from DJ, SMJ |
| 5 | *Two Cures* | Aidan Hart | With contributions from DJ, SMJ |
| 10 | *Transfiguration* | Donald Jackson | In collaboration with AH |
| 11 | *"Listen to Him"* | Sally Mae Joseph | |
| 13 | *"Hear O Israel"* | Hazel Dolby | |
| 16 | *Carpet Page* | Sally Mae Joseph | |
| **LUKE** | | | |
| 1 | *Magnificat* | Sally Mae Joseph | |
| 2 | *Gloria in Excelsis* | Sally Mae Joseph | |
| 2 | *Nunc Dimitiis* | Hazel Dolby | |
| 9 | *"You shall love the Lord"* | Hazel Dolby | |
| 15 | *Luke Anthology* | Donald Jackson | With contributions from SMJ, AH |
| 24 | *Decoration* | Sally Mae Joseph | |
| 24 | *Carpet Page — Tree of Life* | Sally Mae Joseph | |
| **JOHN** | | | |
| 6 | *"I am" sayings* | Thomas Ingmire | |
| 7 | *Woman taken in Adultery* | Aidan Hart | With contributions from DJ, SMJ |
| 21 | *Decoration* | Sally Mae Joseph | |
| 21 | *Carpet Page* | Sally Mae Joseph | |
| **ACTS** | | | |
| 2 | *Decoration* | Sally Mae Joseph | |
| 5 | *Life in the Community* | Aidan Hart | In collaboration with DJ |
| 15 | *The Life of Saint Paul* | Donald Jackson | In collab. with AH, contributions from AJ |
| 27 | *"To the ends of the earth"* | Donald Jackson | With contributions from SMJ, AJ |
| 28 | *"You will be my witness"* | Donald Jackson | With contributions from AJ |

*Scribes:* Sue Hufton, Donald Jackson, Sally Mae Joseph and Brian Simpson
*Hebrew Script:* Christopher Calderhead (Notes), Donald Jackson, Izzy Pludwinski (Consultant)
*Natural History Illustrations:* Chris Tomlin
*Computer Graphics:* Vin Godier

# PENTATEUCH

*Interpretive illuminations, incipits and special treatments in this volume are the work of Donald Jackson, except:*

| CHAPTER | ILLUSTRATION | ARTIST | NOTES |
|---|---|---|---|
| **GENESIS** | | | |
| 2 | *Garden of Eden* | Donald Jackson (DJ) | With contributions from Chris Tomlin (CT) |
| 3 | *Adam and Eve* | Donald Jackson | With contributions from CT |
| 29 | *Jacob's Ladder* | Donald Jackson | In collaboration with CT |
| 34 | *Jacob's Dream* | Donald Jackson | With contributions from CT |
| 50 | *Carpet Page* | Sally Mae Joseph (SMJ) | |
| **EXODUS** | | | |
| 19 | *Ten Commandments* | Thomas Ingmire | |
| **LEVITICUS** | | | |
| 19:2 | *"You shall be holy"* | Sally Mae Joseph | |
| 19:18 | *"You shall not take vengeance"* | Sally Mae Joseph | |
| 19:34 | *"The alien who resides"* | Sally Mae Joseph | |
| **NUMBERS** | | | |
| 6:24 | *"The Lord bless you"* | Suzanne Moore | |
| 20:12 | *"You did not trust"* | Thomas Ingmire | |
| 21:8 | *"Make a poisonous serpent"* | Thomas Ingmire | |
| **DEUTERONOMY** | | | |
| 6:4-5 | *"Hear O Israel"* | Hazel Dolby | |
| 30:19-20 | *"Choose life"* | Suzanne Moore | |
| 33 | *Death of Moses* | Donald Jackson | In collaboration with AH, contributions from SMJ |
| 34 | *Menorah decoration* | Sally Mae Joseph | |

*Scribes:* Sue Hufton, Donald Jackson, Sally Mae Joseph and Brian Simpson
*Hebrew Script:* Donald Jackson, Izzy Pludwinski (Consultant and Scribe)
*Natural History Illustrations:* Chris Tomlin
*Computer Graphics:* Vin Godier

# PSALMS

*The Frontispiece and all book headings in this volume are the work of Donald Jackson.*

| | | |
|---|---|---|
| Psalms 1–41 | Book I | Brian Simpson |
| Psalms 42–72 | Book II | Sally Mae Joseph |
| Psalms 73–89 | Book III | Donald Jackson |
| Psalms 90–106 | Book IV | Donald Jackson |
| Psalms 107–150 | Book V | Sally Mae Joseph |
| Psalm 150 | *"Praise the Lord"* | Sally Mae Joseph |
| Psalms 6, 32, 38, 51, 102, 130, 143 | Penitential Psalms | Donald Jackson |

*Raised and burnished gilding throughout:* Sally Mae Joseph
*Psalm Numbers:* Brian Simpson
*Computer Graphics:* Vin Godier

## ART AND PHOTO CREDITS

## ACKNOWLEDGEMENTS

IT IS FOUR YEARS since I began to write *Illuminating the Word: The Making of The Saint John's Bible*. Many people have helped with the research and production of this book, and I am grateful to all of them.

Donald Jackson opened the Scriptorium to me and sat for many hours of interviews. He put his staff at my disposal and gave me intimate access to the project as it unfolded. He shared his hopes, dreams and frustrations about the project and trusted me to tell this story. I could never have written the book without his help.

Mabel Jackson has always been a thoughtful and generous host. On my many trips to Wales, she made me feel at home and made sure I had everything I needed to do my work. Her quiet dedication to the project is often expressed behind the scenes and it is invaluable.

Sally Mae Joseph provided me an insider's view of the workings of the Scriptorium. I value her friendship more than I can express.

Other members of the Scriptorium team helped me collect reference material, make photocopies and pull out pages of the manuscript for me to see. Early in my involvement, Mark L'Argent and Olivia Edwards aided the research. In more recent years, Rebecca Cherry has fielded many of my phone calls and an alarmingly large flow of e-mail.

Jo White was the person who first suggested I should be the one to write this book. She made the introductions and helped me with details of my contract.

Saint John's Abbey provided me a place to work on many visits to Collegeville. The resources of the monastery and university were made available with great generosity. The staff at the Hill Monastic Manuscript Library was particularly helpful.

The monks at Saint John's welcomed me as a guest several times within the monastic enclosure. Their hospitality reminded me that the monastery is not simply a big institution—it is their home.

The leaders of the abbey and university took time out of very busy schedules to grant me interviews. I am grateful to Abbot John Klassen, OSB, and President Dietrich Reinhart, OSB, for giving me their time and supporting the writing of this book.

While I was living in England, my boss, the Reverend Andrew McKearney, gave me great flexibility to arrange short trips to Wales in order to do my research.

Betsy Jennings Powell—who has no background in calligraphy—read the entire typescript as a favor to me. Her careful attention to detail and sensitive comments on the text helped me make the book as accessible as possible to the general reader.

Fact-checking and proofreading by Margaret Arnold, Daniel Durken, OSB, Donald Jackson, Sally Mae Joseph, Carol Marrin, Mary Schaffer and John Taylor helped purge the text of errors. Any mistakes which remain are entirely my own.

Margaret Arnold and Wayne Torborg helped sort through many hundreds of images as we prepared the book. Wayne's expertise with digital imagery proved invaluable in sorting the wheat from the chaff.

All of those who sat for interviews, either in person or by telephone, were extremely generous with their time and their insights into the project. I hope I have captured not only their words but the spirit of our conversations.

ACKNOWLEDGEMENTS

216

Finally I owe a debt of gratitude to Carol Marrin, director of the Bible Project. Carol's enormous efficiency and her willingness to embark on the huge learning curve of putting this book together have been an inspiration. I have relied on her good humor and deep common sense throughout my work.

CHRISTOPHER CALDERHEAD

## PRODUCTION CREDITS

Editor: *Christopher Calderhead*

Copy Editors: *Daniel Durken, OSB, and John Taylor*

Production Managers: *Margaret Arnold and Colleen Stiller*

Proofreaders: *Sue Morey and James Wagner*

On-Press Proofing: *Dave Peterson*

Digital imaging, retouching, scanning and pre-press work: *ColorMax, Paynesville, Minnesota*

Printer: *Regent Publishing Services, Ltd.*

Designer: *Jerry Kelly*